THE GREAT DERBY MATCHES

LIVERPOOL
VERSUS
EVERTON

Forewords by Ian St John and Kevin Ratcliffe

MICHAEL HEATLEY
AND IAN WELCH

DIAL HOUSE

First published 1996

ISBN 07110 2450 2

© Michael Heatley and Ian Welch 1996

Published by Dial House

an imprint of Ian Allan Ltd, Terminal House, Station Approach, Shepperton, Surrey TW17 8AS.
Printed by Ian Allan Printing Ltd, Coombelands House, Coombelands Lane, Addlestone, Weybridge, Surrey KT15 1HY.

PICTURE CREDITS

Aerofilms:
23.

Colorsport:
5, 7, 8, 9B, 11, 12B, 13, 15, 16, 17BL, 18, 22, 24, 26-27, 28, 30T, 33, 34, 35, 36, 38, 40, 41R, 43, 44, 47, 48, 49T, 50, 51, 53, 54, 55, 57, 58, 59L, 60, 62, 63, 64, 66L, 67, 69, 70, 71, 72, 73T, 76L, 78, 79, 80, 81, 83, 84, 85, 86, 87, 88, 89, 93, 94, 96, 97, 98, 101, 104, 105, 106, 107, 109BR, 110, 111, 113, 114, 115, 117, 118, 119, 122, 123, 127, 128, 129, 130, 131, 132, 135, 136, 137, 139, 140B, 147TR, 147B, 149, 154, 156, 157, 159, 160.

Empics:
Cover M, Cover BL, Cover BM, Cover BR, Back Cover, 17BR, 20, 21, 25, 28-29, 45T, 46, 52, 56T, 61T, 65L, 68, 74R, 75, 77, 82, 90, 91, 92, 95, 100, 102, 103, 112, 116, 120, 121, 124, 125, 126, 141, 142, 143, 144, 145, 148, 150, 151, 152, 153, 155, 158.

N Fissler Collection:
10L, 12T, 14, 17T, 19, 45B, 49B, 56B, 59R, 61B, 65R, 66R, 70L, 74L, 108, 109TL, 109TR, 109BL.

DM Turner Collection:
Cover TL, Cover TR, 9T, 10R, 32, 37, 39, 41L, 42, 73B, 99, 133, 134, 138, 140T, 147TL.

CONTENTS

FOREWORD

When I came down from Scotland and signed for Liverpool in 1961, my first game was a derby against Everton – and I hadn't a clue what I'd got myself into! The one major difference between the Merseyside and other derbies is that you could, if you wanted to, just give the tickets out at random and fans of both sides would be sitting next to each other. The reason they don't do it is that people have their preferences: the Kopites will always want to be on the Kop and the Gwladys Street End at Goodison the same.

The fans go along to watch the game as committed followers of the teams, but as mates of the guys they're going with who wear the other colour. There's families too: fathers and sons, one red one blue... brothers, pals, cousins, it's unique. You couldn't do that in Manchester, London or Sheffield, and it says something about the football tradition.

The build-up in the city is great because everybody you meet is talking about the game – if they're not asking for a ticket! They're telling you what they're going to do to us or what we should be doing to them. Then afterwards, of course, there's the post-mortem...

I don't see why the Merseyside derby can't stay the top fixture in England. Liverpool have built up a huge support from outside the city through 30 years of success. They get great support from everywhere. Everton are the biggest-supported club in the city as far as the locals are concerned: they've always had the edge with that, but it's dwindled over the years as people have moved away because of work.

But what Everton have got, like Liverpool, is a great stadium and a good financial structure behind them. The rivalry is still as keen as ever – not a bitter rivalry, but a keen one – and I'm sure that will remain. One thing's for certain: if you go to a derby match in ten years' time you'll still not be able to get a ticket for it!

Enjoy the book.

Ian St John

Ian St John

Everybody talks about derbies, yet the only one that's on a par with the Merseyside derby is Celtic v Rangers. That's atmospheric because of the divide in the city between Catholic and Protestant – but having no other edge than red and blue it's remarkable what sort of atmosphere an Everton-Liverpool game generates. And it's definitely the fans that make it that way. It's a friendly atmosphere, but there's something there on derby day, something completely different.

You'll be on the pitch and all of a sudden you see two thousand fans in the Kop – Everton fans. They work with Liverpool fans all week: why can't they stand together on Saturday? On Monday, though, half of them don't go to work. Depending on the result, it's just the Liverpool or Everton fans who are in!

You have to play in one of these games to understand what it's like. On a derby day you very rarely hear anything specific from the crowd… yet it's so noisy you can't hear yourself talk to your team-mates! Lads come up from London, Birmingham and even Manchester and it adds another dimension to their football. Managers don't really wind you up much for these games – you shouldn't need it.

League form has nothing in the least to do with results. You know you're going to get a hard game and anything can happen: every match is like a Cup tie, very hectic. There's few derbies where both teams have settled down and played a passing game. They're good games to remember but not always the best games in the world to play in.

I suppose out of my 30 derbies for Everton I must have captained them in 20-odd. Just to play in them would have been an achievement, but to lead the team out at Wembley and captain them against Liverpool was a great honour. I think I saw about three or four captains off at Liverpool: Phil Thomson, Phil Neal, Graeme Souness, Alan Hansen… amazing, really!

I think the Merseyside derby will carry on being the biggest in England by far: I've certainly not experienced an atmosphere like it anywhere else. I've only been back to Goodison once since I left – being a manager, I don't really get the time – but this book brings it all back to me. I hope it revives memories for you too.

Kevin Ratcliffe

INTRODUCTION

As a five year-old child in Liverpool at the beginning of the 1960s, I recall being greeted at the school gates by a pair of older boys. They seemed to be interrogating the new arrivals as they passed by. What could this be – some kind of initiation ceremony? It was, in a way, but the question each lad was asked was simply this: are you Liverpool or Everton?

Somehow the 25-a-side matches with a tennis ball and coats for goals seemed to be evenly matched – and that's how it's remained since the first ever derby was played between 22 men with a regular-size ball back in 1894. Statistics suggest Liverpool have the edge, but try telling that to 11 men in blue who set out twice a year, sometimes more, to slay the Red dragon! Those who have starred in derbies over the years haven't all been born and bred in Merseyside, but each and every one has reported that there's no other feeling like a Liverpool v Everton confrontation to stir the blood.

When it was suggested to Everton manager Joe Royle that beating Liverpool didn't make a season, he responded with a remark that inferred the questioner didn't know what she was talking about. The response may have been less than chivalrous, but Royle knows what it's like to contest these matches as a player and a manager – something he has in common with Catterick, Paisley, Dalglish, Kendall, Souness and many others. Interestingly, his current counterpart Roy Evans never played in a League derby – but then neither did Bill Shankly!

The city of Liverpool has turned out many world-famous musicians as well as footballers over the years, and it's no coincidence that sport and music found their first meeting point on the terraces of Anfield and Goodison. The adaptation of popular hits to sing the praises (or otherwise) of those on the pitch is now an accepted part of the game in this country, and it all stemmed from Merseyside. Since then, TV's *Match Of The Day* has reinforced the Mersey connection by using the Lightning Seeds' 'Life Of Riley' as a theme for their Goal of the Month competition...but that's another story.

All statistics in this book have been compiled by Ian Welch and relate to the period up to and including the 18 November 1995 match (apart from players' career records in Chapter 4 which end with the 1994-95 season). Any corrections or amendments will be gladly and gratefully received. The book is dedicated to three Evertonians, David and Julian Heatley and Geoff Eccles: the writer is not prepared to disclose his own youthful allegiance to avoid accusations of bias!

This venture would not have been possible without Neil Fissler's research into the Greatest Games, Simon Joslin's ice-cool design, Ian St John and Kevin Ratcliffe's introductions and memories, plus the recollections of sundry other ex-derby warriors (Messrs Reid and Bracewell by courtesy of Rob Mason).

Dennis Turner and Alan Kinsman have also helped by supplying memorabilia and proofreading skills respectively. My thanks, and that of my co-author and statistician Ian Welch go to them all, and to our publisher Simon Forty for his continued faith and support.

Michael Heatley
Ian Welch

All local derbies are, by definition, hard-fought affairs. Whether you're in Manchester, Glasgow, London or Liverpool, no quarter will be given and no prisoners taken. Yet few derby matches are played in the same uniquely humorous spirit as the Merseyside clash between Liverpool and Everton. The city's penchant for ready wit is well chronicled, having turned out a wealth of professional funnymen from Jimmy Tarbuck to Alexei Sayle. But on derby day, every one of the supporters packed into Goodison Park or Anfield is ready and willing to add their own page to the history of the fixture.

Not that it's always been that way. How could it be, when a dispute with Everton had led to Liverpool's foundation? It was Everton, indeed, who had been the first tenants at Anfield Road in 1884, and it was a split in the ranks in 1892 that saw them decamp across Stanley Park to find a new home at Goodison.

John Houlding, the self-made brewer, publican and city councillor who'd steered the fortunes of the club until then, had bought the ground from a fellow brewer called John Orrell, and was calling all the shots: the players even used his

Right: John McKenna was Liverpool's manager and chairman, as well as President of the Football League.

Below: Everton's First Division Champions of 1927-28. Back row, left to right (players only): O'Donnell, Brown, Hardy, Hart, McDonald. Front row: Millington, Irvine, Dean, Dominy, Troup, Virr.

pub, the Sandon Hotel, as changing rooms. When he more than doubled the rent, Everton's response had left him with a ground but no team. His reaction was to give the city of Liverpool a second club, and Merseyside's footballing rivalry began.

Everton had been one of the dozen founder members of the Football League when that most august of competitions opened in 1888: their proud Latin motto read 'Nil Satis Nisi Optimum' (not satisfied unless the best). It took them only until the second season to mount a Championship challenge, though in the event it was Preston North End who romped away with the honours... and the Double, to boot. The Toffees had made the title their own in the 1890-91 season, with outstanding performances from three future England internationals: John Holt,

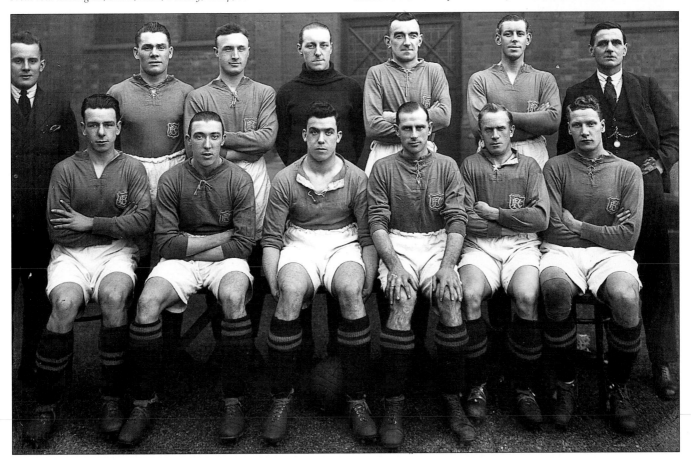

Edgar Chadwick (who would later play for Liverpool) and Alf Milward. Of the trio, only Holt missed a single game.

But success had brought in the crowds, no mean feat in a city still very much dominated by the rugby football code. And John Houlding took advantage of this by raising the rent 150 per cent between 1887 and 1889 alone. The leader of Everton's rent rebellion was one George Mahon, a rugby fan who'd been converted to the round-ball game. He was also the organist at St Domingo's, the church whose football section Everton had comprised before adopting autonomy and

a new name in late 1879. Under his leadership a limited company was founded, with £500 capital, which promptly set up its stall across Stanley Park.

Liverpool, also a limited company, was as close to a ready-packaged club as you could get, with professional players and a ground of First Division standard from the very beginning. Even so, the Football League had doubts about the viability of a rival to Everton, who'd been founder members and attracted crowds of thousands. So the new club was destined to play its first season in the Lancashire League, topping it on goal average, before election to the Second Division was secured in 1893.

Again, the new team – managed by Irishman John McKenna – carried all before it, and by winning through the ancient precursor of the play-offs, the so-called Test Match system, finally took their place alongside Everton in the footballing élite. With the city's dockers now working just a five and a half day week, Saturday afternoons could now be spent at one of two top-class footballing emporia.

The stage was set for the first League derby between the teams, which took place at Goodison Park on 13 October 1894. Already the needle was apparent, with Liverpool taking a week out to train at Hightown while Everton retained its normal routine. And despite their seeming nonchalance it was the Blues who drew first blood in a 3-0 win – the crowd of 44,000, including the Lord Mayor of Liverpool, was at that time the biggest ever seen at a

League game. Perhaps seen is the wrong word to use, since the game ended in semi-darkness.

The return saw honours even at 2-2, with Liverpool apparently unlucky not to shade the result in front of a partisan 30,000 crowd. But the Reds found the First Division somewhat inhospitable and subsided into the play-off zone: a single-goal reverse against Second Division Champions Bury subsequently saw them return whence they'd come.

If it was the Everton scarves that were flying over Merseyside at this point, then Liverpool soon bit back, manager McKenna making good his vow that the club would be in the top flight once again within the year. A 106-goal record haul took them up with some ease in 1896, putting the Merseyside derby back on the agenda. And that – give or take the odd gap, most notably in the 1950s and early 1960s – is exactly where it's been for Liverpool and Everton supporters during the century that followed.

Initially, despite that debut derby defeat, it was Liverpool whose star was in the ascendant. The club also boasted new colours, red replacing the former blue and white quarters used in the 1898 campaign. Prior to that, they'd finished their first season back in the top flight above their rivals, and in 1899 were unlucky not to clinch the Double. It was that season that they became the first club to complete a Merseyside double, two goals by McCowie – one of a plethora of Scots around which the team was built – giving them their first win at Goodison. The Championship was won for the first time in 1901, the year before club founder Alderman John Houlding died. It is worth noting that players of both sides carried his coffin at the funeral.

There's long been a widely held misconception that, like Celtic and Rangers in Glasgow, the supporters of Liverpool and Everton aligned themselves with the Catholic and Protestant faiths. Little evidence exists to support this theory, though Houlding – a strong supporter of the Orange Order – may unwittingly have inspired one side of the equation. Everton's staff in the 1950s contained a large proportion of players from the Republic of Ireland, but such tenuous links hardly stand up.

While other city rivals, notably Tottenham and Arsenal, had to wait the best part of a century to be drawn together in the FA Cup, the first Merseyside derby in the competition was staged as early as 1902, the first of three such meetings in five years. Everton must have felt they'd done the difficult part when they emerged from Anfield with a draw, but the Reds scored twice at Goodison without reply – the first an own goal from Walter Balmer – to send the red half of the 50,000 crowd home happy.

Everton had already reached the Cup Final in 1897 but were on that occasion vanquished by Aston Villa, who'd accounted for Liverpool in the semis. Had things finished differently, the result could, conceivably, have been the first all-Merseyside Cup Final, but it would be the best part of a century before this would come about. Until then, clashes such as the 1902 clash already mentioned and the Toffees' First-Round win in 1904-05

A. GELDARD

Opposite top: Liverpool FC 1922-23, after their second consecutive Championship. Back row, left to right: Wadsworth, Connell (trainer), McNab, Scott, Walsh, unknown director, Bromilow. Front row, Longworth, Gilhespy, Forshaw, McKinlay, Chambers, Hopkin.

Opposite bottom: Goodison legend Dixie Dean with team-mate O'Donnell.

Top right: Albert Geldard joined Everton as an 18 year old in November 1932.

Right: Centre-forward Albert Stubbins, a record £12,500 signing from Newcastle United, repaid his manager's faith with 75 goals in 161 League appearances in a Liverpool shirt.

would intersperse League fare. Such was the success of the city of Liverpool's dynamic duo that they'd claim the Double in 1906 – Liverpool the League, Everton the Cup. On the way to the Crystal Palace, the Toffees overcame their neighbours at Villa Park in a semi-final game where, the *Liverpool Echo* reported 'the roads were congested and the ground full by 2.00pm… the hardware capital was astonished.'

From then until the outbreak of war, both teams enjoyed most success on their opponent's ground. From 1907, Liverpool won six and drew one of nine away League matches, while Everton won at Anfield seven times in succession. John McKenna, the club's first manager who also served as chairman in two spells, remained the man in charge. 'Honest John' would also become President of the Football League, in which role he would serve for over a quarter of a century.

The very last peacetime season saw Liverpool help their neighbours to the

League title, but only indirectly. The Reds' 2-0 victory against Oldham ensured a second title for Everton, who'd gone into the fixture a point ahead of the Boundary Park side but had played one more game. Everton would hold the Championship trophy until 1920.

The war years saw both Liverpool and Everton playing in the Lancashire League, one of several regional competitions set up to compensate for the lack of Football League fare. In the years from 1916 to 1919 Everton finished fourth, fifth, third and first in the unfortunately-named Lancashire Section Principal Tournament, while Liverpool were winners in 1917, second (1918), third (1919) and sixth (1916).

As war clouds subsided, it was Liverpool who shone first. A derby double in 1920-21, achieved within a week in front of an aggregate 100,000 crowd, gave an indication of glories to come, the *Liverpool Football Echo* reporting that, on Forshaw's winning goal in the first match against then-table toppers Everton, 'the Kop rocked like a volcano'. Everton subsided into a mid-table position, while the fourth-placed Reds finished the following season top of the pile: ironically, both derbies in 1921-22 were tame 1-1 draws.

Liverpool retained their title under postwar manager David Ashworth, but a hat-trick was to prove beyond them and Ashworth moved on to Oldham. Over at Goodison Park, the arrival of a young centre-forward who'd come to their notice from over the water at Tranmere, was to tip the balance of Merseyside power very much in their favour. He was, of course, William Ralph Dean, better known (though to his disgust) as Dixie due to his dark hair. Liverpool had concentrated their scouting efforts on Scotland, and it was suggested that they had missed the potential star striker who'd been under their noses all the time.

Thanks largely to the newcomer, the Championship trophy wore blue ribbons in 1928 and 1932, though bizarrely the two wins were divided by a season in the Second Division that postponed derby hostilities for 12 months. Liverpool had the satisfaction of spiking Double dreams in January 1932 when a Dean goal at Goodison proved insufficient to halt the Reds' Cup progress.

Interestingly, the scores that stand out among the inter-war statistics were all registered by Liverpool – a 7-4 win in October 1932 against the reigning Champions and a team that later that season would lift the FA Cup, and a 6-0 win in 1935 with Fred Howe bagging four and Gordon Hodgson the remaining pair. This remains the clearest-cut game in terms of margin of victory between the two sides, and incidentally came at the start of a purple scoring patch for the Reds that saw them score 20 goals in four home matches with just two conceded.

Everton's fifth Championship was won in 1938-39, the season that would turn out to be the last before the declaration of war. The 60,000 who gathered at Goodison in October 1938 to see the Toffees triumph 2-1 sang 'God Save The Queen', certain in the knowledge that Chamberlain's appeasement had ended the threat of conflict. As things turned out, Everton would once again hold the trophy for the duration of World War – the next seven years, as it transpired. Once peacetime football

Above: A joint programme for the Everton-Liverpool fixture of October 1932.

Right: It was Tommy Lawton who had the task of filling Dixie Dean's boots – and a good job he did with 65 goals in 87 League appearances for the Toffees.

Right: Cliff Britton had just taken Burnley from the Second Division to third place in the top flight and the FA Cup Final when he returned to Merseyside in 1948. His Goodison tenure, however, was not as successful – the club spent three seasons in the Second Division after relegation in 1950-51 and 11th was his best position in the First Division as manager.

Bottom right: Dublin-born Jimmy O'Neill played ten seasons at Goodison, earning 17 caps for the Republic of Ireland side.

resumed, the silverware would only pass the short distance across Stanley Park.

Again, though, there would be an interregnum where hastily organised regional competitions would take the place of Football League fare. The guest system saw players of many other clubs wear the red and blue jerseys, including Frank Soo (Stoke) and Abe Rosenthal (Tranmere) for Everton while Liverpool fielded the likes of keepers Sam Bartram (Charlton) and Frank Swift (Manchester City). Even Cliff Britton – a long-serving Evertonian, if no-longer a first-team regular – pulled a red shirt over his head.

Most significantly, the final game of the 1941-42 season, a 4-1 Liverpool defeat of Everton, saw a familiar figure wearing the Number 4 shirt. It was Bill Shankly, still registered with Preston but guesting for the team he would lead to glory as manager two decades later. How fitting it should have been a derby, albeit a wartime one, which saw him pull on a red jersey.

The immediate postwar era has become known in retrospect as English football's golden age. Attendances nationwide reached new levels, as the country welcomed back their sporting heroes. And the 18 September 1948 derby brought Goodison's all-time attendance record, 78,299 cramming in to witness a 1-1 draw. The following season's corresponding game, played in the August sunshine, topped the 70,000 mark – 70,812 to be precise – while 71,150 passed through the turnstiles on 16 September 1950. Those figures still rate ninth and fifth in the all-time rankings.

Liverpool had been first to make a mark, splashing out a record fee of £12,000 to Newcastle for Albert Stubbins and pipping Everton in the process. Legend has it the Geordie goal ace – English football's top scorer in wartime football – tossed a coin to decide where he would continue his career. He'd link with Billy Liddell, a Scots winger signed as a teenager in 1938 who had no time to make his mark in pre-war football. Gaining Scottish wartime international caps, he helped Merseyside-born Jack Balmer set a record of three consecutive hat-tricks as the Reds secured their fifth Championship in 1947.

Their derby record that year of a 0-0 draw and 0-1 defeat was less impressive, but they had a third bite at the cherry when Everton visited Anfield for the Liverpool Senior Cup Final. Unfortunately, the Reds' rivals for the Championship, Stoke City, were due to complete their League programme against Sheffield United. A poor winter had put the fixtures a fortnight out of kilter, but the fact remained that a win for Stoke (without Stan Matthews that day) would take the title.

The game at Bramall Lane kicked off a quarter of an

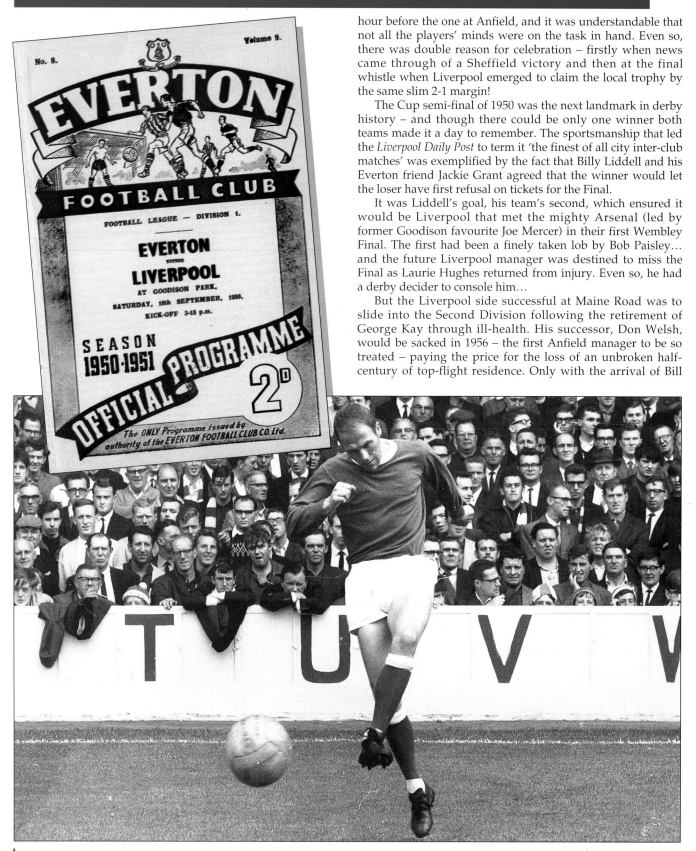

hour before the one at Anfield, and it was understandable that not all the players' minds were on the task in hand. Even so, there was double reason for celebration – firstly when news came through of a Sheffield victory and then at the final whistle when Liverpool emerged to claim the local trophy by the same slim 2-1 margin!

The Cup semi-final of 1950 was the next landmark in derby history – and though there could be only one winner both teams made it a day to remember. The sportsmanship that led the *Liverpool Daily Post* to term it 'the finest of all city inter-club matches' was exemplified by the fact that Billy Liddell and his Everton friend Jackie Grant agreed that the winner would let the loser have first refusal on tickets for the Final.

It was Liddell's goal, his team's second, which ensured it would be Liverpool that met the mighty Arsenal (led by former Goodison favourite Joe Mercer) in their first Wembley Final. The first had been a finely taken lob by Bob Paisley… and the future Liverpool manager was destined to miss the Final as Laurie Hughes returned from injury. Even so, he had a derby decider to console him…

But the Liverpool side successful at Maine Road was to slide into the Second Division following the retirement of George Kay through ill-health. His successor, Don Welsh, would be sacked in 1956 – the first Anfield manager to be so treated – paying the price for the loss of an unbroken half-century of top-flight residence. Only with the arrival of Bill

Shankly would their previous status be restored.

For Liverpudlians and Evertonians, then, the 1950s would be all but barren of derby memories – though the previously-mentioned Liverpool Senior Cup gave them the chance to meet on a quasi-competitive basis each year, it was hardly the 'real thing'. Yet one truly meaningful game stood out as an oasis in this fixtureless desert. And it's one all true Blues will want to forget. The FA Cup Fourth Round draw saw Liverpool visit Goodison and overturn the form-book to emerge 4-0 victors. But even this was to end in anti-climax for the Reds who promptly flopped at home to Huddersfield the following round.

Everton had been one of the last of the League's leading clubs to appoint a manager: Theo Kelly (1939-48) had given way to former player Cliff Britton, but he never recovered from a three-season spell in the Second Division (while Everton were relegated for only the second time, Liverpool remained in the First). Ian Buchan and Johnny Carey would follow before Harry Catterick's 1961 arrival brought the promise of good times to come.

Goodison's floodlights were christened by a visit from Liverpool on 9 October 1957 when the Blues had seen off their visitors 2-0 in a match that celebrated the 75th anniversary of the foundation of the Liverpool County FA. Three weeks later, the Reds gained revenge with a 3-2 win while inaugurating their floodlights.

There have been many friendlies, testimonials and non-League games over the years: indeed though 1980s stalwart Kevin Ratcliffe is credited with 30 appearances, this takes no account of the 'extras'. He recalls the Screen Sport Super Cup,

of which more later, in particular detail. 'We played two games against Liverpool in it, and to be honest we could have done without them. I think we played Liverpool about six or seven times one year. It was a bit like the Scottish League.'

Talk of Scotland evokes the Shankly era – and it was the second coming of William Shankly, following his wartime introduction to Anfield, that lit the red touch paper for a Merseyside revolution. Quietly rebuilding his team with the likes of Yeats and St John, he secured promotion in 1961-62, since when derby fixtures have continued unbroken.

The return of League meetings for the Merseyside clubs after an 11-season absence from the Merseyside sporting calendar meant that the 22 September 1962 clash at Goodison was massively over-subscribed. A 72,488 crowd, Everton's fifth highest ever, saw an honourable draw fought out, though

Opposite top: The programme for the September 1950 clash at Goodison described it as 'the civil war of Liverpool…the armistice will be signed at 4.55pm'.

Opposite bottom: Ironically one of Bill Shankly's former players at Huddersfield Town, Ray Wilson signed for Everton in July 1964 and two years later earned a World Cup Winner's medal at Wembley.

Above: Liverpool's Championship-winning side of 1963-64.
Back row, left to right: Ferns, Milne, Strong, Lawrence, Moran, Furnell, A'Court, Lawler, Byrne.
Front row: Arrowsmith, Wallace, Callaghan, Hunt, Yeats, St John, Melia, Thomson.

Liverpool keeper Jim Furnell was so nervous he dropped the ball before a minute had been played! The return the following Easter finished in similar fashion in front of another full house nearing 56,000.

The city of Liverpool's two clubs certainly seemed intent on proving that while the Beatles were blazing Merseybeat worldwide with almost religious fervour, the gospel of good football would not be far behind. Liverpool's fans were first to modify the Fab Four's songs and start a tradition of community singing that remains with them – and all football – to this day.

At Everton, former Goodison playing favourite Harry Catterick, who had cut his managerial teeth at Sheffield Wednesday, was summoned to replace Johnny Carey whose three years in charge, while unspectacular, had brought Roy Vernon, Alex Young and Jimmy Gabriel to the club.

Catterick built on that foundation with the panache of the centre-forward he once was, and proved a capable if less controversial counterpart to Bill Shankly. Indeed, his side would take the Championship in 1962-63. Liverpool won the title three years later, the same season as Everton took the FA Cup in a 3-2 Wembley thriller against Catterick's former charges Sheffield Wednesday, setting up the clubs' first meeting in the Charity Shield. Held at Goodison Park, the first Mersey meeting in the traditional season curtain-raiser between League Champions and Cup winners was won by a single Roger Hunt goal.

Hunt, who like Goodison star Ray Wilson, had been a member of the victorious England World Cup team that year, was well served by the wing-play of Ian Callaghan and Peter Thompson. Both would win England caps, and their pinpoint accuracy won high praise from Everton's record-breaker Dixie Dean. 'If I'd played with those two feeding me the crosses,' he said, 'I'd have scored 100 League goals – never mind 60!'

There'd been a 5-0 win at Anfield in 1965 that ranked as the best of Shankly's reign, and was destined to go down in folklore as a classic piece of kidology. The boss dropped hints to assistant Bob Paisley that he should get the best odds he could on a Liverpool win, adding that he'd been spying on Everton's Bellefield training ground from the window of his house nearby.

'Catterick has got them running lap after lap,' he exclaimed in a stage whisper. 'They'll be knackered by Saturday!' Come the day, Shankly had stood at his usual vantage point as the team bus came in, returning to the dressing room to deliver his verdict. 'They can hardly walk,' he crowed, 'they look shattered.' Liverpool went out onto the park feeling ten feet tall... little knowing that Shankly would have had to scale his roof to enjoy an uninterrupted view of their rivals training!

In 1968, the 'big freeze' meant that Goodison had to wait until 3 February to stage a home match – and inevitably it was their neighbours who proved the 'first-footers' of the year. Howard Kendall, later to boss the Blues in two widely differing spells, broke the ice with the only goal. 'It gave me a

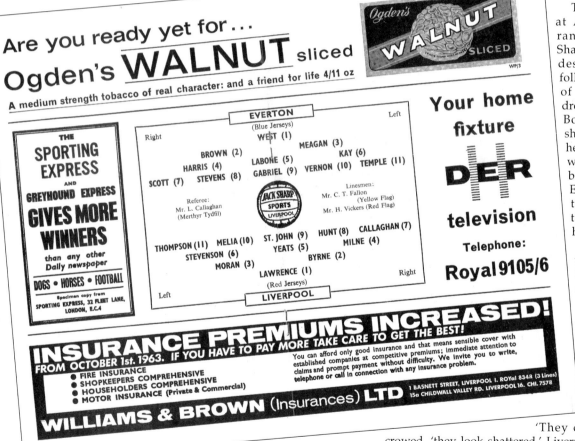

Above: The team line-ups for the 8 February 1964 clash at Goodison which finished 3-1 to Everton. Note the advertisement for former player Jack Sharp's sports shop.

Opposite: The inimitable Bill Shankly whose 15-year reign at Anfield took the club to previously unimagined heights. He retired in 1974 and died seven years later.

tremendous feeling,' he later recalled. It wouldn't prove as easy as a manager: Kendall only became a winner against Liverpool at the eighth attempt, including a 5-0 drubbing at Goodison!

It's hard to remember when the demand for tickets hasn't exceeded the space available – and in this post-Taylor Report era, that's likely to remain so for the foreseeable future. The Kop's seating was the biggest change to Anfield ever made since the most famous popular end in the world acquired its roof in 1928, the better to funnel sound onto the pitch.

Harry Catterick's preference for cultured football led to Goodison being dubbed the School of Science. He built 1970's title-winning team across the middle of the field with the trio of Kendall, Ball and Harvey while Shankly fashioned his around the backbone of keeper Lawrence, centre-half Yeats and centre-forward St John. The two approaches were total contrasts and in keeping with the managers' characters, ensuring some fascinating clashes when the teams did battle. Shankly's 'big three' were Scots like himself, flashing back to the 'team of the Macs' that had served Liverpool so well earlier on.

Yet the 1970s, a sporting decade that has since been over-rehabilitated thanks to glam-rock soundtracks and *Minder* voice-overs, brought little flair to the all-Mersey affair. Four boring 0-0 draws in a row in 1974 and 1975 accompanied the transition of power from Shanks and Catterick to Paisley and Bingham (both, incidentally, former players), and it was fair to say the derby match lost just a *little* of its lustre.

Both men had sides to rebuild, the glory teams of the 1960s having grown old and tired. Liverpool were served

notice of impending change after losing to lower-division Watford in the 1970 FA Cup, while Harry Catterick's team suffered a double blow in 1971 – going out of the European Cup to Greek side Panathinaikos on away goals and returning to England to lose the 1971 FA Cup semi-final to Liverpool by a 2-1 margin.

In derby terms, there was little to raise the temperature following that 1971 clash until the balls in Lancaster Gate's velvet bag set up a fourth semi-final meet in 1977. While '71 saw a change of scene to Old Trafford, it was back to Maine Road for a pulsating encounter which will live in folklore due to referee Clive Thomas disallowing what seemed to be a perfectly good winning goal from Bryan Hamilton. The replay went Liverpool's way, as had the semi-finals they'd contested

in 1950 and 1971 – but as in both those cases they were destined not to lift the silverware. Defeat by Manchester United was also to deprive them of a unique treble, though the League and European Cup would prove some consolation.

David Johnson brought up a unique derby double in April 1978, when his single goal beat Everton. Seven years earlier he'd scored the only goal of the game for Everton, his first club in what, even then, remained the Blues' last League win against their neighbours. As it happened, Andy King would end Everton's winless spell later in the year while Johnson would flit back across Stanley Park to appear yet again in a blue shirt. His one derby appearance in this second period as an Evertonian was in a remarkable game in November 1982 which saw the Toffees trounced 5-0. Keeper Neville Southall

HISTORY OF THE FIXTURE

tasted the axe after this most hurtful of humiliations, and it was ironic that Ian Rush, the executioner in chief, would in 1995 share coaching duties for the Welsh national team with the man he relegated to the reserves.

But Southall and friends had the last laugh in 1985 when Everton's League win was a crushing blow to the team that regarded itself as the top dogs of Merseyside. Liverpool trailed in second, 13 points behind – the largest ever points margin between first and second. Both derbies that year ended 1-0 to the Toffees. For good measure, Everton brought home the European Cup Winners' Cup in the last pre-Heysel season, and had it not been for Manchester United winning the FA Cup Final would have pulled off an unique treble.

The following year Everton ended runners-up – creditable for any other team, but they'd let an eight-point lead slip… to Liverpool, of all people, who made matters worse by taking the Cup to complete the Double. The winning goal came at

Above: Everton's Connolly and Dobson organise a free-kick, April 1976, with referee Clive Thomas in attendance.

Opposite: Programme for the 1984 Charity Shield (top) and the Everton team that won it (bottom left). Back row: Richardson, Reid, Bailey, Steven, Ratcliffe, Southall. Front row: Heath, Mountfield, Sharp, Stevens, Bracewell.

Opposite bottom right: Ray Atteveld, one of several derby foreigners.

Chelsea from Kenny Dalglish, now elevated to player-manager.

Two seasons later, the result was the same but the roles were reversed. It looked for most of the season as if the Reds were going to run away with the title, a nine-point lead established. Everton seemed to have little chance, injuries having taken their toll. But seven wins in succession gave the Toffees a fighting chance as Liverpool lost its way and ended the season empty-handed for just the third time in 15 years.

The Football League Cup, otherwise known as Hardaker's Folly after the man whose vision it was, could hardly have been termed a runaway success. Indeed, Liverpool and Everton initially declined the invitation to enter, in common with other leading clubs, considering it less as a potential crowd-puller as unwanted extra fixtures. The introduction of a one-legged Wembley Final and a place in Europe for the victors changed all that, and it was this that brought the first meeting of the teams on Wembley's hallowed turf. Even the first Charity Shield the pair had contested, in 1966, had been played at Goodison.

The League (Milk) Cup Final of 1984, then, was the match Merseyside had waited nearly a century for… but the result in the pouring rain was an anti-climactic scoreless draw. The lack of goals was probably not surprising, since the Merseysiders boasted two of the meanest defences in the League. No-one

16

wanted to lose this game, so the result was perhaps the best one. And the combined chants of 'Merseyside' that rose from the terraces confirmed that this had been no ordinary fixture, these were no ordinary supporters.

The replay was staged four days later at Maine Road, 52,089 Merseysiders making the pilgrimage down the East Lancs Road. Maybe coats could have been put down in Stanley Park... It was always likely that one goal would be enough to decide things, and it was an undistinguished Graeme Souness effort that skidded past Southall to settle the destination of the silverware.

There was a period in the 1980s when the teams seemed to be meeting almost too regularly, giving rise to the impossible thought that the fixture might be devalued. The Screen Sport Super Cup, devised as a 'consolation' to the clubs which would not be playing in Europe after Heysel, was an example.

Ironically, the two-legged Final would be contested in late 1986 by Liverpool the club that had voluntarily withdrawn from Europe, and Everton, whose Championship would normally have guaranteed it the right to compete in the European Cup. It would turn out to be the first and last Final of an unwanted competition – yet as Liverpool boss Kenny Dalglish noted, 'This is another derby game and as such the competition will be keen... it's certain that when there is a trophy at stake neither Liverpool nor Everton want to do their neighbours any favours.'

The 1980s also brought two Cup Final meetings, both of which are profiled in detail elsewhere. There were those who wondered why a local contest should have to transport itself 200 miles south to be decided, but that was to miss the point. The fact that Liverpool and Everton had reached the Final of the country's most prestigious competition more than justified half of the city taking a day trip to Wembley. And there was now a real international flavour to Merseyside derbies: not one player in Liverpool's 1986 starting line-up was qualified to play for England.

Coming as it did after Hillsborough, the second FA Cup game re-established some sense of normality to a city that had, perhaps, taken the Shankly aphorism about football being more important a matter than life or death too literally until

then. Yet there was a sense of resentment from the blue side of the city that somehow they were expected to roll over and let Liverpool win it 'for the fans'.

The 1989 Cup Final had, by chance, been preceded two and a half weeks earlier by a League encounter that still managed to draw nearly 46,000. It was Liverpool's first competitive game since Hillsborough, and the Goodison crowd was hushed for a respectful pre-kick-off silence in honour of those who had lost their lives. As the season panned out, the dropped points cost

Liverpool the Double – but under the circumstances it hardly mattered.

As Everton boss Colin Harvey summed up in his programme notes, Hillsborough was a tragedy both sides shared. 'Football people round the country have always marvelled at the way Everton and Liverpool supporters could gather together as both friends and rivals at derby matches. This was a special quality in happy times, and in the last two and a half weeks it has been a great strength in tragedy.'

More than religion, racism has reared its head in the derby divide. Neither club had black players on its staff, though Howard Gayle had shone brightly if briefly as a substitute in the 1981 European Cup semi-final, bamboozling the Bayern defence after coming on for Dalglish. But he had never been anywhere near a first-team regular, while Everton's Cliff Marshall made even less of a mark.

Yet the fact that this was an issue was highlighted by the Toxteth riots in 1981: Liverpool was a proudly multi-racial city, yet neither team in any way reflected that cultural diversity. All this changed in 1987 with the signing of John Barnes, one of

the most naturally gifted footballers of his generation, who had been marked down for superstardom after scoring a superb individual goal for England in Brazil's Maracana stadium. Dalglish's first aim had been to import a player with sufficient charisma to mask the departure of Ian Rush to Juventus. But with Barnes he got a whole lot more.

Unfortunately, Barnes got a whole lot of abuse from Everton fans, whose taunts included throwing bananas on to the pitch. Blues skipper Kevin Ratcliffe believes Barnes' understated reaction did himself and the anti-racist cause a great service. 'I think John's done a lot to calm things down in that area by not going overboard about things like that even though he's been upfront about the racism thing. He's done a good job.'

From even the most bigoted Liverpool fans' point of view it left little room for manoeuvre. Their best player was black, and they took to Barnes in a way that left the way clear for future signings like Mark Walters and David James to flourish. On the Goodison side, Nigeria's flamboyant Daniel Amokachi and the less eyecatching but enviably cool skills of Rochdale-born Earl

Barrett have ensured that both Merseyside clubs now more accurately reflect a cross-section of society. It is to be hoped that their fan following, still predominantly white, may one day do so too.

In a bizarre parallel to the racial situation, players previously reviled for equally illogical reasons could win instant forgiveness once wearing the right colour shirt. Though the Kop had always picked on him in his previous visits in the service of Chelsea, Southampton and Coventry, fiery Scot David Speedie made himself an instant folk hero by scoring twice on his Anfield debut against Everton in early 1991.

The Liverpool team of 1987-88 had looked as if it would create new records with an unbeaten start that equalled Leeds United's record of 29 games. A draw at Derby County brought them level, but the next game – almost inevitably – took them to Goodison. A single goal by Wayne Clarke, ironically the younger brother of Leeds striker Allan, a stalwart of the record-setting team, was enough to settle matters after Bruce Grobbelaar had dropped the ball at his feet. It was their fourth competitive meeting of the season, the final score two wins apiece.

The Merseyside derby has always excited outside interest, from as far back as Liverpool's Scots-based 'team of the Macs'. But from the 1980s onwards the mix of players on the pitch would become even more cosmopolitan. Everton boasted such exotic names as Warzycha (Poland), Atteveld (Holland) and Preki (former Yugoslavia), while Liverpool put Kozma (Hungary), Bjornebye (Norway) and Piechnik (Denmark) alongside long-serving Zimbabwean Bruce Grobbelaar. Strangest of all perhaps was Jan Molby, a Dane who now speaks perfect Scouse!

Even before this influx of outside talent, the clubs' support from outside the city was booming as never before, aided by the replica shirt and souvenir business. Both clubs have made merchandising a prime plank of their revenue-rasing game plan – Goodison opened a new gift shop in 1995 – and have authorised magazines dedicated to their own players.

As Ian St John hinted in his introduction, the city of Liverpool is now somewhat less populated than it was, and this has meant a more than proportionate reduction in Everton's fan following within the city boundaries. Liverpool, since the Shankly era, have enjoyed wider worldwide popularity, though in the 1990s their position was usurped by Manchester United. All this adds up not only to money and publicity for the clubs, but an enhanced interest in the times in the season when they meet.

In the normal run of things no quarter is given or expected by either side in a derby game, but the rugged challenges can exact a price. Early 1991 saw the teams meeting in consecutive weeks in the League and then the FA Cup. Both matches saw Liverpool lose players, Ronnie Whelan and then

Opposite: The tragedy that occurred at Hillsborough during the 1989 FA Cup semi-final in which 95 (eventually 96) Liverpool supporters lost their lives inevitably spilled over to the Final at Wembley, where perimeter fencing was removed as a mark of respect.

Right: The programme of the 3 May 1989 derby, contested weeks before the Wembley meeting, showed a photo of Anfield's gates, emphasising that Liverpool's sorrow was shared by all Merseyside.

HISTORY OF THE FIXTURE

Steve McMahon, for the remainder of the season – though McMahon was generally felt to have been the architect of his own misfortune due to a reckless challenge. Even in 1995 a late challenge on the keeper was enough to provoke a dozen-player scrimmage, though nothing too serious resulted.

In the long history of Merseyside derbies, which game has been the greatest of all time? All depends how long in the tooth you are, of course, on how many games you have to choose from – but in living memory, many people's money will be on the FA Cup Fifth Round Replay of 1991.

There'd been no clue of the drama to come in the scoreless first game, when McMahon's injury, sustained while challenging John Ebbrell, was the most memorable incident. Peter Beardsley was recalled for David Speedie, scoring twice to underline his opinion of his controversial absence. Yet Everton equalised both these goals and Ian Rush's third, while John Barnes' extra-time strike was nullified by a second goal from Tony Cottee.

The 4-4 draw had a sensational sting in the tail when Anfield legend Kenny Dalglish revealed it was his last match in charge. Ironically, it would be the man who succeeded him, Graeme Souness, who ran into heart problems, because this pulsating 120 minutes had absolutely everything.

Four Liverpool goals had inspired four Everton ripostes, confirming as if confirmation were needed that the Merseyside derby remained one of football's most passionately contested fixtures.

Everton enjoyed an unhappy early 1990s, and it was the death of John Moores, the pools millionaire who had major shareholdings in both clubs over the years, that proved the catalyst for change. A dual injection of boardroom resources – courtesy of Peter Johnson, the self-made businessman whose hamper business had turned Tranmere into Merseyside's third force – and managerial talent would prove a long-overdue shock to the system.

The hapless Mike Walker, out of his depth after walking out of small-town Norwich, was replaced by a returning son of Goodison. Like Harry Catterick, he was a former centre-forward who picked up managerial experience elsewhere before heeding the call to revive faded fortunes.

The timing of Joe Royle's return to Goodison Park in November 1994 put him under immediate pressure. Not only was the team he inherited bottom of the table, but his very first game was the visit of Liverpool!

Royle had experienced the local derby no fewer than ten times as a player, and doubtless advised his men accordingly – but it was a derby debutant, Scotsman Duncan Ferguson on loan from Rangers, who emerged as the hero of the hour. Playing in Royle's central striking position, he scored – with Paul Rideout – in a 2-0 win.

He would miss the derby fixture of exactly a year later due to a jail sentence, but that game threw up two more derby heroes in flying wingers Anders Limpar and Andrei Kanchelskis. The cosmopolitan duo ensured an Everton win at Anfield for the first-time in ten years: the last had been engineered by Gary Lineker, now a TV pundit (like other derby veterans Ian St John, Andy Gray, Alan Hansen and Michael Robinson).

Yet Kanchelskis, a record signing from Manchester United, earned the description 'red hot – no, *blue* hot!' from a delighted Joe Royle after he popped two goals in at the Kop End. It was a wonderful way for the manager to celebrate his first anniversary.

And as if to prove there's no greater delight than a native Merseysider putting one over on his neighbour, Dave Watson came off the pitch with a look of ecstasy on his face. 'He's got the kind of smile,' commented Royle, 'you're going to need an operation to get rid of.' Odds were it would stay there until the return at Goodison, several months away.

The fans' forum has been the *Liverpool Echo*, whose pink sports edition on a Saturday night is the traditional soapbox for those wishing to trumpet triumphs or decry defeats. The paper first got involved in footballing matters when the teams had been drawn together in the FA Cup semi-final of 1906. Daily reports on the teams were accompanied by a competition for the best footballing poems or stories, and it was the response received that convinced them Merseyside's footballing rivalry was something that would win them readers.

And stories there are in abundance. When Gordon West was playing in front of the Kop towards the end of his reign as Everton's Number 1, he responded to some typically barbed chant by blowing them a kiss. They, in turn, presented him with a handbag!

He would surely agree with the editorial in the programme for the 63rd League meeting between the teams in October 1932. 'There are some events along life's way-sides,' they wrote, 'that never pale. And an Everton-Liverpool meeting is one of them. Today, all roads will lead to Goodison: the stage is set for yet another mighty, pulsating struggle for supremacy.'

May it always be so...

Opposite: The signing of John Barnes in 1987 paved the way for Merseyside's multi-racial derbies of today. When Kenny Dalglish agreed his transfer from Watford, he claimed that 'The fact John happens to be the first black player Liverpool have bought had not crossed my mind.'

Above: Dalglish shows the strain in less happy times. His shock decision to quit in 1991 was made after the emotion of a Mersey derby.

THE SCORE TO DATE

League	P	W	D	L	F	A
Liverpool	153	56	45	52	208	190
Everton	153	52	45	56	190	208

FA Cup	P	W	D	L	F	A
Liverpool	20	9	5	6	34	24
Everton	20	6	5	9	24	34

League Cup	P	W	D	L	F	A
Liverpool	4	2	1	1	2	1
Everton	4	1	1	2	1	2

Charity Shield	P	W	D	L	F	A
Liverpool	3	1	1	1	2	2
Everton	3	1	1	1	2	2

War Games	P	W	D	L	F	A
Liverpool	51	26	9	16	111	97
Everton	51	16	9	26	97	111

Total	P	W	D	L	F	A
Liverpool	231	94	61	76	357	314
Everton	231	76	61	94	314	357

In statistical terms, Liverpool look to have a distinct overall edge. Yet take away the war games, which in many cases weren't contested by the clubs' true players, and the picture becomes rather more interesting. The League situation, taken on its own, is a particularly close-run thing with just four wins in it.

Below: Liverpool and Everton teams join forces at the end of the 1984 Milk Cup Final, the first occasion on which the chant of 'Merseyside' was heard from both sets of supporters. Fittingly, the match was a 0-0 draw – though Liverpool won the replay at Maine Road by a single Souness goal.

2:THE GROUNDS

The most often overlooked piece of the complex jigsaw that is football in Merseyside is, perhaps, Stanley Park – the quarter-mile wide strip of public space opened in 1870 that today separates Anfield, home of Liverpool Football Club, from Goodison Park where Everton have played for the past century. If you've read the history of the fixture chapter, you'll know that Everton called Anfield home for some eight years to 1892 – but Stanley Park was in reality its very first home.

Liverpool of course, stayed put when Everton left Anfield. And though its ground had to play second fiddle to its newer rival for many years – it was Goodison that was selected to stage World Cup games in 1966 – it since has emerged as an enviable state-of-the-art stadium in its own right.

Yet there's been a price to pay: the unthinkable was to become fact in 1994 when the Kop, that most celebrated of popular ends, bowed to the Taylor Report as Anfield became an all-seater stadium.

In 1996, its capacity was 41,000 – 1,000 greater that its rival across the Park, though some 20,000 less than in its heyday. And as if to celebrate the ground's coming of age, it was chosen to be one of England's eight European Championship venues – symbolically, three decades after Goodison's taste of World Cup glory.

Liverpool has always played at Anfield, but as previously hinted Everton used several venues after forming in November 1879 as St Domingo Football Club. It was still using the south-east corner of Stanley Park, the players carrying out the goalposts from Park Lodge in nearby Mill Lane, when the club played its very first local rivals, Bootle. Success prompted a move to an enclosed ground at Priory Road in the autumn of 1883, but the club was forced to move again after just a season

Below: Goodison Park in 1950, with St Luke the Evangelist Church visible in the foreground between the Gwladys Street and Main Stands, and Stanley Park to the top right.

because its landlord, one Mr Cruitt, was annoyed by the excitement and noisiness of the fans!

Anfield became Everton's home in September 1884 – but, as described elsewhere, it was vacated in 1892 after a dispute with the landlord over rent, leaving it vacant for the newly-formed red side of the city. The annual rent for the first year was £100, Everton having been quoted £250 by landlord John Houlding for the privilege of staying put!

The first 3,000-seater Main Stand went up three years later after Liverpool had claimed the Second Division title, and its distinctive Tudor-style gable, displaying the name of the club, stood guard over Anfield's pitch until the 1970s. The Anfield Road End got its first stand in 1903, the famous Kop banking (named after the Spion Kop in South Africa, where many Merseyside soldiers perished in the Boer War) emerging three years later.

There are many Kops across the country, but the term has always been most closely associated with Anfield. Liverpool have traditionally claimed to have the first Kop (although Arsenal may dispute this) and the supporters are renowned for their fervent, yet sporting, support.

In 1907-08 came first reports of communal singing, though this wasn't from home fans but Blackburn Rovers supporters standing on the Kop!

Few delays had been brooked when Everton left Anfield and set about establishing themselves at Mere Green Fields, the new site they'd purchased for the sum of £8,000 just a few hundred yards away.

It was clearly going to be difficult to build a stadium before gate receipts had started flowing in, and it was fortunate that club member James Clement Baxter, a doctor, was in hand to provide a vital bridging loan of £1,000. Without this, the work of building a stadium from scratch could never have been completed on time.

Three stands – one covered holding 3,000 and the others 4,000 apiece – were erected by local Walton firm Kelly Brothers in time for the visit of Bolton in September 1892, less than six months after the parting of the ways. The newly-named Goodison had been christened in August by the FA's Lord Kinnaird, and such was the excitement that 12,000 fans assembled to celebrate the event.

Their enthusiasm was rewarded by Everton players who played not football but a number of different activities in an impromptu sports day. Such was the standard of the ground that it hosted the Notts County v Bolton FA Cup Final two years later and the England v Scotland fixture the following season. Though Anfield had also hosted internationals, it was clear this rival had designs on its status.

The Park End double-decker Stand was built on the south side at a cost of £13,000 in 1907, making Goodison the only ground in the country to boast such a two-tier structure (it would later, in 1971, become the first with a three-tier unit), while the Main Stand was erected on the Goodison Road side two years later. This involved the investment of £28,000 and included offices and changing rooms, while at the same time the terracing was concreted and improved at a cost of £12,000. The outlay was soon to bring its reward: the 1910 FA Cup Final Replay between Newcastle and Barnsley was staged at Goodison, while the Main Stand would endure unchanged into the 1970s.

In 1926 a double-decker stand replaced the wooden structure that had stood on the Bullens Road side, an expenditure of £30,000 being sanctioned. Trainers' dugouts, now a familiar sight, were also introduced in the 1930s: though the first to be seen in England, they were a copy of Aberdeen's innovation observed at first hand in a pre-season friendly.

The building of a new £50,000 stand on the Gwladys Street End in 1938 meant that Everton were now the only club in Britain to boast a ground with four double-decker stands. Its completion was greeted by the visit of King George VI, whose father King George V had been the first monarch to visit a League ground when he visited Goodison in 1913.

Not to be outdone, Anfield had also welcomed George V and his wife Queen Mary in 1921, the royal couple – up for the Grand National – swelling a 41,892 crowd who'd gathered to see Wolves defeat Cardiff in an FA Cup semi-final. The ground had meanwhile acquired a third stand, a barrel-roofed affair on the Kemlyn Road, while in 1928 the Kop was covered and extended to hold just under 30,000 – the largest covered end of its type in the League.

Everton's stadium suffered bomb damage during World War II, the ground having been used as a training area by the Territorial Army. It was repaired with the help of £5,000 from the War Damages Commission, and in 1948 the ground welcomed 78,299 for a Merseyside derby – still the all-time attendance record.

Goodison's Main Stand finally disappeared in 1971 – a sad day for traditionalists and football ground historians, for it had indeed been a landmark. Its replacement was no less impressive, however – a three-decker seating 10,000 spectators.

Opposite: The Shankly Gates at Anfield, bearing the famous words 'You'll Never Walk Alone'.

Below: The last Merseyside derby at Anfield before the refurbishment of the Kop turned it into an all-seater stadium.

THE GROUNDS

Also included in this £1 million development were modernised dressing rooms, a gym, treatment room, a laundry and – pre-dating football's corporate age – a restaurant. With colour TV now the norm, new floodlights were also installed along the top of the stands, Bullens Road acquiring a new roof in the process.

Other improvements were less dramatic: the entrance from Stanley Park had been built in preparation for the 1966 World Cup. Goodison hosted three matches from a group comprising Brazil, Portugal, Hungary and Bulgaria, plus the astonishing quarter-final when Portugal beat South Korea 5-3 and the West Germany v USSR semi-final.

Few problems were encountered in complying with the Taylor Report; the Gwladys Street End, Everton's own Kop, was rebuilt, covered and seated, so that by 1993 only 2,000 of Goodison's 38,500 capacity were standing places. A £1.3 million Football Trust grant permitted the development of a new stand at the Park End, making Goodison Park an all-seater venue.

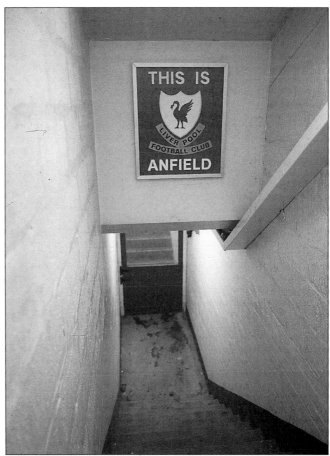

The players' tunnel (above) leading out onto the Anfield pitch (left).

The catalyst for Anfield's redevelopment was the arrival of Bill Shankly in 1959. As he laid the foundations for a club that was to dominate domestic and European football for years to come, so Liverpool upgraded their ground to mirror the on-field success. And the newly installed sign above the players' tunnel to the pitch from the dressing room, proclaiming 'This Is Anfield', would be enough to cause even the most hardened professional a few butterflies.

In 1963, a year after the club gained promotion to the top flight, the Kemlyn Road Stand was pulled down and replaced by a 7,000 all-seater stand at a cost of £350,000. Ten years later a new Main Stand was officially opened by HRH the Duke of Kent and new floodlights installed along the rooves of the side stands. These state-of-the-art £100,000 lights replaced the £12,000 system of four free-standing pylons erected in 1957, for which Everton had been invited to contest the first floodlit friendly (the hosts winning 3-2). Goodison's lights had been christened in similar manner just three weeks earlier, triggering suspicions of a behind-the-scenes race.

The role of Liverpool's greatest ever manager in helping finance those ground improvements has never been doubted. And his reign is commemorated by the Shankly Gate at the Anfield Road entrance to the car park behind the Main Stand, named in his honour and opened by his widow Nessie following his death in 1981. Across the top of the ornate iron gates read the words: 'You'll Never Walk Alone'. To the left of these gates a plaque has been erected to commemorate those supporters who lost their lives at Hillsborough in 1989: their

names are all recorded, while an eternal flame burns in their honour.

A new entrance and ticket office, which projected from the Main Stand on to the car park, was opened in August 1979. During the next close season an under-pitch heating system was laid and the paddock terrace in the Main Stand converted into an all-seater area (capacity 2,350), which meant raising part of the terracing. In May 1982 work began on adding 4,000 seats to the terraced Anfield Road End, which gave the ground a capacity of 45,000 (21,850 seats).

In the summer of 1992 (the club's centenary year) a second tier (4,604 seats) was added to the Kemlyn Road Stand, which was renamed the Centenary Stand. A car park replaced the row of houses which had to be demolished to make way for the development. The club offices are also located on this side of the ground.

Anfield's international history started as far back as 1883 when Everton were still in residence, with England beating Ireland 7-0. More recently, the ground will be remembered as host for the crucial Wales v Scotland World Cup qualifier in 1977. Kenny Dalglish, who had arrived at Liverpool only months earlier, scored for Scotland in a 2-0 win. And in late

Opposite: The Anfield memorial to the supporters who lost their lives in the tragedy at Hillsborough.

Below: The Bullens Road Stand at Goodison Park in 1985.

THE GROUNDS

1995 it was selected for the European Championship play-off between the Republic of Ireland and Holland.

Anfield had gone all-seater in 1994 when the Spion Kop was converted into a 12,400 all-seater stand. Chunks of the famous terrace were sold off to raise money for the Liverpool University Hospital. The flagpole which had for so long graced the Kop's Kemlyn Road corner was re-sited in the club forecourt. And what an important piece of history it was, having been salvaged from the *Great Eastern*, one of the world's first iron ships scrapped in Liverpool's docks towards the end of the last century.

A shared ground will clearly never happen – yet there was one notable occasion when both sides of the city reverberated as one. That was the FA Cup Fifth Round derby in March 1967, watched by over 100,000 fans. Goodison held 64,318, while over at Anfield a further 40,169 watched it at Anfield on closed circuit television making a total of 104,487.

Everton fans making the short journey across Stanley Park for the Merseyside derby have always been allocated the Anfield Road End which, since it was seated, accounts for 3,200 out of a total Anfield capacity of 41,000. Over at Goodison, Reds followers had to adjust to a new viewpoint after the last piece of Everton's redevelopment jigsaw was finally put into place in 1994-95. The opening of the 6,500-capacity Park Stand

on the site of the former visitors' terracing meant Liverpool fans were re-sited in the section of the Bullens Road Stand nearest their old haunt. A total of 1,200 in the Upper and 1,500 in the Lower tier gave them a comparable allocation to that enjoyed by their counterparts at Anfield.

Some have claimed that the atmosphere since the grounds went all-seater compares unfavourably with the days of old, even on derby day. In terms of sheer numbers, 'only' 40,818 saw the 153rd Liverpool v Everton fixture in November 1995, some 15,000 less than squeezed in for the corresponding fixture two decades earlier. Yet to put matters in perspective the clash was the best attended of the day, ahead of both Manchester United and the north London derby of Tottenham and Arsenal.

It's true the all-seated configuration has ended the swaying, communal Kop of old – yet come 2.50pm, as 'You'll Never Walk Alone' is played over the tannoy, the scarves are held aloft as ever. And the comparative ease of access means fans are less likely these days to find their neighbour relieving himself *in situ*!

The size and shape of the venues may have changed over the years, as indeed has the city in which they're situated, but some things remain immutable traditions. The Everton Toffee Lady still walks round the pitch perimeter dispensing free confectionery – 'one of the few things you can still get for free in the Premier League,' according to one local wit – while the Blues still run out to the tune of the long-defunct TV cop show *Z-Cars*.

A day out to either Merseyside ground is always an event – especially if it's a derby day. The Church of St Luke the Evangelist that pokes out almost apologetically between the Gwladys Street and Main Stands at Goodison even opens to sell modestly-priced refreshments on a matchday. Perhaps it recognises that for Liverpool and Everton fans football is up there alongside religion as a motivating and unifying force for good.

Left: Work is carried out on the lower level of the Centenary Stand at Anfield, with the all-seater Kop in the background.

Top: Blue view – the players' tunnel at Goodison Park.

13 OCTOBER 1894
FOOTBALL LEAGUE DIVISION 1

EVERTON	3
LIVERPOOL	0

The first meeting of Merseyside's two great rivals in a League game saw an estimated 44,000 people pack Goodison Park, with many more climbing to any vantage point outside to see the game. The Lord Mayor was among those present to see what the *Liverpool Echo* called 'The great football match'.

The gates were opened an hour and a quarter before kick-off, with a schoolboys' match between Liverpool and Nottingham as pre-match entertainment. Though the visitors wore white, Liverpool's schoolboys wore blue rather than red.

Newly-promoted Liverpool won the toss and elected to kick off in what was only their ninth game in the top flight: they were still seeking their first win, with four draws and four defeats to show.

The Reds had left the city for a week's intensive training while Everton stayed at home, and it looked as if the latter approach would pay off as the home side dominated early play.

After ten minutes Liverpool conceded a free-kick which was taken by left-half Billy Stewart. He found McInnes with a perfect cross, and the Number 8 wrote himself into the history books by scoring the first ever derby goal.

Yet the visitors were paying their high-flying hosts scant respect, and after one challenge from a Liverpool player goalscorer McInnes needed to be helped from the field of play. But he came back and had a hand in creating the second goal of the afternoon.

Bell took the ball from midfield and played it out to McInnes on the flank. He played it in to right-winger Latta who shot home from a tight angle to put the Blues two up.

Everton thought they had pulled another goal clear when Hartley netted with only a few minutes remaining, but the referee had spotted an infringement and the strike was disallowed.

With the light fading fast, the Blues got the goal which ended any hopes of a Liverpool comeback. Left-winger John Bell picked up the ball on the edge of the box before shooting towards goal.

Goalkeeper McCann looked to have the shot well covered until it took a cruel deflection and cannoned off a Liverpool full-back into the net.

Everton ended the season as runners-up to Sunderland, while Liverpool, for all their high hopes, were relegated having won only seven of their 30 matches. Even so, they made a better fist of the return at Anfield on 17 November, drawing 2-2 in front of a 30,000 crowd.

Although they were reportedly the better side, Liverpool could only show a goal by inside-left Doyle Hannah – one of two Scots brothers in the side – to answer Everton goals from their own Caledonian duo Bob Kelso and Alex Latta.

The visitors, however, lost their composure and conceded a last-minute penalty with which Reds captain Jimmy Ross coolly levelled the scores.

It would not be until November 1895 that hostilities would be resumed. The stage had nevertheless been set for a century of rivalry which, initially, would last until Liverpool's second relegation in 1904 and in the longer term to this day.

> '**L**iverpool had spent all last week at Hightown training for this grand match, while Everton were content to undergo their preparation at home. Kicking off at 2.15, the game was to be a very one-sided affair with the Blues running out winners by three goals to nil, much to the delight of the home crowd. Spectators had packed every part of the ground to witness this epic battle.'
> *Liverpool Daily Post*, Monday 15 October 1894

FOOTBALL LEAGUE DIVISION ONE

EVERTON	3
McInnes, Latta, Bell	
LIVERPOOL	0

Attendance: 44,000

Everton:
Cain, Adams, Parry, Boyle, Holt, Stewart, Latta, McInnes, Southworth, Hartley, J Bell.

Liverpool:
McCann, A Hannah, D McLean, McCartney, McQue, McBride, Kerr, Ross, McVean, Bradshaw, H McQueen.

17 NOVEMBER 1895

FOOTBALL LEAGUE DIVISION ONE

LIVERPOOL	2
D Hannah, Ross (*pen*)	
EVERTON	2
Kelso, Latta	

Attendance: 30,000

Liverpool:
M McQueen, A Hannah, D McLean, McCartney, McQue, J McLean, McVean, Ross, Bradshaw, D Hannah, Drummond.

Everton:
Cain, Kelso, Parry, Boyle, Holt, Stewart, Latta, McInnes, Hartley, Chadwick, J Bell.

3 OCTOBER 1896

FOOTBALL LEAGUE DIVISION ONE

EVERTON	2
Hartley, Milward	
LIVERPOOL	1
Ross	

Attendance: 45,000

Everton:
Briggs, Storrier, Arridge, Boyle, Holt, Stewart, J Bell, Taylor, Hartley, Chadwick, Milward.

Liverpool:
Storer, Goldie, Wilkie, McCartney, McQue, Holmes, McVean, Ross, Allan, Becton, Bradshaw.

21 NOVEMBER 1896

FOOTBALL LEAGUE DIVISION ONE

LIVERPOOL	0
EVERTON	0

Attendance: 30,000

Liverpool:
Storer, Goldie, Wilkie, McCartney, Neill, Holmes, McVean, Geary, Allan, Michael, Bradshaw.

Everton:
Menham, Storrier, Arridge, Boyle, Holt, Stewart, Taylor, J Bell, Cameron, Chadwick, Milward.

25 SEPTEMBER 1897

FOOTBALL LEAGUE DIVISION ONE

LIVERPOOL	**3**
Cunliffe, McQue, Becton	
EVERTON	**1**
Taylor	

Attendance: 30,000

Liverpool:
Storer, A Goldie, Wilkie, McCartney, McQue, Cleghorn, Marshall, Walker, Cunliffe, Becton, Bradshaw.

Everton:
McFarlane, Meecham, Barker, Boyle, Holt, Robertson, Taylor, Cameron, Hartley, Chadwick, J Bell.

16 OCTOBER 1897

FOOTBALL LEAGUE DIVISION ONE

EVERTON	**3**
Williams 2, L Bell	
LIVERPOOL	**0**

Attendance: 40,000

Everton:
McFarlane, Meecham, Storrier, Boyle, Holt, Robertson, Taylor, Williams, L Bell, Cameron, Divers.

Liverpool:
Storer, A Goldie, Wilkie, McCartney, Holmes, Cleghorn, Marshall, Walker, Cunliffe, Becton, Bradshaw.

24 SEPTEMBER 1898

FOOTBALL LEAGUE DIVISION ONE

EVERTON	**1**
Proudfoot	
LIVERPOOL	**2**
McCowie 2 (1 pen)	

Attendance: 45,000

Everton:
Muir, Balmer, Molyneux, Boyle, Owen, Taylor, Clarke, L Bell, Proudfoot, Kirwan, Gee.

Liverpool:
Storer, A Goldie, Dunlop, Howell, Raisbeck, W Goldie, Marshall, McCowie, Walker, Morgan, Robertson.

21 JANUARY 1899

FOOTBALL LEAGUE DIVISION ONE

LIVERPOOL	**2**
Walker, Robertson	
EVERTON	**0**

Attendance: 30,000

Liverpool:
Storer, A Goldie, Dunlop, Howell, Raisbeck, W Goldie, Cox, Walker, Allan, Morgan, Robertson,

Everton:
Muir, Balmer, Molyneux, Boyle, Taylor, Hughes, L Bell, Proudfoot, Crompton, Chadwick, Kirwan.

GREATEST GAMES

25 JANUARY 1902
FA CUP FIRST ROUND

LIVERPOOL	**2**
EVERTON	**2**

Liverpool and Everton's first meeting in the FA Cup would go to a replay before the Reds finally reached the Second Round. But there was much expectation as 25,000 people packed into Anfield to see Liverpool win the toss and play against the wind.

The home side had the better of play in the first period, Scotsman George Fleming forcing a save from Kitchen. But Everton improved the longer the half went on, with Bell in particular testing Perkins in the Liverpool goal.

Everton dangerman Sandy Young headed over from close range before Jack Sharp opened the scoring with an angled drive. Everton, encouraged, pushed forward again, and only poor finishing prevented them from going even further ahead.

But things didn't go according to plan and a rash challenge cost them the lead just before the interval, Robertson netting from the spot.

The visitors started the second half well and Taylor beat Perkins only to see his shot narrowly miss the target. Balmer was in good form at the back, keeping Liverpool at bay, while Sharp had a goal effort saved at the other end.

The tie was mostly contested in midfield, which limited the number of chances that fell to each side. Nevertheless, it was Liverpool that went ahead for the first time in the game after Cox crossed for Hunter to fire home. Everton then earned a replay when Sharp headed home a Young free-kick to level the scores.

In the replay at Goodison Liverpool attacked from the start, but it was Everton that started to assert itself, cheered on by a 20,000 crowd. Kitchen was tested by McGuigan in

an opening period played at a frantic pace.

Both goals resulted from free-kicks after sloppy defending from Everton. The first was credited to Raisbeck, though some said Balmer got the final touch. Then Wolstenholme handled and Hunter's free-kick beat Kitchen to ensure Liverpool a ticket to the next round. Unfortunately, that was where the Cup quest ended, losing 4-1 to Southampton.

Below: Alex Raisbeck arrived at Liverpool for £350 in May 1898 from Stoke. It was his free-kick that caught out the Everton defence for the first goal in the replay.

GREATEST GAMES

1 APRIL 1904
FOOTBALL LEAGUE DIVISION 1

EVERTON	5
LIVERPOOL	2

Only three players have ever scored four goals in a Merseyside derby, and Scotsman Sandy Young was the first. Both his successors, Fred Howe in 1935 and Ian Rush in 1982, have been Liverpool players. But April Fool's Day 1904 belonged to the blue side of the city as Young became the first to complete the feat and push third from bottom Liverpool further into trouble.

Matchday was also Good Friday, though it turned out to be anything but that from Liverpool's point of view. They went one down after just three minutes when Sam Wolstenholme opened the scoring with a long-range effort. Only good form from West and Dunlop in the Reds' defence prevented further goals in the first quarter of play.

Surprisingly, Liverpool then pulled level against the run of play after a Cox run at the Everton defence resulted in a cross which Robbie Robinson headed home.

Everton was much the better team, but was held at bay by some strong defending. But it was only a matter of time being another goal came. Hardman made ground down the left, centring for Young to nip in and score in typically opportunist fashion.

Cox tried to pull the strings for the beleaguered Reds in the second half and was rewarded when he stabbed the ball home during a melée. But at the other end scrappy play provided Young with Everton's third, though he needed several tries to beat Cotton as the ball rebounded crazily.

Everton looked like scoring whenever they broke forward into the Liverpool half. And when West headed sideways, Young gave Cotton no chance after receiving the ball at his feet. Worse was to come after Jack Sharp was fouled by Hughes on the edge of the

area. The resulting free-kick picked out Young, who fired home his fourth.

To make matters worse for Liverpool, Raybould blasted wide of the target after they were awarded a penalty kick right on time. It would have given the score more respectability, but Everton deserved this most emphatic of victories after the previous game that season had been drawn. They finished third, while Liverpool, 17th, were as expected relegated.

Above: Sandy Young's four-goal haul in this match wrote his name in the record books. Surprisingly, he was unable to reproduce this form with his post-Everton clubs Spurs, Manchester City and Burslem Port Vale.

23 SEPTEMBER 1899
FOOTBALL LEAGUE DIVISION ONE

LIVERPOOL	1
Robertson	
EVERTON	2
Settle, Taylor	

Attendance: 30,000

Liverpool:
Perkins, A Goldie, Dunlop, Howell, Raisbeck, W Goldie, Cox, C Wilson, Parkinson, Morgan, Robertson.

Everton:
Muir, Balmer, Molyneux, Wolstenholme, Boyle, Blythe, Taylor, J Sharp, Toman, Settle, Schofield.

20 JANUARY 1900
FOOTBALL LEAGUE DIVISION ONE

EVERTON	3
Settle 2, Blythe	
LIVERPOOL	1
Raybould	

Attendance: 30,000

Everton:
Muir, Eccles, Balmer, Wolstenholme, Blythe, Abbott, J Sharp, Taylor, Proudfoot, Settle, Gray.

Liverpool:
Perkins, A Goldie, Dunlop, Howell, Raisbeck, W Goldie, Raybould, Satterthwaite, Walker, Morgan, Robertson.

22 SEPTEMBER 1900
FOOTBALL LEAGUE DIVISION ONE

EVERTON	1
McDonald	
LIVERPOOL	1
Raybould	

Attendance: 50,000

Everton:
Muir, Balmer, Watson, Wolstenholme, Booth, Abbott, J Sharp, McDonald, Proudfoot, Settle, Turner.

Liverpool:
Perkins, J Robertson, Dunlop, Wilson, Raisbeck, W Goldie, Cox, Walker, Raybould, Satterthwaite, T Robertson.

19 JANUARY 1901
FOOTBALL LEAGUE DIVISION ONE

LIVERPOOL	1
Cox	
EVERTON	2
Taylor 2	

Attendance: 18,000

Liverpool:
Perkins, J Robertson, Dunlop, Wilson, Raisbeck, W Goldie, Cox, Walker, Raybould, McGuigan, T Robertson.

Everton:
Muir, Eccles, Crelley, Wolstenholme, Booth, Abbott, J Sharp, Taylor, Proudfoot, Settle, Turner.

33

14 SEPTEMBER 1901

FOOTBALL LEAGUE DIVISION ONE

LIVERPOOL	2
White, Raybould	
EVERTON	2
Settle, J Sharp	

Attendance: 30,000

Liverpool:
Perkins, Glover, Dunlop, Wilson, Raisbeck, Goldie, Bowen, White, Raybould, McGuigan, Cox.

Everton:
Muir, Balmer, Watson, Boyle, Booth, Abbott, J Sharp, Taylor, Proudfoot, Settle, J Bell.

11 JANUARY 1902

FOOTBALL LEAGUE DIVISION ONE

EVERTON	4
Settle 2, J Bell, Young	
LIVERPOOL	0

Attendance: 25,000

Everton:
Kitchen, Balmer, B Sharp, Wolstenholme, Booth, Abbott, J Sharp, Taylor, Young, Settle, J Bell.

Liverpool:
Marshall, Glover, Dunlop, Fleming, Raisbeck, Goldie, Cox, Walker, Raybould, McGuigan, T Robertson.

25 JANUARY 1902

FA CUP FIRST ROUND

LIVERPOOL	2
T Robertson (*pen*), Hunter	
EVERTON	2
J Sharp, Young	

Attendance: 25,000

Liverpool:
Perkins, JT Robertson, Dunlop, Wilson, Raisbeck, W Goldie, T Robertson, Hunter, McGuigan, Fleming, Cox.

Everton:
Kitchen, Balmer, Eccles, Wolstenholme, Booth, Abbott, J Sharp, Taylor, Young, Bowman, J Bell.

30 JANUARY 1902

FA CUP FIRST ROUND REPLAY

EVERTON	0
LIVERPOOL	2
Raisbeck, Hunter	

Attendance: 20,000

Everton:
Kitchen, Balmer, B Sharp, Wolstenholme, Booth, Abbott, J Sharp, Taylor, Young, Bowman, J Bell.

Liverpool:
Perkins, Dunlop, JT Robertson, Wilson, Raisbeck, W Goldie, T Robertson, Hunter, McGuigan, Davies, Cox.

GREATEST GAMES

31 MARCH 1906
FA CUP SEMI-FINAL
(played at Villa Park)

EVERTON	2
LIVERPOOL	0

Everton won the right to contest their third FA Cup Final after coming out top in the battle of the forward lines played out in front of a 37,000 crowd at Villa Park, Birmingham. Merseyside had come to the Midlands for the day, supporters of both sides mingling in the city centre before the game.

Liverpool had stayed in Tamworth overnight, but it was Everton, who travelled down on the day, who proved sharper in possession: their superior understanding would prove crucial in the second half against opponents lacking regulars Cox and Raybould.

Even so, it was Everton custodian Billy Scott who saw more of the action at his end of the pitch in the early stages than his opposite number Sam Hardy. Ulsterman Scott, who recommended his younger brother Elisha to Liverpool, showed no further favours, bringing off two spectacular saves – firstly taking the ball off the toes of Carlin when he was lining up a shot, the other diving full-length to stop Raisbeck's goalbound header. Liverpool, according to one match report, kicked hard but their distribution let them down.

Everton's Harry Makepeace was giving his forwards good service from midfield, and Sharp, Hardman and Bolton all had good games. Sandy Young wasn't on song, however, wasting many chances by wandering offside.

As mentioned, Liverpool was handicapped by the absence of left-sided players Jack Cox and Sam Raybould, their replacements Parkinson and Carlin seemingly unable to get the Reds' game going. Everton's first goal came from Abbott, a low shot from just outside the penalty area not long after left-back Crelley had recovered from being knocked out by a Liverpool drive.

Harold Hardman's second then ensured it would be Everton and not its neighbours who would go on to beat Newcastle United in the Final (Sandy Young, unimpressive on this occasion, would score the only goal of the game).

The Blues had the better of the season's League encounters as well, winning 4-2 at Goodison Park and drawing 1-1 at Anfield. Yet it was Liverpool, under manager Tom Watson, who would end up top of the League with 51 points, following up the previous term's Second Division Championship and crowning the first great season of Merseyside football.

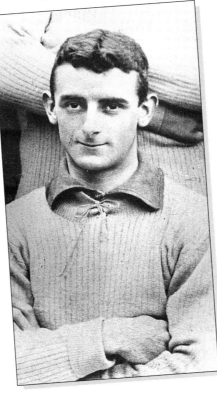

Left: Harold Hardman, scorer of Everton's second goal in the encounter, won four England caps with Everton before moving to Manchester United in 1908. He would be a United director for 50 years.

GREATEST GAMES

9 APRIL 1909
FOOTBALL LEAGUE DIVISION 1

EVERTON	**5**
LIVERPOOL	**0**

Everton recorded its biggest ever win over Liverpool to date when they crashed five past their arch-rivals. But the score wasn't a true reflection of events, with Liverpool having more than its share of chances.

It was only very poor finishing in front of goal which denied them at least one consolation strike. But at the end of the day the Reds came away with nothing, and custodian Sam Hardy must take some of the blame. He looked stale at the end of a hard season, and never lived up to many critics' rating as one of the best goalkeepers of all time. At the other end Billy Scott did all that was asked of him without really being tested.

Everton began the scoring after eight minutes. The visitors' defence lost the flight of the ball and this freed Coleman, whose weak shot was enough to beat Hardy.

Liverpool could have levelled the score, but wasted two clear-cut opportunities, Goddard blazing his shot out of the ground and then Hewitt allowing Scott to dispossess him after racing clear of the Everton defence.

Freeman added a second goal for Everton with a carbon copy of their first; then just before half-time Hewitt produced a good save from Scott after Goddard had crossed well.

Freeman wasted a good chance before White's long drive eluded Hardy, then White drove in another shot which the keeper only half-pushed clear. Turner delightedly tapped in the fourth from close range. Everton was deadly near goal, and Freeman wrapped things up near the end with his second of the game.

The Blues' previous best scores in derby games had both come at Goodison: 4-0 in 1902 and 5-2 two years later. But it was the third successive time they had managed to shut out the Reds, who would only score three more times in the next three meetings.

Above: Billy Scott, an eight-year veteran in the Goodison goal, kept a clean sheet on this occasion. His ability between the posts was a significant factor in Everton finishing second this season.

---

27 SEPTEMBER 1902

FOOTBALL LEAGUE DIVISION ONE

EVERTON	**3**
Abbott, Brearley, Young	
LIVERPOOL	**1**
Raybould (pen)	

Attendance: 40,000

Everton:
Kitchen, Henderson, W Balmer, Taylor, Booth, Abbott, J Sharp, Brearley, Young, Sheridan, J Bell.

Liverpool:
Perkins, Glover, Dunlop, Parry, Raisbeck, Goldie, Goddard, Livingstone, Raybould, Morris, Cox.

---

10 APRIL 1903

FOOTBALL LEAGUE DIVISION ONE

LIVERPOOL	**0**
EVERTON	**0**

Attendance: 28,000

Liverpool:
Platt, Glover, Dunlop, Parry, Raisbeck, Goldie, Goddard, Livingstone, Raybould, Chadwick, Cox.

Everton:
Kitchen, W Balmer, Crelley, Wolstenholme, Booth, Abbott, J Sharp, Taylor, Young, Settle, J Bell.

---

10 OCTOBER 1903

FOOTBALL LEAGUE DIVISION ONE

LIVERPOOL	**2**
Morris 2	
EVERTON	**2**
Sheridan 2	

Attendance: 30,000

Liverpool:
Platt, J McLean, Fleming, Parry, Raisbeck, Hughes, Goddard, Buck, Parkinson, Morris, Cox.

Everton:
Kitchen, Henderson, Crelley, Wolstenholme, Booth, Abbott, Taylor, McDermott, Young, Sheridan, Hardman.

---

1 APRIL 1904

FOOTBALL LEAGUE DIVISION ONE

EVERTON	**5**
Young 4, Wolstenholme	
LIVERPOOL	**2**
Robinson, Cox	

Attendance: 40,000

Everton:
Kitchen, W Balmer, Crelley, Wolstenholme, Booth, Abbott, J Sharp, Taylor, Young, McDermott, Hardman.

Liverpool:
Cotton, West, Dunlop, Parry, Raisbeck, Hughes, Goddard, Robinson, Raybould, J Hewitt, Cox.

2 FEBRUARY 1905

FA CUP FIRST ROUND

LIVERPOOL	1
Parkinson

EVERTON	1
Makepeace

Attendance: 28,000

Liverpool:
Doig, West, Dunlop, Parry, Raisbeck, Fleming, Goddard, Robinson, Parkinson, Raybould, Cox.

Everton:
Roose, R Balmer, Crelley, Makepeace, Taylor, Abbott, J Sharp, McDermott, Young, Settle, Hardman.

8 FEBRUARY 1905

FA CUP FIRST ROUND REPLAY

EVERTON	2
Hardman, McDermott

LIVERPOOL	1
Goddard

Attendance: 40,000

Everton:
Roose, R Balmer, Crelley, Makepeace, Taylor, Abbott, J Sharp, McDermott, Young, Settle, Hardman.

Liverpool:
Doig, West, Dunlop, Parry, Raisbeck, Fleming, Goddard, Carlin, Parkinson, Raybould, Cox.

30 SEPTEMBER 1905

FOOTBALL LEAGUE DIVISION ONE

EVERTON	4
Abbott, Hardman, Settle, J Sharp

LIVERPOOL	2
Hewitt, Goddard

Attendance: 40,000

Everton:
Scott, R Balmer, Crelley, Makepeace, Taylor, Abbott, J Sharp, McDermott, Young, Settle, Hardman.

Liverpool:
Doig, West, Murray, Parry, Raisbeck, Bradley, Goddard, Robinson, Hewitt, Raybould, Cox.

31 MARCH 1906

FA CUP SEMI-FINAL
(played at Villa Park)

EVERTON	2
Abbott, Hardman

LIVERPOOL	0

Attendance: 37,000

Everton:
Scott, R Balmer, Crelley, Makepeace, Taylor, Abbott, J Sharp, Bolton, Young, Settle, Hardman.

Liverpool:
Hardy, West, Dunlop, Parry, Raisbeck, Bradley, Goddard, Robinson, Parkinson, Carlin, Hewitt.

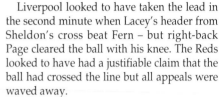

GREATEST GAMES

20 DECEMBER 1919
FOOTBALL LEAGUE DIVISION 1

EVERTON	0
LIVERPOOL	0

The first meeting of the Merseyside giants after World War I ended goalless, and it was only the fifth time in the history of the fixture that these two sides had failed to score.

Liverpool, who looked the better side, did everything but beat Fern in the Everton goal. The Reds were quicker to the ball, particularly in the first period, while their steadiness in defence saw them well on top. It wasn't until they got into the final third of the field that they looked short of ideas.

Everton did raise its game towards the closing stages, but the visitors came through unscathed to claim a valuable point in their climb to fourth in the table. The Blues would only just avoid relegation by two points, ending the campaign in 16th place.

Liverpool looked to have taken the lead in the second minute when Lacey's header from Sheldon's cross beat Fern – but right-back Page cleared the ball with his knee. The Reds looked to have had a justifiable claim that the ball had crossed the line but all appeals were waved away.

Everton's best chance fell to Clennell, but his volley produced a good save from Campbell. Then the visitors hit back, Lacey linked up well with Sheldon and forced one of several fine saves from Fern.

Liverpool were hindered at the start of the second half when centre-forward Chambers picked up an injury. With substitutes as yet unheard-of, he was switched to outside-right with Lacey coming into the middle, but Chambers was eventually obliged to come off with 12 minutes left.

Liverpool redoubled its efforts to break the deadlock despite its depleted ranks, and Page was again needed to clear off the line after Pearson had hooked the ball past Fern from close range.

Jones and Chedgzoy looked ill-paired in a below-par home performance. Left-wing duo Clennell and Harrison were unusually subdued, while centre-forward Kirsopp lacked leadership skills. Even so, Chedgzoy looked to step up the tempo for Everton late on and forced a good save from Campbell, but the game still ended goalless.

Had Liverpool not been handicapped by losing Chambers they could well have broken the deadlock. But dangerman Lacey seemed a lot quieter when he was moved into the centre, much to struggling Everton's relief.

Left: Tom Fern proved himself a worthy successor to Billy Scott with performances such as this clean sheet. His goalkeeping had helped Everton to the Championship in 1915, and his career at Goodison lasted until 1924.

7 OCTOBER 1922
FOOTBALL LEAGUE DIVISION 1

LIVERPOOL	**5**
EVERTON	**1**

Former shipyard worker Harry Chambers wrote himself into the history books when he became the first Liverpool player to score a hat-trick against Everton. This was the first occasion five goals had been scored by the Reds in the 28 years Merseyside's big two had been meeting in League combat.

Chambers had scored a brace two years before, and this time around went one better as Liverpool won at home against the team from across Stanley Park for only the fifth time. Even more creditable was the fact that this was their third game in eight days following an FA Cup replay in midweek.

The Reds started strongly with Johnson heading Hopkin's cross onto the top of the net. Fern was handed an early test by Chambers, but saved well from the Liverpool forward. At the other end Scott received a sharp reminder that there were two teams on the pitch, making a good save from Fleetwood's long-range effort.

Johnson saw a golden chance go begging when a Forshaw cross was dropped at his feet two yards out, but his shot was cleared. Everton immediately broke away and some uncertain Liverpool defending presented Williams with the chance to score.

Scott was on his toes to stop Forbes after McKinlay's misplaced back-pass let him in. Liverpool pulled level when Fred Hopkin, who looked offside, won a corner which he took himself. Chambers met the flag kick to score with his head.

A fierce drive from McNab put Liverpool ahead before Johnson set up a one-two between Chambers and Lacey, the former scoring. Two minutes later Chambers completed his hat-trick with a curling shot. Fern then failed to collect a cross, allowing birthday boy Bromilow to score a fifth.

Bromilow and Hart were later reduced to passengers through injury, while Williams brought a wonderful save from Scott near the end.

Liverpool would build upon this display to win the title by six clear points from Sunderland, new manager Matt McQueen

having taken over from David Ashworth part-way through the season. Their rivals, still managed by a committee, recovered to finish fifth despite losing the return game, played a week later, by a single goal.

Opponents Sam Chedgzoy (Everton, above) and Harry Chambers (Liverpool, right) enjoyed differing fortunes in this derby fixture. Little wonder Chambers, born in Newcastle, rejoiced in the nickname of 'Smiler' – he scored a hat-trick.

13 APRIL 1906
FOOTBALL LEAGUE DIVISION ONE

LIVERPOOL	**1**
West (pen)	
EVERTON	**1**
Taylor	

Attendance: 33,000

Liverpool:
Hardy, West, Chorlton, Parry, Raisbeck, Bradley, Goddard, Carlin, Hewitt, Raybould, Parkinson.

Everton:
Scott, W Balmer, R Balmer, Black, Taylor, Abbott, J Sharp, Bolton, Young, Cook, Hardman.

29 SEPTEMBER 1906
FOOTBALL LEAGUE DIVISION ONE

LIVERPOOL	**1**
Parkinson	
EVERTON	**2**
Young 2	

Attendance: 40,000

Liverpool:
Hardy, Saul, Dunlop, Robinson, Raisbeck, Bradley, Goddard, Parkinson, Hewitt, Carlin, Cox.

Everton:
Scott, W Balmer, Crelley, Makepeace, Taylor, Abbott, J Sharp, Bolton, Young, G Wilson, Hardman.

29 MARCH 1907
FOOTBALL LEAGUE DIVISION ONE

EVERTON	**0**
LIVERPOOL	**0**

Attendance: 45,000

Everton:
Scott, W Balmer, R Balmer, Makepeace, Taylor, Abbott, J Sharp, Settle, Young, G Wilson, Hardman.

Liverpool:
Hardy, Saul, Dunlop, Parry, Raisbeck, Bradley, Goddard, Robinson, Raybould, Hewitt, Cox.

5 OCTOBER 1907
FOOTBALL LEAGUE DIVISION ONE

EVERTON	**2**
Makepeace, Settle	
LIVERPOOL	**4**
J Hewitt, Raisbeck, Cox, C Hewitt	

Attendance: 40,000

Everton:
Scott, W Balmer, R Balmer, Makepeace, Taylor, Abbott, J Sharp, Bolton, Young, Settle, Hardman.

Liverpool:
Hardy, West, Saul, Chorlton, Raisbeck, Bradley, Goddard, C Hewitt, J Hewitt, Robinson, Cox.

17 APRIL 1908

FOOTBALL LEAGUE DIVISION ONE

LIVERPOOL	0
EVERTON	0

Attendance: 35,000

Liverpool:
Hardy, West, Rogers, Parry, Raisbeck, Bradley, Goddard, McPherson, J Hewitt, Orr, Cox.

Everton:
Scott, R Balmer, Maconnachie, Makepeace, Taylor, Adamson, Couper, Coleman, Freeman, Young, Donnachie.

3 OCTOBER 1908

FOOTBALL LEAGUE DIVISION ONE

LIVERPOOL	0
EVERTON	1
Barlow	

Attendance: 40,000

Liverpool:
Hardy, Saul, West, Chorlton, Harrop, Bradley, Goddard, Parkinson, Hewitt, Orr, Bowyer.

Everton:
William Scott, R Balmer, Maconnachie, Harris, Taylor, Makepeace, J Sharp, Coleman, Freeman, Young, Barlow.

9 APRIL 1909

FOOTBALL LEAGUE DIVISION ONE

EVERTON	5
Coleman, Freeman 2, White, Turner	
LIVERPOOL	0

Attendance: 45,000

Everton:
William Scott, R Balmer, Maconnachie, Harris, Taylor, Makepeace, J Sharp, Coleman, Freeman, White, Turner.

Liverpool:
Hardy, Crawford, Chorlton, Harrop, Raisbeck, Bradley, Goddard, Robinson, Hewitt, Orr, Uren.

2 OCTOBER 1909

FOOTBALL LEAGUE DIVISION ONE

EVERTON	2
Coleman, Freeman	
LIVERPOOL	3
Goddard, Stewart, Parkinson	

Attendance: 45,000

Everton:
William Scott, R Balmer, Maconnachie, Harris, Clifford, Makepeace, J Sharp, Coleman, Freeman, Young, Turner.

Liverpool:
Hardy, Chorlton, Crawford, Robinson, Harrop, Bradley, Goddard, Stewart, Parkinson, Orr, McDonald.

GREATEST GAMES

6 FEBRUARY 1926
FOOTBALL LEAGUE DIVISION 1

EVERTON	3
LIVERPOOL	3

For the second time in the season the Merseyside derby threw up a six-goal thriller. Liverpool had won the first game at Anfield in September 5-1 after a Forshaw hat-trick. He'd also notched three in the game before that, a 5-0 win against Manchester United, so was clearly the man in form: given their scoring touch and Forshaw's 27 League goals in 32 games, it was a surprise that Liverpool could only finish seventh.

Yet as the fog rolled off the Mersey, Everton took them all the way in what was a Titanic struggle. With both sides out of the FA Cup, they were able to give 100 per cent to this game. A heavy pitch took everything possible out of both sets of players.

Everton's Northern Ireland international Bobby Irvine opened the scoring after just two minutes, but Cyril Oxley levelled.

Forshaw, still on cloud nine after his earlier hat-trick, added a second to give his side the lead again. But Chedgzoy cut in from the wing to put Everton back in the game with a shot that beat Scott hands down. Everton wasn't finished, however, and Troup's cross picked out Dean at the far post. His header left Hardy standing.

Liverpool hit straight back and inevitably it was Forshaw who snatched them a share of the points. A cross from the wing found him unmarked in the area and his header hit the back of the net after taking a defection.

Everton looked the better of the two sides going forward with Dean at his brilliant best. But the visitors looked the better team overall and defended stoutly despite letting in three goals.

Liverpool keeper Elisha Scott enjoyed a private duel with his close friend Dean, showing good form as the Everton Number 9 threatened to run riot, while left-back McKinlay was outstanding, particularly in the second half.

Above: Forfar-born winger Alec Troup, whose cross created Everton's final equaliser for Dean, was the architect of many goals for the famous centre-forward. Despite measuring only five foot five inches, his value to the team was considerable.

GREATEST GAMES

25 FEBRUARY 1928
FOOTBALL LEAGUE DIVISION 1

LIVERPOOL	**3**
EVERTON	**3**

Dixie Dean marked his 100th appearance for the Blues with a well-taken hat-trick. In time, he would set a record of 34 career hat-tricks which still stands today.

He pulled Everton level after 17 minutes with a strong accurate shot after Riley had failed to hold Weldon's effort. Liverpool had taken the lead after only five minutes when defenders Kelly and O'Donnell were caught pushing too far forward. Hopkin took advantage to shoot home from the left-hand side of the area.

Dean notched his second five minutes before half-time, Weldon trapping the ball in midfield before playing it forward for the striker to run on to. He completed his hat-trick on the hour when O'Donnell took the ball off Liverpool striker Race's toe. He found right-winger Ted Critchley, whose cross was headed home with Riley off his line.

The game was a real nailbiter, with the result in doubt until the final whistle. An injury to right-back Lucas forced Liverpool into a reshuffle: he moved to outside-right, Edmed to centre-forward, Chambers to centre-half and Jackson into the vacant full-back slot.

Race forced a fine fingertip save from Hardy, before the home side pulled one back in the 73rd minute through Bromilow. Lucas nearly equalised despite his leg injury before the Reds finally salvaged a point when McKinlay hit a long free-kick beyond the Everton defence.

Hardy came and failed to collect: the ball looked to have crossed the line before Hodgson got the final touch to ensure the draw.

Everton stayed top of the League on goal difference, and would still be there at the end of the season. And the man they chiefly had to thank was Dean, who set his never-to-be-beaten record of 60 League goals in 39 League games. Liverpool, whose manager Matt McQueen had retired through ill-health ten days before this match was played, finished just one point clear of relegation in 16th place.

While full-back Tommy Lucas (far right) would hold few happy memories of this game, having sustained an injury, hat-trick man Dixie Dean (right) would add the newspaper cutting to his growing collection.

"DIXIE" DEAN

PLAYER'S CIGARETTES.

T. LUCAS.

---

12 FEBRUARY 1910

FOOTBALL LEAGUE DIVISION ONE

LIVERPOOL	**0**
EVERTON	**1**
Freeman	

Attendance: 40,000

Liverpool:
Beeby, Chorlton, Rogers, Robinson, Harrop, Bradley, Goddard, Stewart, Parkinson, Orr, McDonald.

Everton:
Walter Scott, Clifford, Maconnachie, Allan, Taylor, Makepeace, J Sharp, White, Freeman, Young, Barlow.

1 OCTOBER 1910

FOOTBALL LEAGUE DIVISION ONE

LIVERPOOL	**0**
EVERTON	**2**
Makepeace, A Young	

Attendance: 40,000

Liverpool:
Beeby, Longworth, Chorlton, Robinson, Peake, McConnell, Goddard, Brough, Parkinson, Gilligan, McDonald.

Everton:
William Scott, R Balmer, Maconnachie, Harris, R Young, Makepeace, Berry, Gourlay, Freeman, A Young, Turner.

27 DECEMBER 1910

FOOTBALL LEAGUE DIVISION ONE

EVERTON	**0**
LIVERPOOL	**1**
Parkinson	

Attendance: 51,000

Everton:
William Scott, Stevenson, R Balmer, Harris, R Young, Makepeace, Berry, Lacey, A Young, Gourlay, Beare.

Liverpool:
Hardy, Longworth, Crawford, Robinson, Harrop, McConnell, Goddard, Stewart, Parkinson, Bowyer, Uren.

4 FEBRUARY 1911

FA CUP SECOND ROUND

EVERTON	**2**
A Young 2	
LIVERPOOL	**1**
Parkinson	

Attendance: 50,000

Everton:
William Scott, Stevenson, Maconnachie, Harris, R Young, Makepeace, Lacey, Gourlay, Magner, A Young, Beare.

Liverpool:
Hardy, Longworth, Crawford, Robinson, Harrop, McConnell, Goddard, Stewart, Parkinson, Orr, Uren.

16 SEPTEMBER 1911

FOOTBALL LEAGUE DIVISION ONE

EVERTON	2
Beare, Gourlay	
LIVERPOOL	1
Parkinson	

Attendance: 40,000

Everton:
William Scott, Stevenson, Holbem, Harris, R Young, Makepeace, Beare, Jefferis, Jordan, Gourlay, Lacey.

Liverpool:
Hardy, Longworth, Crawford, Robinson, Lowe, McConnell, Goddard, Gilligan, Parkinson, Orr, Uren.

20 JANUARY 1912

FOOTBALL LEAGUE DIVISION ONE

LIVERPOOL	1
Gilligan	
EVERTON	3
Beare, T Browell, Jefferis	

Attendance: 35,000

Liverpool:
Hardy, Longworth, Pursell, Robinson, Peake, Lowe, Goddard, Bovill, Gilligan, Stewart, Uren.

Everton:
William Scott, Stevenson, Maconnachie, Harris, Fleetwood, Makepeace, Beare, Jefferis, T Browell, Bradshaw, Davidson.

5 OCTOBER 1912

FOOTBALL LEAGUE DIVISION ONE

LIVERPOOL	0
EVERTON	2
T Browell, Gault	

Attendance: 46,000

Liverpool:
Campbell, Longworth, Pursell, Lowe, Ferguson, McKinlay, Goddard, Stewart, Miller, Parkinson, Lacey.

Everton:
Caldwell, Stevenson, Holbem, Harris, Fleetwood, Makepeace, Beare, Gault, T Browell, Bradshaw, Davidson.

8 FEBRUARY 1913

FOOTBALL LEAGUE DIVISION ONE

EVERTON	0
LIVERPOOL	2
Parkinson 2	

Attendance: 40,000

Everton:
Caldwell, Holbem, Maconnachie, Harris, Fleetwood, Makepeace, Beare, Jefferis, Houston, T Browell, Davidson.

Liverpool:
Campbell, Longworth, Crawford, Lowe, Ferguson, Peake, Goddard, Metcalfe, Miller, Parkinson, Lacey.

GREATEST GAMES
9 JANUARY 1932
FA CUP THIRD ROUND

EVERTON	1
LIVERPOOL	2

Liverpool recovered from being a goal down in 60 seconds to leave Goodison Park with a ticket to the Fourth Round of the Cup. Yet it was the home side who were the players in form, on their way to a second Championship in consecutive years – this time the First Division, after bouncing back from relegation to the Second in the best way possible.

An early goal seemed to confirm a gap in class against a side that would finish just tenth. But a match which nearly became a foregone conclusion ended as one of the most entertaining seen all season.

Everton won the toss and played with the wind at their backs. When Liverpool pivot Bradshaw hesitated, Dixie Dean – a hat-trick hero last time the teams met – seized on the opportunity.

But Liverpool refused to crumble, and their form improved as the game went on. Although Critchley on Everton's right used his pace against McDougall to good effect, his fellow forwards were unable to take advantage of the chances presented. And when they did hit the target they found Elisha Scott, in the Liverpool goal, in good form despite his initial task of picking the ball out of the net.

It wasn't until the end of the half that Liverpool enforced its superiority. Five minutes before the interval McRorie took a free-kick 40 yards out. Everton failed to clear and Gordon Gunson, the Reds' best forward, scored with a neat shot.

Liverpool started the second half in much the same way as it ended the first but even with a light shower the high standard of entertainment was maintained. Jackson at the back kept his team in the game with some clever anticipation and sure dealing with Everton attacks.

Bradshaw recovered from his early mistake to keep Dean quiet, but the rest of the Everton forwards weren't enjoying the best of form. Toffees left-winger Stein missed an open goal and Dean slipped while lining up a shot. The Liverpool attack, on the other hand, was now into its stride with balding inside-left Dave Wright at the centre of most things created.

Liverpool then broke away four minutes from time, Gunson and Wright combining to set up the winner for Gordon Hodgson. Sadly for the Reds, they'd meet their match against Chelsea in the Sixth Round after further wins against Chesterfield and Grimsby, yet the warm glow of a derby win remained.

Left: South-African born of English parents, Gordon Hodgson notched the winner in this Cup tie from the inside-right position.

GREATEST GAMES

11 FEBRUARY 1933
FOOTBALL LEAGUE DIVISION 1

LIVERPOOL	**7**
EVERTON	**4**

Liverpool pulled a major surprise in this game when it plumped for youth against its local rivals. It was expected that experienced players would have been picked on the big occasion, but manager George Patterson's gamble paid dividends as the speed of the youngsters proved to be Everton's undoing in a game of non-stop football.

Yet it was a tried and tested derby marksman, Dixie Dean, who opened the scoring after eight minutes, seizing upon a miskick by home centre-half Bradshaw to score.

The equaliser came from winger Harold Barton, who outstripped the Everton defence for speed before guiding the ball over Sagar's head. Liverpool then went ahead after good work by Roberts: his pass released Hanson who finished coolly, despite looking offside.

The Reds were by now well on top and swept though the Everton defence almost at will. Full-backs Cresswell and Cook were caught out many times by the swiftness of the Liverpool forwards, and it was the former who inadvertently helped on a free-kick to present Morrison with the chance for Liverpool's third just before half-time.

Everton then pulled a goal back, Geldard twice beating Jackson and, with the choice of any one of three players to pass to, picked out Johnson. But Liverpool was still rampant and added two more through Taylor and Barton.

Everton was still not finished, and skipper Dean set a fine example to his team-mates when, on 75 minutes, he nodded home his 16th derby goal after Stein's corner had picked him out. There were three more goals, the first for Liverpool from Roberts. Team-mate Barton completed his hat-trick a few minutes from the end although Stein scored a fourth for the Blues at the death.

Everton had won the earlier match 3-1 with a double strike from Dean, evening up the local honours, but it would prove an undistinguished season in League terms for Liverpool and Everton who, divided by two points, finished 14th and 11th respectively. Goodison fans had the consolation of a Cup victory against Manchester City – and no prizes for guessing who scored their first goal in a 3-0 win...

Outside-right Harold Barton (left) and left-back Warney Cresswell (far left) were in direct opposition in this memorable match. It's clear who came out on top, Liverpool's winger recording a hat-trick.

---

20 SEPTEMBER 1913

FOOTBALL LEAGUE DIVISION ONE

EVERTON	**1**
Wareing	
LIVERPOOL	**2**
Lacey 2	

Attendance: 40,000

Everton:
Mitchell, Stevenson, Maconnachie, Harris, Wareing, Grenyer, Beare, Jefferis, T Browell, Bradshaw, Harrison.

Liverpool:
Campbell, Speakman, Crawford, Fairfoul, Lowe, Ferguson, Goddard, Stewart, Miller, Gracie, Lacey.

17 JANUARY 1914

FOOTBALL LEAGUE DIVISION ONE

LIVERPOOL	**1**
Metcalfe	
EVERTON	**2**
Parker 2	

Attendance: 35,000

Liverpool:
Campbell, Longworth, Crawford, Fairfoul, Lowe, Ferguson, Sheldon, Dawson, Metcalfe, Gracie, Lacey.

Everton:
Fern, Thompson, Maconnachie, Harris, Fleetwood, Makepeace, Palmer, Jefferis, Parker, Bradshaw, Harrison.

3 OCTOBER 1914

FOOTBALL LEAGUE DIVISION ONE

LIVERPOOL	**0**
EVERTON	**5**
Parker 3, Clennell 2	

Attendance: 32,000

Liverpool:
Campbell, Longworth, Pursell, Bratley, Fairfoul, Ferguson, Sheldon, Metcalfe, Nicholl, McKinlay, Lacey.

Everton:
Fern, Thompson, Maconnachie, Fleetwood, Galt, Makepeace, Chedgzoy, Jefferis, Parker, Clennell, Palmer.

6 FEBRUARY 1915

FOOTBALL LEAGUE DIVISION ONE

EVERTON	**1**
Clennell	
LIVERPOOL	**3**
Sheldon, Nicholl, Pagnam	

Attendance: 30,000

Everton:
Fern, Thompson, Maconnachie, Fleetwood, Galt, Makepeace, Chedgzoy, Kirsopp, Parker, Clennell, Palmer.

Liverpool:
E Scott, Longworth, Pursell, Lacey, Lowe, McKinlay, Sheldon, Banks, Pagnam, Miller, Nicholl.

20 DECEMBER 1919

FOOTBALL LEAGUE DIVISION ONE

EVERTON	0
LIVERPOOL	0

Attendance: 40,000

Everton:
Fern, Page, Weller, Brown, Fleetwood, Grenyer, Jones, Chedgzoy, Kirsopp, Clennell, Harrison.

Liverpool:
Campbell, Longworth, Bamber, Bromilow, W Wadsworth, McKinlay, Sheldon, Lacey, Chambers, Lewis, Pearson.

27 DECEMBER 1919

FOOTBALL LEAGUE DIVISION ONE

LIVERPOOL	3

Lewis, T Miller 2

EVERTON	1

Parker

Attendance: 48,000

Liverpool:
Campbell, Longworth, Pursell, Bamber, W Wadsworth, McKinlay, Sheldon, Lacey, T Miller, Lewis, H Wadsworth.

Everton:
Fern, Thompson, Weller, Brown, Wareing, Grenyer, Chedgzoy, Jefferis, Parker, Rigsby, Donnachie.

23 OCTOBER 1920

FOOTBALL LEAGUE DIVISION ONE

LIVERPOOL	1

Forshaw

EVERTON	0

Attendance: 50,000

Liverpool:
McNaughton, Lucas, McKinlay, Bamber, W Wadsworth, Bromilow, Sheldon, Forshaw, Johnson, Chambers, H Wadsworth.

Everton:
Fern, Thompson, McDonald, Fleetwood, Brewster, Grenyer, Jones, Kirsopp, Peacock, Reid, Harrison.

30 OCTOBER 1920

FOOTBALL LEAGUE DIVISION ONE

EVERTON	0
LIVERPOOL	3

Johnson, Chambers 2

Attendance: 55,000

Everton:
Fern, Downs, McDonald, Fleetwood, Brewster, Grenyer, Chedgzoy, Crossley, Peacock, Reid, Harrison.

Liverpool:
Scott, Longworth, McKinlay, Lacey, W Wadsworth, Bromilow, Sheldon, Forshaw, Johnson, Chambers, H Wadsworth.

GREATEST GAMES

7 SEPTEMBER 1935
FOOTBALL LEAGUE DIVISION 1

LIVERPOOL	6
EVERTON	0

This 6-0 scoreline remains the biggest margin of victory between Liverpool and Everton in derby history. The esteemed Ted Sagar in the Blues' goal had never seen anything like it – anything, that is, apart from the 7-4 win three years earlier!

Yet Everton started as if it intended to wipe the floor with its neighbours. It was only the third game of the season, and Dixie Dean must have fancied his chances after opening his account in a 4-0 opening-day win against Derby. But Liverpool was no easy meat, as Fred Howe proved on the quarter-hour with a glancing header from Carr's clever cross. Gordon Hodgson's snap shot just before the 30-minute mark made it two, and the same player rifled in a third five minutes or so later.

Howe had scored a fourth just before the break, and from then on Liverpool were playing exhibition stuff against a demoralised enemy. Everton fans could – and did – point to two unfortunate injures, a chipped bone in the toe and a groin strain suffered by Dean and Williams respectively, but by the time these were sustained the match was already over as anything but a spectacle.

Howe hadn't given up hope of his hat-trick, however, and doubled his tally in the last four minutes to accelerate the departure of the visiting supporters who had already abandoned the Anfield Road End. His four goals represented a Liverpool record in derby matches, and equalled Sandy Young's quartet in 1904.

The Reds then embarked on a scoring spree that saw them score 20 goals in four home matches with just two conceded. Yet the very next result to this was a 0-6 reverse at Maine Road, and this oscillating form cost manager George Patterson his job at the end of a season when they finished 19th. Everton, who drew the January return, could do only three places better.

Both Everton's Cliff Britton (right) and Reds full-back Ernie Blenkinsop (top) won international honours for England in the 1930s, though both were in opposition on this occasion.

GREATEST GAMES

25 MARCH 1950
FA CUP SEMI-FINAL
(Played At Maine Road)

EVERTON	0
LIVERPOOL	2

Despite dominating British football for many years, it wasn't until the mid 1980s that Liverpool reached the FA Cup Final on a regular basis. The second time it did so was in 1950, 36 years after its first appearance, and on this occasion fate decreed that its near neighbours should be the final hurdle between the Reds and a Wembley date with Arsenal.

There had been much talk about an all-Merseyside final, but this match – played at neutral Maine Road – was the nearest the city would get for another two decades. And it was Everton that had started most promisingly, with forwards Fielding and Wainwright staunchly supported by their wing-half-backs. And for a time it looked as if Liverpool would stumble at the semi-final stage once again.

Yet the Blues failed to turn their domination into goals, lacking a centre-forward who was able to finish. Future manager Harry Catterick was wearing the Number 9 shirt, but did not make it onto the scoresheet.

The Mersey tide turned when, after 25 minutes, Fagan crossed from the right: Stubbins' header beat goalkeeper Burnett, only for Moore to clear off the goalline. This close shave seemed to jolt Everton into life, and they retaliated immediately at the other end of the pitch. Fielding and Wainwright set up a good chance for Eglington, but he shot wide of the target.

Five minutes later Liverpool was ahead. Payne's centre was punched clear by Burnett under pressure from Liddell, but Bob Paisley – who'd moved up from his regular left-half position, a piece of opportunism that later earned him a flea in his ear from manager George Kay – seized upon the opportunity and lobbed the ball over Burnett's head into the net.

Everton again tried to hit back, and forced three corners in as many minutes but found they had nothing to show for their efforts. Then after 62 minutes Liverpool came again. Baron rode a strong tackle before flicking the ball towards goal, and left-half Farrell unaccountably tried to play a short ball out of defence.

In stepped Liddell, quick as a flash, to intercept – and, with a left-foot shot, found the net via the inside of the far post. This ended any hopes Everton had of reaching Wembley, leaving the Manchester stage to Liverpool and its exultant supporters. Sadly, however, its Wembley quest would end in tears with a 0-2 reverse.

Left: Such was the mastery of Scots winger Billy Liddell, who scored in this encounter, that the press often christened his club 'Liddellpool'.

6 OCTOBER 1923	
FOOTBALL LEAGUE DIVISION ONE	
EVERTON Chadwick	1
LIVERPOOL	0
Attendance: 51,000	

Everton:
Fern, McDonald, Livingstone, Brown, McBain, Hart, Chedgzoy, Irvine, Cock, Chadwick, Troup.

Liverpool:
Scott, Parry, McKinlay, McNab, W Wadsworth, Pratt, Lacey, Forshaw, Walsh, Chambers, Hopkin.

13 OCTOBER 1923	
FOOTBALL LEAGUE DIVISION ONE	
LIVERPOOL Walsh	1
EVERTON Chedgzoy, Cock	2
Attendance: 50,000	

Liverpool:
Scott, Lucas, McKinlay, McNab, W Wadsworth, Pratt, H Wadsworth, Forshaw, Walsh, Chambers, Hopkin.

Everton:
Fern, McDonald, Livingstone, Brown, McBain, Hart, Chedgzoy, Irvine, Cock, Chadwick, Troup.

4 OCTOBER 1924	
FOOTBALL LEAGUE DIVISION ONE	
EVERTON	0
LIVERPOOL Rawlings	1
Attendance: 53,000	

Everton:
Harland, Raitt, Livingstone, Brown, McBain, Hart, Chedgzoy, Irvine, Cock, Chadwick, Troup.

Liverpool:
E Scott, Lucas, McKinlay, McNab, W Wadsworth, Bromilow, Rawlings, Forshaw, Johnson, Shone, Lawson.

7 FEBRUARY 1925	
FOOTBALL LEAGUE DIVISION ONE	
LIVERPOOL Shone, Hopkin, Chambers	3
EVERTON Chadwick	1
Attendance: 56,000	

Liverpool:
E Scott, Lucas, McKinlay, McNab, W Wadsworth, Pratt, Rawlings, Chambers, Johnson, Shone, Hopkin.

Everton:
Harland, Raitt, McDonald, Brown, McBain, Reid, Chedgzoy, Irvine, Cock, Chadwick, Troup.

GREATEST GAMES

29 JANUARY 1955
FA CUP FOURTH ROUND

EVERTON	**0**
LIVERPOOL	**4**

Second Division Liverpool brushed aside its fancied local rivals in clinical fashion to reach the Fifth Round of the FA Cup. Everton, currently the only Merseyside team in the top division, had been many people's tip to lift the trophy at Wembley in May: Liverpool wasn't given a hope.

Yet it was the Reds who settled after withstanding early pressure and took the lead after just 17 minutes. Geoff Twentyman's free-kick found Jackson, whose cross picked out Billy Liddell: the wonder winger controlled the ball with his chest before scoring.

In contrast to their sluggish hosts, Liverpool was quick in the tackle and direct with its play. Liddell had a fine game, giving Jones the roasting of his life with his fellow wide-man Brian Jackson having the better of Lello and Rankin.

The Blues played little good football, lacking co-ordination and being guilty of over-elaboration: Dave Hickson, the critics' tip as a potential matchwinner, was marked out of the game by Laurie Hughes. Twentyman looked the best defender on view, with only left-winger Eglington posing the Liverpool defence any problems.

In the 29th minute Liverpool went further ahead when Twentyman put in another free-kick. Liddell and Anderson both missed it, but Alan A'Court had his wits about him and ran on to beat O'Neill from close range. The third goal was the result of an error by O'Neill when the Everton keeper failed to hold Jackson's shot: John Evans was on hand to put the result beyond doubt.

Evans completed the scoring with his second 19 minutes later when he was found by a brilliant Jackson cross, his header giving O'Neill no chance. By this time, Goodison was emptying fast, leaving the red and white-scarved hordes to acclaim their heroes.

Sadly for their jubilant fans, Liverpool could not continue this rich vein of form, and were humbled at home by Huddersfield in the next round. Yet though it would be seven more seasons before top-flight derbies resumed, this was a Saturday to paint the town red.

Right: Lancashire-born winger Alan A'Court was not a prolific scorer, breaking into double figures in only one of his 12 first-team seasons at Anfield, but he was happy to make the scoresheet against Everton.

GREATEST GAMES

22 SEPTEMBER 1962
FOOTBALL LEAGUE DIVISION 1

EVERTON	**2**
LIVERPOOL	**2**

A last-minute goal from Roger Hunt ensured the points were shared in the first Merseyside derby in 11 years at Goodison Park. With only seconds left on the watch of Middlesbrough referee Howey, outside-left Alan A'Court sent over a looping centre and Kevin Lewis headed the ball down for Hunt to roll it into the net.

Evertonians in the 73,000 crowd could hardly believe their eyes as the Liverpool Number 8 beat home keeper Gordon West, capitalising on a spell of desperate Liverpool attacking that had seemed likely to go unrewarded.

The roof had been raised less than a minute after the kick-off when Everton had the ball in the back of Jim Furnell's net. The Liverpool keeper dropped the ball as he tried to bounce it and Roy Vernon was on hand to tap it home. Much to everyone's amazement, however, the referee awarded a free-kick against the scorer for an apparent infringement.

Stevens had another goal ruled out for offside six minutes later as Vernon, Young and Gabriel maintained the pressure. The breakthrough came when Reds full-back Gerry Byrne was adjudged to have handled – and, though the decision seemed a little harsh, Vernon decisively dispatched the spot-kick beyond Furnell.

Kevin Lewis levelled for Liverpool five minutes before the break, having earlier been denied by West. When Ian Callaghan hooked the ball into the box, the winger-turned-spearhead made no mistake with his second chance of the half.

The frantic pace of the action inevitably relented in the second period, but though Liverpool looked to be having the better of things it was the visitors who would fall behind for the second time just after the hour when Vernon's blocked shot fell to Johnny Morrissey. The left-winger, who had been a Liverpool player until three months ago, made no mistake from close range.

The visitors then staged a late rally, with Callaghan looking the most dangerous forward on the park as Melia and A'Court

prompted from midfield. Yet all this effort looked unlikely to bear fruit until Hunt's last-gasp equaliser against a team that would go on to take the League Championship in Harry Catterick's second full season in charge. Liverpool's eighth place after promotion was less spectacular but praiseworthy.

Top: Roy Vernon, who joined Everton in February 1960, was known for his ability to strike a dead ball with precision and power.

Right: The match programme for this derby draw.

15 OCTOBER 1927

FOOTBALL LEAGUE DIVISION ONE

EVERTON	1
Troup	
LIVERPOOL	1
Edmed	

Attendance: 65,729

Everton:
Taylor, Cresswell, O'Donnell, Kelly, Hart, Virr, Critchley, Forshaw, Dean, Weldon, Troup.

Liverpool:
Riley, Lucas, McKinlay, McMullan, Jackson, Bromilow, Edmed, Hodgson, Devlin, Reid, Pither.

25 FEBRUARY 1928

FOOTBALL LEAGUE DIVISION ONE

LIVERPOOL	3
Hopkin, Bromilow, Hodgson	
EVERTON	3
Dean 3	

Attendance: 56,447

Liverpool:
Riley, Lucas, McKinlay, Morrison, Jackson, Bromilow, Edmed, Hodgson, Race, Chambers, Hopkin.

Everton:
Hardy, Cresswell, O'Donnell, Kelly, Hart, Virr, Critchley, Forshaw, Dean, Weldon, Troup.

29 SEPTEMBER 1928

FOOTBALL LEAGUE DIVISION ONE

EVERTON	1
Troup	
LIVERPOOL	0

Attendance: 55,415

Everton:
Davies, Cresswell, O'Donnell, Kelly, Hart, Virr, Ritchie, Dunn, Dean, Weldon, Troup.

Liverpool:
Scott, Jackson, Done, Morrison, Davidson, Bromilow, Edmed, Hodgson, Whitehurst, McDougall, Hopkin.

9 FEBRUARY 1929

FOOTBALL LEAGUE DIVISION ONE

LIVERPOOL	1
Race	
EVERTON	2
Griffiths, White	

Attendance: 55,000

Liverpool:
Riley, Jackson, Done, Morrison, Davidson, Bromilow, Edmed, Clarke, McFarlane, Race, Salisbury.

Everton:
Davies, Common, O'Donnell, Kelly, Griffiths, Hart, Ritchie, Dunn, White, Easton, Troup.

GREATEST GAMES

25 SEPTEMBER 1965
FOOTBALL LEAGUE DIVISION 1

LIVERPOOL	5
EVERTON	0

Liverpool hadn't beaten Everton by such a convincing margin for over 30 years – but the Blues argued that they did so against an under-strength team.

The Reds were without full-back Lawler, but the visitors lost flu victim Derek Temple on the morning of the game.

A second reshuffle was indicated when defensive kingpin Brian Labone went off at half-time to be replaced by a midfielder, Gerry Glover. At that point, the Blues were only one goal down and still in the game.

But Liverpool, who'd been overturned 4-0 at home just 12 months earlier, had waited two years for an outright victory, while Everton had won only once away from Goodison Park in four attempts since the start of the season.

West was on his toes from the start, making saves from Yeats, Hunt and Thompson inside the first five minutes: Hunt also hit the post as Liverpool continued to pour forward. Smith also hit an upright before midfielder Milne scooped the ball over the bar.

The deadlock was finally broken in the 34th minute. Full-back Tommy Wright held back his tormentor Peter Thompson, and from the resulting free-kick Smith dived in to head the ball past West.

Everton hit back immediately, Lawrence diving at the feet of Pickering and saving from Young, while Ray Wilson went close with a free-kick. Four minutes before the interval Gabriel's effort looked goalbound but produced a good save from Lawrence.

Ex-Red Johnny Morrissey, called into the squad to replace Temple at the last moment,

looked Everton's most dangerous player despite it being his first game of the season, but had very little support.

Then the the dam burst – and ironically it was West, the first-half hero, who presented Hunt with an easy chance by going down too early. Three minutes later the keeper was lobbed by Stevenson after Thompson's centre had been deflected to him.

Hunt then netted his second, bending to nod Stevenson's pass beyond West, while strike partner Ian St John headed his first goal of the season from Callaghan's cross in the last minute.

Despite Labone's potentially critical absence, only an Everton fan could complain about a result which reflected the teams' end-of-season standings. Liverpool won their second Championship under Shankly, while Everton, fourth the previous term, slumped to 11th.

Above right: Whole-hearted performances such as this two-goal display made England forward Roger Hunt a Liverpool legend in his decade at Anfield.

GREATEST GAMES

13 AUGUST 1966
FA CHARITY SHIELD

EVERTON	**0**
LIVERPOOL	**1**

Cup winners met League Champions at Goodison – and it was Liverpool who took the new season's first trophy when Roger Hunt's ninth-minute strike settled the matter.

The England striker was found 25 yards out by Thompson after good work down the left by Byrne and Callaghan – and before Gordon West could move a muscle he was picking the ball out of the net.

If truth were told, the Reds could have added a hatful more, such was their domination. Stevenson, Smith and St John were in full control of the midfield, leaving Everton – nominally the home team – with no option but to defend.

England defenders Wilson and Labone – the former, like Hunt, still basking in the golden glow of a World Cup winners' medal – managed to repel most of what Liverpool could throw at them, but could do nothing to stop the early goal.

At the other end, Young and Trebilcock, the Wembley FA Cup-winning strike force just three months earlier, were kept on a tight leash by Yeats and Smith, and it was nearly half an hour before Tommy Lawrence was truly tested.

Gerry Glover, making one of only three appearances for the Blues, freed Trebilcock with a through ball, but his shot was pushed away by Lawrence. Full-back Wright had

Everton's only other chance of note, but sent a typical defender's shot into the side netting.

Liverpool then started to relax but remained firmly in control, much to the dismay of home fans in the 63,000 crowd, and in truth many of the Liverpool players will have faced a bigger challenge in practice matches at Melwood then their city rivals could offer.

By a quirk of the Football League fixture list, the first competitive derby of the season would come just a fortnight later at the same venue, by which time Harry Catterick had shaken up his side sufficiently to produce a quite different result.

Dropping Glover, Scott and Trebilcock in favour of Pickering, Morrissey and big-money signing Alan Ball, he conjured up a 3-1 win, Ball (2) and substitute Brown the scorers.

The season, which would end almost exactly even in League terms with Liverpool fifth and Everton sixth, saw two more clashes – a scoreless Anfield return on New Year's Eve and a 1-0 Everton victory in the FA Cup Fourth Round, Ball again the scorer.

Below: Liverpool 1966-67.
Back row, left to right: Strong, Lawler, Lawrence, Byrne, Smith.
Front row: Callaghan, Hunt, Milne, Yeats, Thompson, St John, Stevenson.

30 JANUARY 1932

FOOTBALL LEAGUE DIVISION ONE

EVERTON	2

Critchley, White

LIVERPOOL	1

Wright

Attendance: 46,537

Everton:
Sagar, Williams, Bocking, Clark, McClure, Thomson, Critchley, White, Dean, Johnson, Rigby.

Liverpool:
Scott, Done, Steel, Morrison, Bradshaw, McDougall, Barton, Hodgson, Wright, McPherson, Gunson.

1 OCTOBER 1932

FOOTBALL LEAGUE DIVISION ONE

EVERTON	3

Dean 2, Critchley

LIVERPOOL	1

Gunson

Attendance: 44,214

Everton:
Sagar, Williams, Cresswell, Britton, White, Thomson, Critchley, McGourty, Dean, Johnson, Stein.

Liverpool:
Scott, Steel, Jackson, Morrison, Bradshaw, McDougall, Barton, Hodgson, Wright, McPherson, Gunson.

11 FEBRUARY 1933

FOOTBALL LEAGUE DIVISION ONE

LIVERPOOL	7

Barton 3, Hanson, Morrison, Taylor, Roberts

EVERTON	4

Dean 2, Johnson, Stein

Attendance: 50,000

Liverpool:
Scott, Steel, Jackson, Morrison, Bradshaw, Taylor, Barton, Roberts, Wright, McPherson, Hanson.

Everton:
Sagar, Cook, Cresswell, Britton, White, Thomson, Geldard, Dunn, Dean, Johnson, Stein.

30 SEPTEMBER 1933

FOOTBALL LEAGUE DIVISION ONE

LIVERPOOL	3

Nieuwenhuys, Hanson, English

EVERTON	2

Johnson, White

Attendance: 54,800

Liverpool:
Riley, Steel, Tennant, Morrison, Bradshaw, McDougall, Nieuwenhuys, Hodgson, English, D Wright, Hanson.

Everton:
Sagar, Cook, Cresswell, Britton, Gee, Thomson, Geldard, Dunn, White, Johnson, Stein.

GREATEST GAMES

3 FEBRUARY 1968
FOOTBALL LEAGUE DIVISION 1

EVERTON	1
LIVERPOOL	0

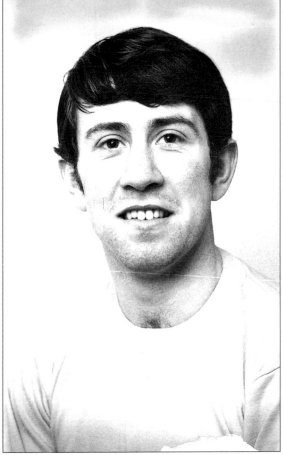

A goal from Howard Kendall settled this Merseyside derby, his strike after half an hour following a superb move that underlined Goodison's reputation as the 'School of Science'. And the schoolmaster in this case was Alan Ball.

He took a pass from Harvey before slipping the ball inside to Husband. The winger's cross curled away from Tommy Lawrence in the Liverpool goal to reach Ball, whose second pass of the move picked out the unmarked Kendall. The midfielder nearly notched a less distinguished second 20 minutes later when his low cross beat Smith and Lawrence, the keeper recovering to stop the ball before it crossed the line.

Liverpool had started the game much the better side, with Callaghan missing two chances in the opening minutes. He also had a hand in a promising move which opened up the home defence after 13 minutes. Thompson, however, headed over with plenty of time and space.

Liverpool sparked into life after the goal, with Roger Hunt shooting wide and newly-arrived centre-forward Tony Hateley (father of future England international Mark) heading over from Callaghan's cross.

Four minutes before half-time Ian St John lobbed the ball forward to Hunt who moved in menacingly on goal. But Gordon West read the danger well, coming out and stopping the England striker at full stretch.

The Reds again forced two corners in the opening moments of a second half which saw three fruitless penalty appeals. Two came from Everton for 'fouls' on Husband and recently-signed midfielder Ernie Hunt, while Liverpool's Hunt also had one denied.

Everton was looking much the better team and was unlucky not to increase its lead when Wright saw a shot come back off the bar. The Reds looked short of ideas, but almost snatched a share of the spoils when Hateley had a close-range shot blocked on the line.

Both teams would finish the season in the top five, Liverpool shading the honours in third place, while Everton reached the Cup Final for the second time in three years.

Above: Goalscorer Howard Kendall would serve Everton as both player and manager, but would never again notch a derby goal.

GREATEST GAMES

21 NOVEMBER 1970
FOOTBALL LEAGUE DIVISION 1

LIVERPOOL	3
EVERTON	2

This game will live long in the memory of the 53,777 who gathered at Anfield to see it. Non-stop running, bonecrunching challenges and courageous performances all went to make this a classic. And it was the Liverpool attack, most of whom had been unknown 12 months earlier, who did enough to secure a 3-2 win.

Yet no-one, whatever colour scarf they wore, would have laid money on such a result after the visitors went two goals up. Ex-Red Johnny Morrissey achieved the near impossible, beating Tommy Smith in a tackle to free Alan Whittle, and the precocious youngster coolly lobbed Clemence to silence the Kop.

And the silence became deafening after a left-wing link-up between Morrissey and Ball. The resulting cross found Royle at the far post and the centre-forward, having lost

marker Larry Lloyd, made no mistake with his head.

Liverpool looked out of sorts, with recently-signed Welshman Toshack looking lost up front in just his second League game in red, but it took a youngster in his first derby, Steve Heighway, to lift his side's fortunes. The graduate from Skelmersdale slipped John Hurst on the left and, cutting inside, hit a shot that evaded no fewer than four defenders *en route* to Rankin's net. Moments later he was at it again, proving as much a thorn in Everton's side as Morrissey had been to his team in the first period. This time, Heighway crossed to provide Toshack with a header that registered his first goal for his new club.

But the excitement wasn't over: the Anfield tumult reached a new crescendo as Toshack flicked-on a free-kick for goalscoring full-back Chris Lawler, a master of the blind-side run, to shoot across goal. The ball entered the net via the foot of the post to cap a remarkable comeback.

Liverpool, a team in transition, would finish fifth, while their neighbours – Champions the previous season – slumped to 14th.

Above: Liverpool's flying winger Steve Heighway turned the course of this game, scoring his side's first and making the equaliser for John Toshack.

Right: The match programme.

10 FEBRUARY 1934
FOOTBALL LEAGUE DIVISION ONE

EVERTON	0
LIVERPOOL	0

Attendance: 52,088

Everton:
Coggins, Williams, Cook, Britton, Gee, Thomson, Critchley, Cunliffe, Johnson, Stevenson, Stein.

Liverpool:
E Scott, Tennant, Done, Morrison, Bradshaw, McDougall, Nieuwenhuys, Hodgson, English, Taylor, Hanson.

15 SEPTEMBER 1934
FOOTBALL LEAGUE DIVISION ONE

EVERTON	1
Dean	
LIVERPOOL	0

Attendance: 43,001

Everton:
Sagar, Cresswell, Cook, Britton, Gee, Thomson, Leyfield, Cunliffe, Dean, Stevenson, Stein.

Liverpool:
Riley, Steel, Blenkinsop, Morrison, Low, McDougall, EV Wright, Hodgson, English, Taylor, Hanson.

20 MARCH 1935
FOOTBALL LEAGUE DIVISION ONE

LIVERPOOL	2
Hodgson 2 (*1 pen*)	
EVERTON	1
Dean	

Attendance: 32,000

Liverpool:
Kane, Cooper, Tennant, Savage, Bradshaw, McDougall, Nieuwenhuys, EV Wright, Hodgson, Johnson, Hanson.

Everton:
Sagar, Jackson, Jones, Britton, Gee, Thomson, Geldard, Cunliffe, Dean, Coulter, Stein.

7 SEPTEMBER 1935
FOOTBALL LEAGUE DIVISION ONE

LIVERPOOL	6
Howe 4, Hodgson 2	
EVERTON	0

Attendance: 48,000

Liverpool:
Riley, Cooper, Blenkinsop, Savage, Bradshaw, McDougall, Nieuwenhuys, Hodgson, Wright, Howe, Carr.

Everton:
Sagar, Williams, Cresswell, Britton, White, Thomson, Geldard, Miller, Dean, Stevenson, Leyfield.

4 JANUARY 1936

FOOTBALL LEAGUE DIVISION ONE

EVERTON	0
LIVERPOOL	0

Attendance: 52,282

Everton:
King, Cook, Jones, Britton, White, Mercer, Geldard, Bentham, Cunliffe, Miller, Gillick.

Liverpool:
Riley, Cooper, Dabbs, Savage, Bradshaw, McDougall, Nieuwenhuys, Wright, Howe, Glassey, Carr.

19 SEPTEMBER 1936

FOOTBALL LEAGUE DIVISION ONE

EVERTON	2

Dean, Stevenson

LIVERPOOL	0

Attendance: 55,835

Everton:
Sagar, Jackson, Cook, Britton, Gee, Mercer, Gillick, Cunliffe, Dean, Stevenson, Coulter.

Liverpool:
Hobson, Dabbs, Blenkinsop, Busby, Bradshaw, McDougall, Nieuwenhuys, P Taylor, Howe, Wright, Hanson.

23 JANUARY 1937

FOOTBALL LEAGUE DIVISION ONE

LIVERPOOL	3

Howe, Taylor, Balmer

EVERTON	2

Stevenson 2

Attendance: 37,632

Liverpool:
Riley, Cooper, Dabbs, Busby, Bradshaw, McDougall, Nieuwenhuys, P Taylor, Balmer, Howe, Hanson.

Everton:
Sagar, Cook, Jones, Britton, Gee, Mercer, Gillick, Cunliffe, Dean, Stevenson, Coulter.

2 OCTOBER 1937

FOOTBALL LEAGUE DIVISION ONE

LIVERPOOL	1

Nieuwenhuys

EVERTON	2

Lawton, Trentham

Attendance: 45,000

Liverpool:
Kemp, Harley, Dabbs, Busby, Rogers, McDougall, Nieuwenhuys, Eastham, Howe, P Taylor, Hanson.

Everton:
Sagar, Cook, JE Jones, Mercer, Gee, Watson, Geldard, Stevenson, Lawton, Dougal, Trentham.

27 MARCH 1971
FA CUP SEMI-FINAL
(Played At Old Trafford)

EVERTON	1
LIVERPOOL	2

A capacity crowd of 63,000 fans, paying £75,000 at the turnstiles, packed into Old Trafford to watch this battle royal between the two Merseyside giants. And it looked as if Everton would be heading to the capital to contest the FA Cup Final in May when it took an early lead.

Joe Royle, who'd already notched 17 goals in a splendid season that would win him his first international cap for England, combined with Johnny Morrissey on the left. Alan Whittle flicked on his pass to set up Alan Ball with an angled drive from close range.

Soon afterwards wonderkid Whittle spurned a chance to wrap the game up, blazing wide despite an unmarked Ball crying out for the ball on the far post. The pocket-size striker had burst onto the scene from the youth ranks the previous season with a haul of 11 goals in 15 League games, but the miss was typical of a less consistent campaign this time round and left his team-mate distinctly unimpressed.

Liverpool, who'd taken three out of four points in the League derbies this season, gradually regained the initiative as Eire international Steve Heighway, swopping wings at will, turned both Everton full-backs inside-out.

Alun Evans was alert to this threat and capitalised by running through the middle to latch onto a Heighway cross and shoot home a quite delightful goal.

Everton's midfielders Kendall and Harvey both had fine games, but when they started to fade so did Everton's hopes. Liverpool sent over wave after wave of attacks, and finally created the chance which won the match 15 minutes from time. Andy Rankin punched clear under pressure from Toshack's aerial threat, but only as far as Evans. He fed Heighway, whose cross from the left found Brian Hall unmarked on the back post. The diminutive midfielder thumped the ball home with undisguised glee, and Liverpool was on its way to Wembley.

Their opponents there (as in 1950) were Double-chasing Arsenal, who were to achieve their aim by taking the game into extra-time and winning it through Charlie George. In League terms, Liverpool who finished fifth to qualify for a place in the European Fairs Cup (where they would lose to Leeds United in a two-legged semi-final) had more reason to be satisfied than Everton, whose final position was 14th.

Below: Alan Ball celebrates his successful strike with fellow midfielders Colin Harvey and Howard Kendall.

13 NOVEMBER 1971
FOOTBALL LEAGUE DIVISION 1

EVERTON	**1**
LIVERPOOL	**0**

Throughout his career, David Johnson made a habit of scoring on his debut – League, FA Cup, League Cup and internationals were all marked with a goal, so it should come as no surprise that he was the scorer of the only goal in his first Merseyside derby.

He did so after a slick four-man move involving Newton, Ball, Kendall and winger Jimmy Husband. His tantalising cross was headed down by Johnson – and, though Ray Clemence pushed his first effort onto the post, the striker made no mistake second time around.

Liverpool had a similar chance after just ten minutes, but failed to put it away. Heighway's corner was headed on by utility man Ian Ross to the unmarked Alun Evans. West managed to pushed his header onto the post, but any chance of a follow-up ended when the keeper, who had a fine game in the Everton goal, grabbed the ball.

Liverpool's cause wasn't helped when they lost centre-half Larry Lloyd with a serious knee injury just before half-time. Up front they missed Kevin Keegan who might have had more of an impact on the game than his replacement Ross. The Blues had their problems as well with Royle and Morrissey missing through injury.

Callaghan missed a great chance to equalise in the final minute when his shot was hit with plenty of power, but inspired West's best save of the afternoon.

Referee Thomas, who'd have a stormy history in derby games of the 1970s, booked two players from each side: Ball and Newton of Everton and Lawler and Toshack of Liverpool.

He also awarded 28 free-kicks to Everton and one less to Liverpool in a niggly game of few chances. Surprisingly it wasn't David Johnson who emerged with man of the match honours but midfielder John McLaughlin, also playing in his first Merseyside derby. Ironically he would be a goalscorer – an own-goal for Liverpool – in the return!

Right: Goalscorer David Johnson, who scored for both sides in Merseyside derbies, rejoined Everton after spells at Portman Road and Anfield. He won eight full England caps whilst with Liverpool.

---

16 FEBRUARY 1938
FOOTBALL LEAGUE DIVISION ONE

EVERTON	**1**
Lawton	
LIVERPOOL	**3**
Balmer, Shafto 2	

Attendance: 33,465

Everton:
Morton, Cook, JE Jones, Britton, TG Jones, Mercer, Geldard, Cunliffe, Lawton, Stevenson, Gillick.

Liverpool:
Riley, Cooper, Ramsden, P Taylor, Rogers, Bush, Nieuwenhuys, Balmer, Shafto, Fagan, Van Den Berg.

1 OCTOBER 1938
FOOTBALL LEAGUE DIVISION ONE

EVERTON	**2**
Bentham, Boyes	
LIVERPOOL	**1**
Fagan (pen)	

Attendance: 64,977

Everton:
Sagar, Cook, Greenhalgh, Mercer, TG Jones, Thomson, Gillick, Bentham, Lawton, Stevenson, Boyes.

Liverpool:
Riley, Cooper, Bush, Busby, Rogers, McInnes, Nieuwenhuys, Taylor, Fagan, Balmer, Van Den Berg.

4 FEBRUARY 1939
FOOTBALL LEAGUE DIVISION ONE

LIVERPOOL	**0**
EVERTON	**3**
Lawton 2, Bentham	

Attendance: 55,994

Liverpool:
Kemp, Cooper, Harley, Busby, Bush, McInnes, Nieuwenhuys, Taylor, Fagan, Balmer, Eastham.

Everton:
Sagar, Cook, Greenhalgh, Mercer, TG Jones, Thomson, Gillick, Bentham, Lawton, Stevenson, Boyes.

21 SEPTEMBER 1946
FOOTBALL LEAGUE DIVISION ONE

LIVERPOOL	**0**
EVERTON	**0**

Attendance: 49,838

Liverpool:
Sidlow, Lambert, Ramsden, Taylor, Hughes, Paisley, Nieuwenhuys, Balmer, Stubbins, Jones, Liddell.

Everton:
Burnett, Saunders, Greenhalgh, Mercer, TG Jones, Bentham, McIlhatton, Fielding, Higgins, Stevenson, Eglington.

29 JANUARY 1947

FOOTBALL LEAGUE DIVISION ONE

EVERTON	1
Wainwright	
LIVERPOOL	0

Attendance: 30,612

Everton:
Sagar, Jackson, Greenhalgh, Bentham, Humphreys, Farrell, McIlhatton, Stevenson, Wainwright, Fielding, Eglington.

Liverpool:
Sidlow, Harley, Lambert, Taylor, Jones, Paisley, Eastham, Balmer, Stubbins, Done, Liddell.

27 SEPTEMBER 1947

FOOTBALL LEAGUE DIVISION ONE

EVERTON	0
LIVERPOOL	3
Balmer, Stubbins, Fagan	

Attendance: 66,776

Everton:
Sagar, Saunders, Greenhalgh, Watson, TG Jones, Farrell, Fielding, Wainwright, Catterick, Stevenson, Eglington.

Liverpool:
Sidlow, Lambert, Hughes, Taylor, Jones, Paisley, Priday, Fagan, Stubbins, Balmer, Liddell.

21 APRIL 1948

FOOTBALL LEAGUE DIVISION ONE

LIVERPOOL	4
Stubbins, Liddell, Brierley, Balmer	
EVERTON	0

Attendance: 55,035

Liverpool:
Sidlow, Jones, Lambert, Taylor, Hughes, Paisley, Liddell, Balmer, Stubbins, Fagan, Brierley.

Everton:
Sagar, Saunders, Hedley, Lindley, TG Jones, Farrell, Higgins, Wainwright, Lello, Stevenson, Eglington.

18 SEPTEMBER 1948

FOOTBALL LEAGUE DIVISION ONE

EVERTON	1
Dodds	
LIVERPOOL	1
Fagan	

Attendance: 78,299

Everton:
Sagar, Saunders, Hedley, Bentham, TG Jones, Watson, Powell, Fielding, Dodds, Stevenson, Boyes.

Liverpool:
Sidlow, Shepherd, Lambert, Taylor, Jones, Paisley, Payne, Balmer, Shannon, Fagan, Liddell.

8 DECEMBER 1973
FOOTBALL LEAGUE DIVISION 1

EVERTON	0
LIVERPOOL	1

Everton's unbeaten home record bit the dust in this pre-Yuletide derby, the 109th meeting between the two clubs. Yet for a long period it seemed the Blues were the most likely to end up on top in what was an evenly-balanced game witnessed by over 56,000 despite the proximity to Christmas.

Mick Buckley and Joe Harper pushed forward at every opportunity, while Clements was in charge of the midfield. Yet they could not convert territorial domination into goal chances, the best effort in the first half being a Buckley shot that Clemence was glad to push away.

The pivotal battle was an aerial one, between two internationals, Joe Royle and Larry Lloyd, and it was the Liverpool stopper who kept his opponent in check for most of the match. Alongside him, Phil Thompson was building his reputation, a slight yet determined home-grown youngster who would come through to captain the side. It was Thompson's first taste of the derby atmosphere as a player, while for Lloyd, soon to move to Nottingham Forest, it would be his last.

Everton started the second half brightly, with a flurry of chances. Bernard's shot took an awkward bounce before being pushed wide by Clemence, then Harper evaded his marker and crossed to find Mick Lyons. The lanky defender, who'd moved up front to augment the attack, rose to find the net with a powerful header only for a linesman's flag to rule out his strike.

Liverpool had gone into the match without key attackers Heighway and Toshack, and their cause was further undermined by the loss of Kevin Keegan through injury: he was replaced by Brian Hall. It was hard to see where a Reds goal would come from, but in the end it came from an unexpected source.

Alan Waddle, recently signed from Third Division Halifax and clearly still adjusting to the pace of the top flight, popped up in the Everton box to meet a Callaghan centre. He stuck out a left leg and the deflection took the ball over the line – much to the disappointment of home keeper Dave Lawson, who'd had little to do on a freezing afternoon. From then on there was only going to be one winner.

Liverpool would finish the season second behind Leeds, a goalless Anfield derby in April denting title hopes, while Everton ended seventh.

Right: Unlucky for some? Though Kevin Keegan featured in 13 Merseyside derbies between 1971 and 1977, injury prevented him from finishing this one.

GREATEST GAMES

3 APRIL 1976
FOOTBALL LEAGUE DIVISION 1

LIVERPOOL	**1**
EVERTON	**0**

As Liverpool raced towards its ninth Championship, flame-haired striker David Fairclough earned himself the tag of 'Supersub' after stepping off the bench to win matches. And he enhanced his reputation no end by replacing John Toshack to win the working man's varsity match.

It was the first time in four attempts that a goal had been scored by either side, there having been a spell of goalless draws in 1974 and 1975. In fact, the last time that Everton found the net against their arch rivals was in November 1971!

Because of the Grand National at nearby Aintree that afternoon, kick-off had been switched to 11.00am – and inevitably much of the passion this game generates was lacking.

None of the Blues' starting line-up had played the last time they scored a goal – and they didn't look like coming close on this occasion. Latchford was isolated in attack, pre-match rumours of Lyons partnering him just eight weeks after undergoing a cartilage operation having proved unfounded.

Yet the home team didn't create that many chances themselves – until, that was, Fairclough entered the action. The 19 year old striker was thrown into the game with 25 minutes left in place of Toshack, and from the start his confidence, pace, balance and skill caused problems for the visitors.

With two minutes left on the clock and a fifth consecutive goalless draw still looking likely, Fairclough was given the ball 40 yards out near the touchline. Off he galloped, beating five opponents before reaching the penalty area – and though keeper Dai Davies cut down the angle, he found the ball skimming past him.

Unbelievably, Liverpool could have had another goal just a minute later as Bryan Hamilton handled on the line. With three penalties scored in his last three games, England defender Phil Neal stepped up to take the spot-kick – only to drive it wide of both Davies and the post.

Everton, who finished a disappointing 11th, would finally break its duck against Liverpool at Anfield five months later – almost five years since its last goal in the fixture.

Above: Supersub David Fairclough is mobbed by delighted team-mates after scoring the winning goal in a close-run derby.

GREATEST GAMES

16 OCTOBER 1976
FOOTBALL LEAGUE DIVISION 1

LIVERPOOL	**3**
EVERTON	**1**

Everton manager Billy Bingham, recovering from an operation, selected his team from his hospital bed – and lived to rue the consequences. Together with his coaches Kenyon and Bernard, he opted to play five players under the age of 23: David Jones (19), Andy King (20), Ken McNaught (21), George Telfer (21) and Ronnie Goodlass (23).

It was the inexperience of the youngsters which proved to be his side's downfall in a game of boys against men. The Blues seemed uncomfortable, while Liverpool looked every inch the Champions they were.

Record buy Bob Latchford, rated by his manager among the best strikers in the League, had a quiet afternoon partnered by Telfer, though a fine save from Clemence denied him a goal with the very last kick of the game.

Before they had really settled, Everton found themselves two down inside the first 12 minutes. John Toshack, who dominated in the air throughout, headed down McDermott's corner kick for Heighway to score. Then Keegan raced through the middle of the Everton defence to win a penalty as Ken McNaught caught him with a late tackle.

Referee Matthewson confirmed the spot-kick, and Phil Neal, who had missed from the spot in the previous Merseyside derby, gave Dai Davies no chance.

Three minutes before the interval Liverpool added a third. Ray Kennedy played a long ball to Keegan, whose cross was headed goalwards by McDermott. McNaught made a clearance from under the bar, but the lurking Toshack was on hand to head home.

Midfielder Martin Dobson pulled a goal back for the visitors three minutes after half-time with what was the goal of the game, giving Clemence no chance from 35 yards. Everton piled on the pressure, and was denied a penalty minutes before time when Neal looked to have handled in the area. This time referee Matthewson said no, and the crowd was denied a grandstand finish.

This was the most entertaining derby for several seasons, following a spate of goalless draws and a single-goal win. Liverpool would retain its title, the second won in Bob Paisley's third season in charge, but even so the return at Goodison in March ended… 0-0!

Below: Though he wasn't actually present at Anfield, Everton boss Billy Bingham – a former player whose managerial tenure lasted between 1973 and 1977 – played a major part in the outcome.

GREATEST GAMES

23 APRIL 1977
FA CUP SEMI-FINAL
(Played At Maine Road)

EVERTON	2
LIVERPOOL	2

This game will forever be remembered for a controversial decision by referee Clive Thomas. Everton fans will never know why he disallowed Bryan Hamilton's last-gasp effort which would have taken the Toffees to Wembley.

Both teams had been hit by injuries. Latchford, Kenyon and Jones were missing for Everton, while Toshack, Callaghan and Thompson had been ruled out of the Reds' line-up.

Liverpool supersub David Fairclough, playing from the start due to the injury crisis, should have scored in the first minute but his shot got held up in the mud and his second attempt landed him on his backside. His Everton counterpart McKenzie caught the eye as he forced a fine save from Clemence: midfielder Mick Buckley also came close.

But Buckley was caught napping in his own penalty box by his Liverpool opposite number Terry McDermott. He took a pass from Keegan and, evading the Evertonian, lofted his shot beyond Dave Lawson.

Everton soon got back into the game, however, when Hughes slipped while trying to stop Pearson. The winger found Martin Dobson and his centre was converted by McKenzie, the ball taking a deflection to wrong-foot Clemence.

Keegan now buzzed around the pitch and forced two good saves from Lawson, Heighway hit top gear on the left wing and Ray Kennedy ran the midfield. It seemed only a matter of time before Liverpool scored.

Lawson's mistake gave Case his chance to head home, but the keeper made amends by saving from ex-team-mate David Johnson. But Everton weren't finished: McKenzie popped up in the area and Clemence was left helpless as Rioch equalised.

Conditions were better for the replay four days later with a dry pitch and Liverpool looked determined to win this game from the very first whistle.

Referee Thomas once again played a hand with the first goal: Pejic was adjudged to have pushed Johnson and Neal smashed home the resulting penalty. Everton felt they too should have had a penalty when Clemence's raised foot made contact with McKenzie, but an indirect free-kick was all they got. A third penalty incident could have resulted in the second half when Buckley appeared to handle.

Smith set up the second Liverpool strike with a long ball out to the left wing, Fairclough sent his cross into the penalty area for Case to convert. From then on, Everton was overrun in midfield, and it was no surprise when a third goal came from Kennedy who had two attempts at converting a Keegan free-kick before scoring.

Liverpool stayed on course for the treble to book an (ultimately unsuccessful) Wembley date with Manchester United. Again, though, it was referee Thomas who made all the headlines.

Left: Ken McNaught dispossesses David Fairclough in this semi-final clash.

12 APRIL 1965

FOOTBALL LEAGUE DIVISION ONE

EVERTON	**2**
Morrissey, Temple	
LIVERPOOL	**1**
Stevenson (pen)	

Attendance: 65,402

Everton:
West, Wright, Brown, Gabriel, Labone, Harris, Scott, Harvey, Pickering, Temple, Morrissey.

Liverpool:
Lawrence, Lawler, Byrne, Milne, Yeats, Stevenson, Callaghan, Hunt, St John, Smith, Thompson.

25 SEPTEMBER 1965

FOOTBALL LEAGUE DIVISION ONE

LIVERPOOL	**5**
Smith, Hunt 2, Stevenson, St John	
EVERTON	**0**

Attendance: 53,557

Liverpool:
Lawrence, Strong (Arrowsmith), Byrne, Milne, Yeats, Stevenson, Callaghan, Hunt, St John, Smith, Thompson.

Everton:
West, Wright, Wilson, Gabriel, Labone (Glover), Harris, Scott, Young, Pickering, Harvey, Morrissey.

19 MARCH 1966

FOOTBALL LEAGUE DIVISION ONE

EVERTON	**0**
LIVERPOOL	**0**

Attendance: 62,337

Everton:
West, Brown, Wilson, Gabriel, Labone, Harris, Scott, Young, Pickering (Wright), Harvey, Temple.

Liverpool:
Lawrence, Lawler, Byrne, Smith, Yeats, Stevenson, Callaghan, Hunt, St John, Arrowsmith, Thompson.

13 AUGUST 1966

FA CHARITY SHIELD

EVERTON	**0**
LIVERPOOL	**1**
Hunt	

Attendance: 63,329

Everton:
West, Wright, Wilson, Gabriel, Labone, Glover, Scott, Young, Trebilcock, Harvey, Temple.

Liverpool:
Lawrence, Lawler, Byrne, Smith, Yeats, Stevenson, Callaghan, Hunt, St John, Strong, Thompson.

28 OCTOBER 1978
FOOTBALL LEAGUE DIVISION 1

EVERTON	**1**
LIVERPOOL	**0**

Andy King scored the only goal of the game that gave his side their first victory over Liverpool for seven years. He was on hand when fellow midfielder Martin Dobson headed the ball down into his path and his sliced effort flew over Clemence into the net.

Intentional or not, his effort entered into the record books as the goal which ended the Toffees' awful run against their most bitter of rivals, even though the visitors did enough to justify a share of the spoils.

Everton had the better of the first half and should have scored when Bob Latchford got on to the end of winger Dave Thomas' cross before getting bundled to the ground.

Everton's goal sparked Liverpool into life, with David Johnson – ironically, the man who scored the winning goal seven years ago when playing for Everton – looking most likely to score again. His strike partner Kenny Dalglish was shackled by Kenyon and Wright, and when he did manage to release Johnson the resulting goal was ruled out for offside.

Everton custodian George Wood pulled off a couple of impressive saves as Liverpool looked to step up a gear, while a catalogue of last-ditch tackles underlined Everton's intention to prove themselves as real Championship challengers.

As it turned out, it would be red ribbons that would adorn the League trophy, though Everton proved they were contenders by finishing fourth – though a massive 17 points behind Liverpool's 68-point haul. Andy King was again on the mark in March 1979, his goal securing a share of the points in a 1-1 draw. Three points out of four against the Champions was enough to put a gloss on the Toffees' season.

Above: Celebrations all round for Everton midfielder Andy King, whose goal proved decisive.

Below: The match programme.

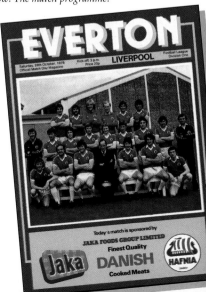

GREATEST GAMES

20 OCTOBER 1979
FOOTBALL LEAGUE DIVISION 1

LIVERPOOL	2
EVERTON	2

A double dismissal in the 70th minute of the 121st Merseyside League derby made the headlines and detracted from what was otherwise a thrilling encounter. Terry McDermott and Garry Stanley became the first players to be sent off in the 85-year history of this fixture.

Liverpool had gone ahead after only nine minutes thanks to Everton skipper Mick Lyons. He tried to steer the ball back to George Wood but lofted the ball fully 40 yards into his own net for one of the fixture's most spectacular goals.

Brian Kidd, a veteran of Manchester and north London derbies, pulled Everton level only for another ex-Gunner, Ray Kennedy, to restore Liverpool's lead.

The home side had the better of play for almost the whole game but missed a succession of chances before a long clearance from keeper Wood bounced awkwardly. Andy King pounced to shoot past Ray Clemence and bring the scores level again.

Two minutes later Stanley tangled with Jimmy Case, and in seconds the situation had degenerated into midfield mayhem. Referee David Richardson promptly sent Stanley and McDermott for an early bath.

Stanley maintained that he had not thrown a punch in his life and hadn't done so then. McDermott was gagged by manager Bob Paisley, but Case said that all he could remember was going for the ball and ending up on the floor with Stanley standing on his leg. No matter who did what to whom, this was an incident never before seen in Mersey derby history.

The return game at Goodison in March was won 2-1 by Liverpool – and though a Phil Neal penalty proved the decisive goal the incidence of foul play was significantly lower.

As for the clubs' fortunes, they could hardly have been more different: Liverpool retained the title, while Gordon Lee's Everton only just escaped relegation in 19th place.

Below: Liverpool's two goalscorers, Ray Kennedy and Mick Lyons, fight an aerial duel. Lyons' own goal is one of five the Reds have accumulated in a century of derby games.

FOOTBALL LEAGUE DIVISION ONE

EVERTON	1
Kendall	
LIVERPOOL	0

Attendance: 64,482

Everton:
West, Wright, Wilson, Kendall, Labone, Harvey, Hurst, Ball (Brown), Royle, Hunt, Husband.

Liverpool:
Lawrence, Lawler, Smith, Strong, Yeats, Hughes, Callaghan, Hunt, Hateley, St John, Thompson.

27 AUGUST 1968

FOOTBALL LEAGUE DIVISION ONE

EVERTON	0
LIVERPOOL	0

Attendance: 63,998

Everton:
West, Wright, Brown, Kendall, Labone, Harvey, Husband, Ball, Royle, Hurst, Morrissey.

Liverpool:
Lawrence, Lawler, Wall, Smith, Yeats, Hughes, Callaghan, Hunt, Hateley, St John, Thompson.

8 OCTOBER 1968

FOOTBALL LEAGUE DIVISION ONE

LIVERPOOL	1
Smith	
EVERTON	1
Ball	

Attendance: 54,496

Liverpool:
Lawrence, Lawler, Wall, Smith, Yeats, Hughes, Callaghan, Hunt, Evans, St John, Thompson.

Everton:
West, Wright, Brown, Kendall, Labone, Harvey, Husband, Ball, Royle, Hurst, Morrissey.

6 DECEMBER 1969

FOOTBALL LEAGUE DIVISION ONE

EVERTON	0
LIVERPOOL	3
Hughes, Brown og, Graham	

Attendance: 57,370

Everton:
West, Wright, Brown, Kendall, Labone, Jackson, Whittle, Ball, Royle, Hurst, Morrissey.

Liverpool:
Lawrence, Lawler, Wall, Strong, Yeats, Hughes, Callaghan, Ross, Thompson, St John, Graham.

GREATEST GAMES

24 JANUARY 1981
FA CUP FOURTH ROUND

EVERTON	2
LIVERPOOL	1

Everton fans had been waiting a long time to celebrate their first FA Cup win over Liverpool since 1967. Two up and seemingly safe, they were forced to hang on for dear life after Jimmy Case's goal set up a dramatic last quarter-hour.

Victory in the FA Cup tastes even sweeter, as derby debutant Kevin Ratcliffe explained. 'It's is a one-off thing and you'd like to go on longer than they do. You don't get a chance to meet them again in that competition, that's always a big spur.'

Everton never let Liverpool get into their stride: with McMahon, Hartford and Ross running the midfield, the Reds' threat was minimal with Lee, McDermott and Souness stifled.

Everton took the lead after only 17 minutes: Hartford made an opening for Eastoe, whose shot glanced off Clemence. Neal tried to clear but fellow full-back Avi Cohen could only get in the way and the ball was in the net.

In a hotly-contested game referee Clive Thomas (who'd refereed another controversial Cup tie in 1977) cautioned five players: McMahon and O'Keefe of Everton and Case, Souness and Cohen of Liverpool.

Varadi grabbed the second goal of the afternoon when O'Keefe took the ball wide of Clemence before crossing it into the far post. The striker's rapture also sparked an amusing moment, as Ratcliffe recalls. 'After he scored he turned away and celebrated in front of the Liverpool fans. Then somebody chucked a pork pie at him and it hit him on the top of the head... quite funny when you look back.'

Fifteen minutes from the end Liverpool wiped the smile off Everton faces when Ray Kennedy squared the ball for substitute Case to rifle the ball past Martin Hodge. But a second goal would not come: for once Liverpool had no answer to Everton's resources of stamina and courage. The Toffees were rewarded by a run to the Sixth Round while Liverpool was left to concentrate on the League, in which it won one derby and drew the other *en route* to fifth spot.

Below: Flamboyant forward Imre Varadi, scorer of Everton's second goal, evades his marker Phil Thompson. This proved the high spot of his Goodison career.

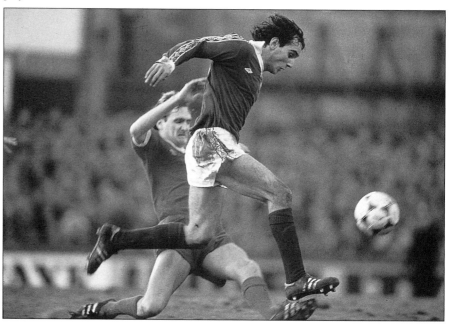

GREATEST GAMES

27 MARCH 1982
FOOTBALL LEAGUE DIVISION 1

EVERTON	**1**
LIVERPOOL	**3**

EVERTON v LIVERPOOL
SATURDAY 27th MARCH 1982 — 3.00 p.m.
FOOTBALL LEAGUE DIVISION ONE
OFFICIAL MATCHDAY MAGAZINE 30p

TODAY'S MATCH IS SPONSORED BY
HAFNIA
Danish Cooked
Meats

Supporters at Goodison for the season's second derby barely had enough time to take their places before both sides had scored. Two goals inside the first three minutes left fans rubbing their eyes in disbelief.

Republic of Ireland midfielder Ronnie Whelan opened the visitors' account with a move he started and ended himself. Having crossed for Craig Johnston to head against the bar, he pounced to ram the ball home after the Everton defence only half-cleared the danger.

But high-flying Liverpool's joy was to prove short-lived. Blues midfielder Kevin Richardson's cross was only punched clear by Grobbelaar, and when the ball came back into the box Sharp poked it home for one of 15 League goals he'd score this season.

Liverpool, who would remain unbeaten to the end of the season in a powerful run that assured them of the title, stepped up a gear in the second half, Johnston beating Richardson

and Ratcliffe before passing to fellow midfielder Sammy Lee. He found Dalglish, who held off two defenders to lay the ball off for Graeme Souness. The Scot's right-foot shot caught Neville Southall unsighted in the home goal to put Liverpool back in front.

The third goal, which made the game safe for Liverpool, was set up for Johnston by the front pair of Rush and Dalglish, though Bruce Grobbelaar had to produce an acrobatic save to deny Sharp a second goal after Trevor Ross had jigged his way past the Liverpool defence.

The corresponding fixture, at Anfield in November, had produced the same scoreline. But while Liverpool had then struggled to fire on all cylinders and Everton, under new manager Howard Kendall, had gone into the game as equals, this second win underlined the Reds' resolve to regain the Championship they'd conceded to Aston Villa the previous campaign. This was the third match of a 16-game run of 13 wins and three draws that helped them do just that.

Above left: Hard-working defender Billy Wright could not stem the Red tide on this occasion. Later this year he was dropped for allegedly being overweight and never played for Everton again.

---

13 NOVEMBER 1971

FOOTBALL LEAGUE DIVISION ONE

EVERTON	**1**
Johnson	
LIVERPOOL	**0**

Attendance: 56,293

Everton:
West, H Newton, McLaughlin, Kendall, Kenyon, Harvey, Johnson, Ball, Husband, Hurst, Jones.

Liverpool:
Clemence, Lawler, Lindsay, Smith, Lloyd (Graham), Hughes, Ross, A Evans, Heighway, Toshack, Callaghan.

4 MARCH 1972

FOOTBALL LEAGUE DIVISION ONE

LIVERPOOL	**4**
Wright og, McLaughlin og, Lawler, Hughes	
EVERTON	**0**

Attendance: 53,922

Liverpool:
Clemence, Lawler, Lindsay, Smith, Lloyd, Hughes, Keegan, Hall, Heighway, Toshack, Callaghan.

Everton:
West, T Wright, McLaughlin, Kendall, Kenyon, Harvey, Husband, Darracott, Johnson (B Wright), Lyons, Whittle.

7 OCTOBER 1972

FOOTBALL LEAGUE DIVISION ONE

LIVERPOOL	**1**
Cormack	
EVERTON	**0**

Attendance: 55,975

Liverpool:
Clemence, Lawler, Lindsay, Storton, Lloyd, Hughes, Keegan, Cormack, Heighway, Boersma, Callaghan.

Everton:
Lawson, T Wright, Newton, Kendall (Lyons), Kenyon, Hurst, Johnson, Bernard, Royle, Harvey, Connolly.

3 MARCH 1973

FOOTBALL LEAGUE DIVISION ONE

EVERTON	**0**
LIVERPOOL	**2**
Hughes 2	

Attendance: 54,856

Everton:
Lawson, T Wright, Styles, Hurst, Kenyon, Darracott, Jones, Kendall, Harper, Lyons, Connolly.

Liverpool:
Clemence, Lawler, Lindsay, Smith, Lloyd, Hughes, Keegan, Hall, Boersma, Heighway, Callaghan.

GREATEST GAMES

6 NOVEMBER 1982
FOOTBALL LEAGUE DIVISION 1

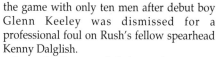

EVERTON	**0**
LIVERPOOL	**5**

This scoreline should surely read Everton 0, Ian Rush 4 (and one other) after the Welsh marksman produced one of the best goalpoaching displays ever witnessed in a Merseyside derby.

Rush's four-goal haul equalled Fred Howe's 47 year-old record for the most goals scored by one Liverpool player against the Old Enemy in one game – Alex Young in April 1904 is the only Evertonian to hold the equivalent record.

And just to rub salt into the wounds of Evertonians they had to play the majority of the game with only ten men after debut boy Glenn Keeley was dismissed for a professional foul on Rush's fellow spearhead Kenny Dalglish.

Long balls out of defence from Alan Hansen set up both Rush's first two goals. Dalglish then provided a cross for defender Mark Lawrenson to slide home a third – a rare goal this for the Eire international, and the only one he'd notch in 18 derby appearances.

Rush completed his hat-trick soon afterwards, Dalglish having set him up: the post denied him first time around, but he made no mistake with the rebound.

By now Rush was walking around Goodison as if it were he and not Everton that owned the place, and it came as no surprise when he added his fourth and Liverpool's fifth. Yet another inch-perfect pass from Hansen set Sammy Lee running at the Everton defence: he found Rush with a through ball, but Blues keeper Southall made the task all too easy by charging out of his goal, presenting his international team-mate with an easy chance.

Rush would finish the season with 24 League goals from 34 appearances as Liverpool retained their title. Everton finished seventh in their second season under Howard Kendall: this would be far and away their heaviest defeat, and their improvement was such that they came away from Anfield in March with a 0-0 draw.

Left: Reds manager Bob Paisley wasn't the only man out of his seat at Goodison as Ian Rush equalled the derby goalscoring record in a stunning away win. Paisley said of his striker: 'You would have to go a long way to find a more complete footballer'.

6 NOVEMBER 1983
FOOTBALL LEAGUE DIVISION 1

LIVERPOOL	3
EVERTON	0

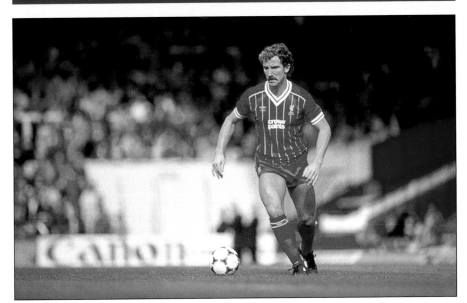

Liverpool's Michael Robinson marked his first Merseyside derby with a goal to put the game beyond Everton. The Republic of Ireland international, who'd play only 30 League games after his transfer from Brighton, was on hand to fire home after a Rush shot failed to reach the goal.

The Welsh striker had already opened his team's account, finishing a move that started inside his own half. Hansen passed to Dalglish who moved inside, evading Alan Harper, and released Steve Nicol on the right wing. His cross from the by-line bounced off an Everton defender into the path of Rush, who made no mistake.

Harper made amends for his part in the earlier goal by clearing from Lee after Grobbelaar's long clearance had enabled Dalglish to set up the midfielder. Yet even at 2-0 Everton looked intent on getting back into the game. Sheedy pushed the ball forward to Sharp, and the Scottish striker chipped the ball goalwards from 30 yards – but Grobbelaar, diving backwards, turned the ball over in typically spectacular style.

Liverpool's third was probably the best goal of the game, Dalglish, Rush and Lawrenson working the ball down the left for Nicol to finish the move in style with a diving header.

Though beaten that time, Neville Southall needed to be on his toes later on to deny Robinson a second on his derby debut. In all, Everton had now failed to beat their arch rivals from across Stanley Park in the League since 1978 – a fact Robinson, in his later incarnation as a TV commentator, would doubtless have picked up on. Their later League meeting at Anfield in March ended one apiece.

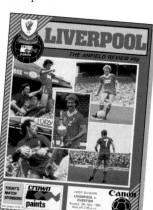

Above: Gritty Scot Graeme Souness always relished the midfield battles that were a feature of Merseyside derbies like this one.

Left: The match programme.

8 DECEMBER 1973

FOOTBALL LEAGUE DIVISION ONE

EVERTON	0
LIVERPOOL	1

Waddle

Attendance: 56,098

Everton:
Lawson, Darracott, McLaughlin, Clements, Lyons, Hurst, Bernard, Harper, Royle, Buckley, Connolly.

Liverpool:
Clemence, Smith, Lindsay, PB Thompson, Lloyd, Hughes, Keegan (Hall), Cormack, Waddle, Boersma, Callaghan.

20 APRIL 1974

FOOTBALL LEAGUE DIVISION ONE

LIVERPOOL	0
EVERTON	0

Attendance: 55,858

Liverpool:
Clemence, Smith, Lindsay, PB Thompson, Cormack, Hughes, Keegan, Hall, Heighway, Boersma, Callaghan.

Everton:
Lawson, Bernard, Seargeant, Clements, Kenyon, Hurst, Harvey, Jones, Latchford, Lyons, Telfer.

16 NOVEMBER 1974

FOOTBALL LEAGUE DIVISION ONE

EVERTON	0
LIVERPOOL	0

Attendance: 57,190

Everton:
Davies, Bernard, Seargeant, Clements, Kenyon, Hurst, Buckley (Pearson), Dobson, Lyons, Jones, Connolly.

Liverpool:
Clemence, Smith, Neal, McDermott, Lawler, Hughes, Keegan, Cormack, Boersma, Kennedy, Callaghan.

22 FEBRUARY 1975

FOOTBALL LEAGUE DIVISION ONE

LIVERPOOL	0
EVERTON	0

Attendance: 55,583

Liverpool:
Clemence, Smith, Neal, Thompson, Cormack, Hughes, Keegan, Hall, Heighway, Toshack, Callaghan.

Everton:
Davies, Bernard, Seargeant, Clements, Kenyon, Hurst, Jones, Dobson, Latchford, Lyons, Telfer (Pearson).

27 SEPTEMBER 1975

FOOTBALL LEAGUE DIVISION ONE

EVERTON	0
LIVERPOOL	0

Attendance: 55,769

Everton:
Davies, McLaughlin, Seargeant, Pearson, Kenyon, Lyons, Buckley, Dobson, Latchford, Smallman, G Jones.

Liverpool:
Clemence, Neal, Lindsay, Thompson, Cormack, Hughes, Keegan, Hall, Heighway, Toshack, Callaghan.

3 APRIL 1976

FOOTBALL LEAGUE DIVISION ONE

LIVERPOOL	1

Fairclough

EVERTON	0

Attendance: 54,632

Liverpool:
Clemence, Smith, Neal, Thompson, Kennedy, Hughes, Keegan, Case, Heighway, Toshack (Fairclough), Callaghan.

Everton:
Davies, Bernard, D Jones, Lyons, McNaught (Kenyon), Buckley, Hamilton, Dobson, Latchford, Connolly, Telfer.

16 OCTOBER 1976

FOOTBALL LEAGUE DIVISION ONE

LIVERPOOL	3

Heighway, Neal (*pen*), Toshack

EVERTON	1

Dobson

Attendance: 55,141

Liverpool:
Clemence, Neal (Fairclough), Jones, Thompson, Kennedy, Hughes, Keegan, McDermott, Heighway, Toshack, Callaghan.

Everton:
Davies, Darracott, Jones, Lyons, McNaught, Bernard (Pearson), King, Dobson, Latchford, Goodlass, Telfer.

22 MARCH 1977

FOOTBALL LEAGUE DIVISION ONE

EVERTON	0
LIVERPOOL	0

Attendance: 56,562

Everton:
Lawson, Darracott, Pejic, Lyons, McNaught, King, Kenyon (Telfer), Dobson, Latchford, Rioch, Pearson.

Liverpool:
Clemence, Neal, Jones, Smith, Kennedy, Hughes, Keegan, Case, Heighway, Fairclough, McDermott.

GREATEST GAMES

25 MARCH 1984
MILK (LEAGUE) CUP FINAL
(Played at Wembley)

EVERTON	0
LIVERPOOL	0

The first ever all-Merseyside Wembley Cup Final ended all-square, leaving both teams to try again at Manchester City's Maine Road ground the following Wednesday night.

To be fair the conditions were not all that one would expect for a high level of football, but Liverpool owed their 39-match unbeaten run in the competition to referee Alan Robinson who turned down a clear-cut penalty appeal.

Just seven minutes into the game Heath challenged Grobbelaar on the edge of the area. When the Everton forward hit the ball towards goal, Hansen got back to seemingly control the ball with his hand. Had the decision gone Everton's way the deadlock would have been broken, perhaps decisively.

Everton missed three chances in the first half: a Sheedy shot was blocked by Lawrenson, Richardson hit the side netting and Reid shot at Grobbelaar after being freed by Sheedy. Everton were rock-like at the back with Ratcliffe and Mountfield well in control. Dalglish threatened briefly, while Kennedy shot over from five yards and Southall saved a Rush volley to justify his wages.

The Cup could have been won late on when Grobbelaar failed to collect Harper's cross and Sharp headed back across goal to Heath when he might have scored himself. Some observers thought the result an anti-climax, but Kevin Ratcliffe saw it differently. 'It was a great occasion, and to come off level was what both sets of supporters wanted. No-one wanted to lose at Wembley on the first time.'

The replay was decided by a single goal

from Graeme Souness, who ensured Liverpool won the Milk Cup for the third successive year and the fourth time overall. Dalglish, Lee, Johnston and Neal were all involved in the move which led to the goal. The Scots international midfielder then rode a tackle on the edge of the box before unleashing a powerful left-foot shot past Southall.

Everton, to their credit, battled for every ball and ran until they dropped. They'd started brightly despite the fact that Sheedy had failed to recover from an ankle ligament injury and was unable to play. It was only their fourth defeat since the New Year, but that was little consolation.

In the 12th minute Grobbelaar scrambled across his goal to stop a Reid shot before Liverpool took the lead. Everton had another chance to take the tie into extra time just before the end when Sharp headed down a deep cross, but Reid and Heath got in each other's way when the net beckoned.

The major surprise was that Ian Rush, with the benefit of a second chance, was unable to continue his record of scoring in every round. Even so, he – like all Liverpool's players and fans – would be rejoicing as they returned down the East Lancs Road.

For Everton, there would be the not inconsiderable consolation of a second trip to Wembley, in which it would beat Watford 2-0 to lift the FA Cup. Liverpool took the title, reinforcing the fact that this had been Merseyside's best all-round year since 1965. It also set up a Charity Shield derby clash, of which more overleaf…

Opposite: Mark Lawrenson dispossesses Everton's Adrian Heath in the first game at Wembley.

Below: Souness scores the replay winner.

Bottom: John Bailey and Sammy Lee do battle in the same game.

23 APRIL 1977

FA CUP SEMI-FINAL
(played at Maine Road)

EVERTON	2
McKenzie, Rioch	
LIVERPOOL	2
McDermott, Case	
Attendance: 52,637	

Everton:
Lawson, Darracott, Pejic, Lyons, McNaught, Rioch, Buckley, Dobson (Hamilton), Pearson, McKenzie, Goodlass.

Liverpool:
Clemence, Neal, Jones, Smith, Kennedy, Hughes, Keegan, Case, Heighway, Fairclough (Johnson), McDermott.

27 APRIL 1977

FA CUP SEMI-FINAL REPLAY
(played at Maine Road)

LIVERPOOL	3
Neal (*pen*), Case, Kennedy	
EVERTON	0
Attendance: 52,579	

Liverpool:
Clemence, Neal, Jones, Smith, Kennedy, Hughes, Keegan, Case, Johnson, Fairclough, McDermott.

Everton:
Lawson, Darracott, Pejic, Lyons, McNaught, Rioch, Buckley, Dobson (King), Pearson, McKenzie, Goodlass.

22 OCTOBER 1977

FOOTBALL LEAGUE DIVISION ONE

LIVERPOOL	0
EVERTON	0
Attendance: 51,668	

Liverpool:
Clemence, Neal, Jones, Hansen, Kennedy, Hughes, Dalglish, Case, Heighway, Toshack, Callaghan.

Everton:
Wood, Jones, Pejic, Lyons, Higgins, Rioch, King, Dobson, Latchford, Pearson, Thomas.

5 APRIL 1978

FOOTBALL LEAGUE DIVISION ONE

EVERTON	0
LIVERPOOL	1
Johnson	
Attendance: 52,759	

Everton:
Wood, Jones, Pejic, Lyons, Darracott, Ross, King, Dobson, Latchford, McKenzie, Thomas.

Liverpool:
Clemence, Neal, Smith, Thompson, Kennedy, Hughes, Dalglish, Case, Heighway, McDermott, Johnson.

28 OCTOBER 1978

FOOTBALL LEAGUE DIVISION ONE

EVERTON	1
King	

LIVERPOOL	0

Attendance: 53,141

Everton:
Wood, Todd, Pejic, Kenyon, Wright, Nulty, King, Dobson, Latchford, Walsh, Thomas.

Liverpool:
Clemence, Neal, A Kennedy, Thompson, R Kennedy, Hansen, Dalglish, Case (McDermott), Heighway, Johnson, Souness.

13 MARCH 1979

FOOTBALL LEAGUE DIVISION ONE

LIVERPOOL	1
Dalglish	

EVERTON	1
King	

Attendance: 52,352

Liverpool:
Clemence, Neal, Hughes, Thompson, R Kennedy, Hansen, Dalglish, Johnson (Fairclough), Case, McDermott, Souness.

Everton:
Wood, Todd, Heard, Lyons, Wright, Ross, King, Dobson, Latchford, Telfer, Thomas.

20 OCTOBER 1979

FOOTBALL LEAGUE DIVISION ONE

LIVERPOOL	2
Lyons og, R Kennedy	

EVERTON	2
Kidd, King	

Attendance: 52,201

Liverpool:
Clemence, Neal, A Kennedy, Thompson, R Kennedy, Hansen, Dalglish, Case, Johnson, McDermott, Souness.

Everton:
Wood, Wright, Bailey, Lyons, Higgins, Ross, Nulty, Stanley, Latchford, Kidd, King.

1 MARCH 1980

FOOTBALL LEAGUE DIVISION ONE

EVERTON	1
Eastoe	

LIVERPOOL	2
Johnson, Neal (*pen*)	

Attendance: 53,018

Everton:
Wood, Gidman, Bailey, Nulty (Eastoe), Lyons, Ross, Hartford, Wright, King, Kidd, McBride.

Liverpool:
Clemence, Neal, A Kennedy, Thompson, R Kennedy, Hansen, Dalglish, Case, Johnson (Fairclough), McDermott, Souness.

GREATEST GAMES

18 AUGUST 1984
FA CHARITY SHIELD

EVERTON	1
LIVERPOOL	0

The second ever Charity Shield to be contested by the two Mersey sides and the first to be played at Wembley (the 1966 fixture was staged at Goodison Park) saw few changes from the sides that had won League and Cup the previous term.

And the crucial difference was in midfield, where Liverpool had still to find a replacement for Graeme Souness, transferred to Italian giants Sampdoria in the summer. By contrast, Everton new boy Paul Bracewell linked well with old stager Peter Reid to provide the bite that Liverpool lacked. Indeed Bracewell looked a steal at £250,000, with Sunderland's loss clearly Everton's gain.

The goal which won the Charity Shield had more than a element of luck about it, and was one the erratic Bruce Grobbelaar wouldn't want to remember. He came from his line to collect Sharp's cross, but the ball ran loose and pinged around pinball-style in the penalty area until the unfortunate keeper got an unwanted final touch.

Liverpool looked short of fire-power up front. Paul Walsh was on the bench even though he hadn't played in the pre-season games, but though he replaced midfielder Lee he couldn't find a way through. Rush had looked alone up front before Walsh's arrival, and couldn't find a way past central defenders Mountfield or captain Ratcliffe.

'We had the better of that game,' claimed the Everton skipper, who in retrospect regarded it as a curtain-raiser to his most successful Goodison campaign. 'We started off pretty well: that's the season we won the League and the European Cup Winners' Cup. We reached Wembley and lost against Manchester United, so it could have been a treble.' Ever the pragmatist, though, he insisted the Charity Shield was well down on his personal list of priorities. 'The most important game is the one after that – the first game of the season.'

Below: Everton skipper Kevin Ratcliffe holds the Charity Shield aloft after the second Wembley meeting of many in the 1980s.

21 SEPTEMBER 1985
FOOTBALL LEAGUE DIVISION 1

EVERTON	**2**
LIVERPOOL	**3**

Everton were down and out of this match almost before it started when Kenny Dalglish opened the scoring after only 20 seconds. The Liverpool player-manager set his side on the road to victory, but confirmation of the result took somewhat longer than might at first have been expected.

The Blues had kicked off full of early-season hope, but eight touches later Neville Southall was picking the ball out of his own net. Not only had Dalglish become the first player-manager to score in the Mersey derby, he'd now established the record for the quickest goal.

Ian Rush added a second, equalling Harry Chambers' record of eight goals in derbies when Ronnie Whelan intercepted Bracewell's back-header. Steve McMahon, playing against his old club for the first time, then thundered home a 25-yarder to give the Reds a 3-0 lead that appeared to be out of Everton's reach.

Manager Howard Kendall had other ideas, however, throwing caution to the wind and playing just three at the back. And the tactic paid immediate dividends when McMahon was caught in possession by Paul Bracewell: his shot was deflected into the path of Graeme Sharp, who crashed the ball in off the bar.

Just seven minutes later, Bracewell was again involved in the move that led to Everton's second. Gary Stevens found Gary Lineker who made no mistake in his first taste of derby action since his £800,000 transfer from Leicester. He would finish the season on 30 League goals, having picked up the players' and sportswriters' Player of the Year awards.

As Everton pressed for a last-gasp equaliser, opposing player-manager Dalglish could have had a hat-trick in the last five minutes, twice beating Southall but firing wide of the target. Nevertheless, he emerged to give the game his own personal seal of approval.

'Two committed teams and sets of supporters as well as the referee made it one of the greatest games I've ever been involved in,' said Dalglish. 'I find the atmosphere generated by these two clubs quite unbelievable.'

Left: The Toffees' top marksman Gary Lineker celebrates – but his smile would be short-lived on this occasion.

Above: The match programme.

FOOTBALL LEAGUE DIVISION ONE

EVERTON	**2**
Hartford, McBride	
LIVERPOOL	**2**
Lee, Dalglish	

Attendance: 52,565

Everton:
McDonagh, Gidman (O'Keefe), Bailey, Wright, Lyons, Stanley, McMahon, Eastoe, Latchford, Hartford, McBride.

Liverpool:
Clemence, Neal, Cohen, Thompson, R Kennedy, Hansen, Dalglish, Lee, Johnson, McDermott, Souness.

24 JANUARY 1981

FA CUP FOURTH ROUND

EVERTON	**2**
Eastoe, Varadi	
LIVERPOOL	**1**
Case	

Attendance: 53,804

Everton:
Hodge, Ratcliffe, Bailey, Wright, Lodge, Ross, McMahon, Eastoe, Varadi, Hartford, O'Keefe.

Liverpool:
Clemence, Neal, Thompson, Irwin, Cohen, R Kennedy, Dalglish (Case), Lee, Fairclough, McDermott, Souness.

21 MARCH 1981

FOOTBALL LEAGUE DIVISION ONE

LIVERPOOL	**1**
Bailey og	
EVERTON	**0**

Attendance: 49,743

Liverpool:
Clemence, Neal, Money, Irwin, R Kennedy, Hansen, Dalglish, Lee, Heighway, Case, Souness.

Everton:
McDonagh, Gidman, Bailey, Wright, Stanley, Ross, McMahon, Eastoe, Varadi (McBride), Lodge, O'Keefe.

7 NOVEMBER 1981

FOOTBALL LEAGUE DIVISION ONE

LIVERPOOL	**3**
Dalglish 2, Rush	
EVERTON	**1**
Ferguson	

Attendance: 48,861

Liverpool:
Grobbelaar, Neal, Lawrenson, Thompson, R Kennedy (Johnson), Hansen, Dalglish, Whelan, Rush, McDermott, Souness.

Everton:
Arnold, Stevens, Bailey, Higgins, Lyons, Lodge, McMahon, O'Keefe, Ferguson, Ainscow (Biley), McBride.

27 MARCH 1982

FOOTBALL LEAGUE DIVISION ONE

EVERTON	1
Sharp	
LIVERPOOL	**3**
Whelan, Souness, Johnston	

Attendance: 51,847

Everton:
Southall, Borrows, Ratcliffe, Higgins, Wright, Richardson, Irvine, Heath, Sharp, McMahon, Ross.

Liverpool:
Grobbelaar, Neal, Lawrenson, A Kennedy, Whelan, Thompson, Dalglish, Lee, Rush, Johnston, Souness.

6 NOVEMBER 1982

FOOTBALL LEAGUE DIVISION ONE

EVERTON	0
LIVERPOOL	**5**
Rush 4, Lawrenson	

Attendance: 52,741

Everton:
Southall, Borrows, Bailey, Keeley, Wright, McMahon, Heath, Johnson (Richardson), Sharp, King, Sheedy.

Liverpool:
Grobbelaar, Neal, Kennedy, Thompson, Johnston, Hansen, Dalglish (Hodgson), Lee, Rush, Lawrenson, Souness.

19 MARCH 1983

FOOTBALL LEAGUE DIVISION ONE

LIVERPOOL	0
EVERTON	0

Attendance: 44,737

Liverpool:
Grobbelaar, Neal, Kennedy, Lawrenson, Whelan, Hansen, Dalglish, Lee, Rush, Johnston, Souness (Hodgson).

Everton:
Arnold, Stevens, Bailey, Ratcliffe, Higgins, Richardson, Irvine (Ainscow), McMahon, Sharp, Heath, Sheedy.

6 NOVEMBER 1983

FOOTBALL LEAGUE DIVISION ONE

LIVERPOOL	3
Rush, Robinson, Nicol	
EVERTON	0

Attendance: 40,875

Liverpool:
Grobbelaar, Neal, Kennedy, Lawrenson, Nicol, Hansen, Dalglish, Lee, Rush, Robinson, Souness.

Everton:
Southall, Harper, Bailey, Ratcliffe, Higgins, Steven, Irvine, Heath, Sharp, King, Sheedy.

GREATEST GAMES

22 FEBRUARY 1986
FOOTBALL LEAGUE DIVISION 1

LIVERPOOL	0
EVERTON	2

To blame Bruce Grobbelaar for Everton's win wouldn't be fair – but than again football isn't always a fair game. Having kept the Reds in the game for 73 minutes, the Clown Prince of goalkeepers then blotted his copybook, letting Kevin Ratcliffe's speculative 25-yarder squirm away from him and roll into the net.

Until then, it had looked as if table-topping Liverpool would increase their three-point lead over Manchester United – even though injuries to Kenny Dalglish and Paul Walsh had meant Jan Molby was pressed into action as a makeshift striker. The Dane looked unhappy with his new-found role and was taken off at half-time, but by then Peter Reid was starting to run the show.

There'd been double drama early on when Grobbelaar pushed away Kevin Richardson's sixth-minute effort. The Everton midfielder then had appeals for a penalty rejected when he looked to have been pulled down by the Liverpool keeper.

Neville Southall needed to be on his toes when Craig Johnston, the Reds' second stand-in striker of the afternoon, was released by Ronnie Whelan. Then Everton defender Pat Van den Hauwe cleared off the line from Ian Rush after he had rounded Southall and headed for goal.

Yet it was Gary Lineker who proved that there's nothing like a thoroughbred striker, notching his 28th goal of the season when he lobbed the advancing keeper 12 minutes from time. It was his only chance of the game, and the way he took it showed why he would top-score in the forthcoming World Cup Finals in Mexico. It also showed why he would take advantage of that high-profile showcase to further his career with Barcelona after just one season at Goodison.

Liverpool went on to win the League, never losing a game after that with an amazing sequence of 11 wins and one draw. For Everton, who would finish the campaign just two points behind the Champions, it was a morale-boost which would set them up for their third competitive meeting of the season at Wembley in May.

Left: Gary Lineker casts a shadow on his shadow, Liverpool's Gary Gillespie, who was powerless to prevent him sealing Everton's win.

Below: The match programme.

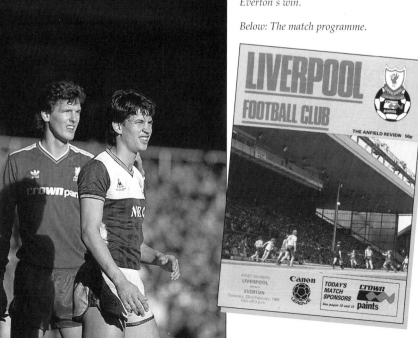

GREATEST GAMES

10 MAY 1986
FA CUP FINAL
(Played at Wembley)

EVERTON	1
LIVERPOOL	3

16 AUGUST 1986
FA CHARITY SHIELD
(Played at Wembley)

EVERTON	1
LIVERPOOL	1

Liverpool's victory at Wembley gave it the distinction of being only the third side this century, after Tottenham and Arsenal, to win both the League Championship and FA Cup in the same season.

And the thanks went to Ian Rush who, not for the first time, saved the Reds from defeat against their keenest rivals. To add to his two goals and Man of the Match display, he had a hand in Craig Johnston's goal which gave Liverpool the lead.

Gary Lineker opened the scoring after 28 minutes, Peter Reid winning the ball from Kenny Dalglish to hit a typically searching 30-yard pass. Lineker ran clear of Alan Hansen, Bruce Grobbelaar blocking his first shot but powerless to stop the second.

Kevin Sheedy and Trevor Steven both shot wide in the first ten minutes of the second

Below: Managers Howard Kendall and Kenny Dalglish lead their teams onto the Wembley pitch for the first Merseyside FA Cup Final.

---

3 MARCH 1984

FOOTBALL LEAGUE DIVISION ONE

EVERTON	1
Harper	
LIVERPOOL	1
Rush	

Attendance: 51,245

Everton:
Southall, Stevens, Bailey, Ratcliffe, Mountfield, Reid, Steven (Harper), Heath, Sharp, Gray, Sheedy.

Liverpool:
Grobbelaar, Neal, Kennedy, Lawrenson, Whelan, Hansen, Robinson, Lee (Nicol), Rush, Johnston, Souness.

25 MARCH 1984

FOOTBALL LEAGUE CUP FINAL
(played at Wembley)

EVERTON	0
LIVERPOOL	0

Attendance: 100,000

Everton:
Southall, Stevens, Bailey, Ratcliffe, Mountfield, Reid, Irvine, Heath, Sharp, Richardson, Sheedy (Harper).

Liverpool:
Grobbelaar, Neal, Kennedy, Lawrenson, Whelan, Hansen, Dalglish, Lee, Rush, Johnston (Robinson), Souness.

28 MARCH 1984

FOOTBALL LEAGUE CUP FINAL REPLAY
(played at Maine Road)

LIVERPOOL	1
Souness	
EVERTON	0

Attendance: 52,089

Liverpool:
Grobbelaar, Neal, Kennedy, Lawrenson, Whelan, Hansen, Dalglish, Lee, Rush, Johnston, Souness.

Everton:
Southall, Stevens, Bailey, Ratcliffe, Mountfield, Reid, Irvine (King), Heath, Sharp, Richardson, Harper.

18 AUGUST 1984

FA CHARITY SHIELD
(played at Wembley)

EVERTON	1
Grobbelaar og	
LIVERPOOL	0

Attendance: 100,000

Everton:
Southall, Stevens, Bailey, Ratcliffe, Mountfield, Reid, Steven, Heath, Sharp, Bracewell, Richardson.

Liverpool:
Grobbelaar, Neal, A Kennedy, Lawrenson, Whelan, Hansen, Dalglish, Lee (Walsh), Rush, Nicol, Wark.

20 OCTOBER 1984

FOOTBALL LEAGUE DIVISION ONE

LIVERPOOL	**0**
EVERTON	**1**
Sharp	

Attendance: 45,545

Liverpool:
Grobbelaar, Neal, Kennedy, Lawrenson, Whelan, Hansen, Dalglish, Robinson, Rush, Wark, Molby.

Everton:
Southall, Stevens, Van den Hauwe, Ratcliffe, Mountfield, Reid, Steven, Heath, Sharp, Bracewell, Harper.

23 MAY 1985

FOOTBALL LEAGUE DIVISION ONE

EVERTON	**1**
Wilkinson	
LIVERPOOL	**0**

Attendance: 51,045

Everton:
Southall, Stevens, Bailey, Ratcliffe, Van den Hauwe, Richardson, Harper, Wilkinson, Gray, Atkins (Wakenshaw), Sheedy.

Liverpool:
Grobbelaar, Neal, Beglin, Molby, Nicol, Hansen, Dalglish, Whelan, Rush, Lee, Wark.

21 SEPTEMBER 1985

FOOTBALL LEAGUE DIVISION ONE

EVERTON	**2**
Sharp, Lineker	
LIVERPOOL	**3**
Dalglish, Rush, McMahon	

Attendance: 51,509

Everton:
Southall, Stevens, Van den Hauwe, Ratcliffe, Marshall (Heath), Harper, Steven, Lineker, Sharp, Bracewell, Sheedy.

Liverpool:
Grobbelaar, Nicol (Neal), Beglin, Lawrenson, Whelan, Hansen, Dalglish, Johnston, Rush, Molby, McMahon.

22 FEBRUARY 1986

FOOTBALL LEAGUE DIVISION ONE

LIVERPOOL	**0**
EVERTON	**2**
Ratcliffe, Lineker	

Attendance: 45,445

Liverpool:
Grobbelaar, Lee, Beglin, Lawrenson, Whelan, Hansen, Gillespie, Johnston, Rush, Molby (MacDonald), McMahon.

Everton:
Southall, Stevens, Pointon, Ratcliffe, Van den Hauwe, Reid, Steven, Lineker, Sharp, Bracewell (Harper), Richardson.

half, but then Liverpool struck with devastating speed. After Kevin McDonald punished full-back Gary Stevens for a sloppy piece of play he found Jan Molby: the Dane sent Rush clear and he side-stepped Bobby Mimms – deputising for the injured Neville Southall – before slotting the ball into an empty net.

Liverpool's second goal came in its next attack six minutes later, Rush turning provider with a pass for Molby. His cross was missed by Dalglish in the middle, but Johnston converted it at the far post.

With Everton pressing hard to get on terms, the destination of the Cup was sealed when Molby and Ronnie Whelan prised open Everton's three-man defence and, with no-one to stop him, Rush fired past Mimms.

It could have been a different story if Lineker had managed to volley a second from Sharp's well-placed pass. But at the end of the day there was no stopping the Red Machine from writing themselves into the history books.

Yet it could all have been so different. Both teams were on course for the Double as they emerged victorious from their respective semi-finals against Southampton (Liverpool) and Sheffield Wednesday. For Everton it all went wrong when they lost 1-0 at Oxford. 'We thought we got let down by the referee on the day,' explains Kevin Ratcliffe, 'and had we won that game we would have won the League. If we'd won against Liverpool we'd have won the Cup, so we were only two games away from the Double.'

As it was, the Blues were bridesmaids on both counts – and that gave rise to a sad post-Wembley ritual, as beaten skipper Ratcliffe explained.

'Both teams had to travel round the city on a coach, it didn't matter what the score was and we realised at the time, me and Alan Hansen, that it was a bad thing because we knew that one team could win the Double. It

Above: Alan Hansen comes out top in a five-man melée featuring Lawrenson, Nicol, Lineker and Sheedy.

Above right: Ronnie Whelan watches Ian Rush equalise in the Charity Shield.

Right: Craig Johnston beats Everton's Mimms to score his side's second Cup Final goal.

would be nice if one could go away with one and one with the other, but we always had the fear that one could be going on that coach with nothing. Peter Reid didn't go, and got a hefty fine: looking back, I wish I hadn't either!

'The fans turned out, but not as many as the Liverpool fans: then again if Peter Reid didn't turn up, who could expect them to?'

By August, however, all this had been forgotten as some 88,000 Merseysiders returned to the capital for the Charity Shield and Wembley was once again turned into a sea of red and blue.

Like a thoroughbred horse race, the two sides matched each other stride for stride and couldn't be separated in a photo finish. Yet it was the introduction of Dalglish in the 65th minute which looked to have given Liverpool the edge.

So when Everton took the lead ten minutes from time with a goal from Adrian Heath, it seemed marginally against the run of play. Despite a lack of first-team opportunities the previous season, the diminutive striker had signed a four-year contract in the summer and was happy to underline his value to the team, pouncing on the ball as the Liverpool defence stood still before sweeping the ball past Hooper.

If Heath owed his place to the departure of Lineker (and manager Kendall's decision not to splash out on a replacement), then Hooper was even more fortunate to be on the pitch, having

substituted for Bruce Grobbelaar in the 57th minute when a stomach strain forced the Zimbabwean out of the action.

Heath's goal looked likely to decide the destination of the Shield, but Ian Rush had other ideas. With just two minutes remaining, he scored his annual goal against the arch rivals – less than two months after scoring twice in the Cup Final.

Dalglish's driven cross beat Mimms and, with one lethal stroke of the foot, Rush pulled his side level as the finishing post beckoned. The entertainment served up by the two teams was of the highest quality, and few – including the five million people watching the game live on television – could argue with the result.

Everton went on to win the Championship for the second time in three years, while though Liverpool finished the season trophyless they and their supporters would return to Wembley the following April for the League Cup Final.

25 APRIL 1987

FOOTBALL LEAGUE DIVISION ONE

LIVERPOOL	3
McMahon, Rush 2	
EVERTON	1
Sheedy	

Attendance: 44,827

Liverpool:
Hooper, Gillespie, Venison, Ablett, Whelan, Hansen, Spackman, Johnston, Rush, Molby, McMahon.

Everton:
Southall, Stevens, Power, Ratcliffe, Watson, Reid, Steven, Heath, Clarke, Snodin, Sheedy.

28 OCTOBER 1987

FOOTBALL LEAGUE CUP THIRD ROUND

LIVERPOOL	0
EVERTON	1
Stevens	

Attendance: 44,071

Liverpool:
Grobbelaar, Lawrenson, Gillespie, Nicol, Whelan, Hansen, Beardsley, Aldridge, Johnston, Barnes, McMahon.

Everton:
Southall, Stevens, Van den Hauwe, Ratcliffe, Watson, Reid, Steven, Heath, Sharp, Snodin, Wilson.

1 NOVEMBER 1987

FOOTBALL LEAGUE DIVISION ONE

LIVERPOOL	2
McMahon, Beardsley	
EVERTON	0

Attendance: 44,760

Liverpool:
Grobbelaar, Gillespie, Lawrenson, Nicol, Whelan, Hansen, Beardsley, Aldridge, Johnston, Barnes, McMahon.

Everton:
Southall, Stevens, Van den Hauwe, Ratcliffe, Watson, Reid, Steven, Clarke (Mountfield), Sharp, Snodin, Wilson.

21 FEBRUARY 1988

FA CUP FIFTH ROUND

EVERTON	0
LIVERPOOL	1
Houghton	

Attendance: 48,270

Everton:
Southall, Stevens, Pointon, Van den Hauwe, Watson, Reid (Harper), Steven, Heath, Sharp, Snodin, Power (Bracewell).

Liverpool:
Grobbelaar, Ablett, Venison, Nicol, Spackman, Hansen, Beardsley, Aldridge, Houghton, Barnes, McMahon.

21 JANUARY 1987
LEAGUE (LITTLEWOODS) CUP FIFTH ROUND

EVERTON	0
LIVERPOOL	1

Liverpool reached the semi-final of the Littlewoods Cup thanks to Ian Rush, but the game was marred by the broken leg suffered by Liverpool's Republic of Ireland international defender Jim Beglin.

It was a bruising encounter, and the highly charged atmosphere was ignited even further when Beglin emerged from a Gary Stevens challenge with a broken leg.

Liverpool were clearly upset by the tackle: trainer Ronnie Moran was furious with the linesman who was close to the incident, while Whelan was cautioned for dissent. Yet though it was Everton who appeared more shaken by the incident, they enjoyed the best chances of the first half, Sharp and Heath shooting narrowly wide.

Kenny Dalglish switched his team around at half-time with Irvine on for McMahon, Lawrenson and Venison moving into midfield and Molby and Whelan dropping back into defence. Everton tried their utmost to raise the tempo of the game, but it was the re-shaped Liverpool who looked the better team.

Irvine outstripped Stevens, who understandably seemed a little subdued, and crossed for Walsh to shoot from the edge of the box. His superb drive beat Southall but came back off the post.

Tempers frayed once again when Sharp was cautioned for elbowing Molby in the face. The Red tide then surged forward through Walsh. He fired in a low shot which was hacked off the line by Stevens after passing through a sea of legs, and a replay seemed inevitable.

Then, with seven minutes remaining, Rush broke the deadlock in all too familiar style, lashing home a fierce left-foot drive as the ball broke in Everton's box to take him to joint second place in terms of goals scored in derby games.

Liverpool went on to reach Wembley for the sixth time in this competition, but were beaten by Arsenal. They did so without Jim Beglin, who would be sidelined for the whole of the following season and, unable to regain his place, would leave Anfield for Leeds on a free transfer in June 1989.

Below left: The Fifth Round programme.

Below: Ex-Evertonian Steve McMahon attempts to stop Adrian Heath as he seeks to equalise Ian Rush's decisive goal which took Liverpool through to the Sixth Round of the Cup.

GREATEST GAMES

25 APRIL 1987
FOOTBALL LEAGUE DIVISION 1

LIVERPOOL	3
EVERTON	1

I an Rush blasted two more goals in his Liverpool career – and not for the first time he broke Everton hearts as he did so. The Welsh international was the difference between both teams, his brace deciding this top of the table clash.

He even had a hand in the first goal of the game which was scored by former Everton star Steve McMahon. Just nine minutes had elapsed when Rush set McMahon up 25 yards out. The combative England international thundered the ball home, leaving Neville Southall helpless. Nigel Spackman, a recent addition to Dalglish's squad from Chelsea, forced a brilliant save from Southall soon afterwards as Liverpool looked to extend their lead.

Not content with performing heroics, the Everton keeper played a part in his side's goal when his long clearance forced Hansen to push deadline signing Wayne Clarke, filling in for the injured Graeme Sharp. The free-kick was lined up 25 yards out, and Mike Hooper in the Liverpool goal was left helpless when Kevin Sheedy's educated left foot made contact with the ball.

Then on the stroke of half-time Rush moved into top gear. Johnston's corner was flicked on and the former Chester forward headed home.

As the second half gathered pace, Southall performed heroics to deny McMahon, racing off his line to stop his former team-mate who had been freed by Ablett's long ball forward. Then it was time for Rush to edge closer to Dixie Dean's record for the most goals scored in Merseyside derbies. He broke down the right before lifting the ball over Southall with just six minutes left.

Yet the last laugh was Everton's as they reversed the previous season's fortunes by finishing one place above their neighbours as Champions. Howard Kendall would bow out on this high – still Everton's post-war peak – to take over at Spanish club Athletico Bilbao.

Above: Two-goal Ian Rush makes his move. The derby fixture's leading goalscorer would take the following season out as he tried his luck in Italian football with Juventus.

---

20 MARCH 1988

FOOTBALL LEAGUE DIVISION ONE

EVERTON	1
Clarke	
LIVERPOOL	0

Attendance: 44,162

Everton:
Southall, Stevens, Pointon, Van den Hauwe, Watson, Reid, Steven, Clarke (Heath), Sharp, Harper, Sheedy (Power).

Liverpool:
Grobbelaar, Gillespie, Ablett, Nicol, Spackman (Molby), Hansen, Beardsley, Johnston, Houghton, Barnes, McMahon.

---

11 DECEMBER 1988

FOOTBALL LEAGUE DIVISION ONE

LIVERPOOL	1
Houghton	
EVERTON	1
Clarke	

Attendance: 42,372

Liverpool:
Hooper, Ablett, Venison, Nicol, Whelan, Burrows, Beardsley, Aldridge (Rush), Houghton, Barnes, McMahon.

Everton:
Southall, Snodin, Van den Hauwe, Ratcliffe, Watson, Bracewell (Reid), Steven, McCall, Clarke, Cottee, Wilson.

---

3 MAY 1989

FOOTBALL LEAGUE DIVISION ONE

EVERTON	0
LIVERPOOL	0

Attendance: 45,994

Everton:
Southall, McDonald, Van den Hauwe, Ratcliffe, Watson, Bracewell, Nevin, Steven, Sharp, Cottee, Sheedy (McCall).

Liverpool:
Grobbelaar, Ablett, Staunton, Nicol, Whelan, Hansen, Beardsley, Aldridge (Rush), Houghton, Barnes, McMahon.

---

20 MAY 1989

FA CUP FINAL
(played at Wembley)

EVERTON	2
McCall 2	
LIVERPOOL	3
Aldridge, Rush 2	

Attendance: 82,800

Everton:
Southall, McDonald, Van den Hauwe, Ratcliffe, Watson, Bracewell (McCall), Nevin, Steven, Sharp, Cottee, Sheedy (Wilson).

Liverpool:
Grobbelaar, Ablett, Staunton (Venison), Nicol, Whelan, Hansen, Beardsley, Aldridge (Rush), Houghton, Barnes, McMahon.

20 MAY 1989
FA CUP FINAL
(Played At Wembley)

EVERTON	2
LIVERPOOL	3

The third Merseyside Cup Final to be staged at Wembley in five years was played in an emotional atmosphere less than eight weeks after the tragedy at Hillsborough that would cost 96 Liverpool fans their lives. The national stadium's perimeter fencing was taken down for the day as a mark of respect, and banners proclaimed the fact that those who could not be there would never be forgotten.

For the neutral observers on live television, the game was a fine spectacle, played in bright sunshine and with all the ingredients of a classic Cup-tie. But it takes two teams to make a game like this and Everton certainly had no intention of just turning up for a day out in the sun – even if the emotional odds were stacked against them.

Liverpool went ahead with their very first attack of the game, Nicol and McMahon combining to set up Aldridge whose deadly right foot made no mistake from close range. The smile on his face suggested it was some kind of atonement for his penalty miss in the previous season's Final that had handed the trophy to Wimbledon. But Liverpool could not relax, and it needed a timely block by Hansen in the Reds' penalty area to deny Sheedy after Grobbelaar had come a long way to miss McDonald's cross.

The introduction of ginger-haired midfielder Stuart McCall as substitute 25 minutes from time pepped up Everton's attacking ideas, but the breakthrough just would not come as Liverpool's incomparable back line held firm. Then, with the referee about to blow for full time and the score still 1-0, Liverpool keeper Grobbelaar only half-saved Pat Nevin's cross and McCall pounced to send the tie into extra time.

At this point, Kenny Dalglish called on his secret weapon – derby demon Ian Rush, who'd been sitting on the bench for the 90 minutes wearing an unfamiliar Number 14 shirt. He came on for John Aldridge, who'd given his all in the heat – and inevitably it was the Welshman, with his fresh legs, who put Liverpool back in front in the first period of extra time. Nicol threaded a ball through to Rush who beat his countrymen Ratcliffe

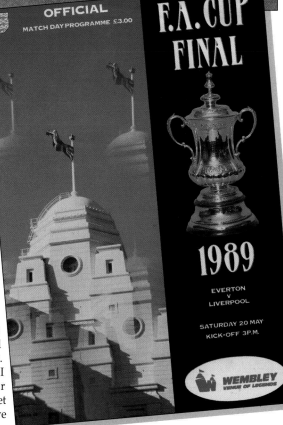

and Southall to thump the ball into the roof of the net.

McCall equalised with a powerful volley from outside the penalty area, but in a game which had twice seen them pinned back though never overhauled Liverpool had the last laugh. And it was a second Rush strike that proved the decider, as he stole in to steer the ball wide of Southall after a move involving Whelan and Barnes.

After events at Hillsborough it seemed unlikely that Everton would come out on top with the whole country almost willing Liverpool to triumph. And that is the way it ended.

Everton captain Kevin Ratcliffe felt 'the Final was disappointing for us because the things that went on were all Liverpool Liverpool Liverpool... it wasn't a joint day. We all felt for Hillsborough and I did my bit by raising money for them, but football's something I get paid for doing and I want to achieve as much as I can. I felt they had a goal start already – we were in a no-win situation that day.'

There was a disappointing finale for Liverpool, too. They may have lifted the Cup, but their Double dream was to be shattered in front of their own fans by Arsenal.

Opposite: Steve McMahon cradles the Cup as Liverpool celebrate.

Top: Stuart McCall takes the match into extra-time with a last-minute equaliser.

Above: The Wembley programme.

17 FEBRUARY 1991

FA CUP FIFTH ROUND

LIVERPOOL	**0**
EVERTON	**0**

Attendance: 38,323

Liverpool:
Grobbelaar, Hysen, Burrows, Nicol, Molby, Ablett, Speedie (Beardsley), Staunton, Rush, Barnes, McMahon (Venison).

Everton:
Southall, McDonald, Ebbrell, Ratcliffe, Watson, Keown, Atteveld, McCall, Sharp, Sheedy (Cottee), Nevin.

20 FEBRUARY 1991

FA CUP FIFTH ROUND REPLAY

EVERTON	**4**
Sharp 2, Cottee 2	
LIVERPOOL	**4**
Beardsley 2, Rush, Barnes	

Attendance: 37,766

Everton:
Southall, Atteveld (McCall), Hinchcliffe, Ratcliffe, Watson, Keown, Nevin (Cottee), McDonald, Sharp, Newell, Ebbrell.

Liverpool:
Grobbelaar, Hysen, Burrows, Nicol, Molby, Ablett, Beardsley, Staunton, Rush, Barnes, Venison.

27 FEBRUARY 1991

FA CUP FIFTH ROUND SECOND REPLAY

EVERTON	**1**
Watson	
LIVERPOOL	**0**

Attendance: 40,201

Everton:
Southall, McDonald, Hinchcliffe, Ratcliffe, Watson, Keown, Atteveld (Nevin), McCall, Sharp, Newell, Ebbrell.

Liverpool:
Grobbelaar, Hysen, Venison (Speedie), Nicol, Molby, Ablett, Beardsley, Houghton, Rush, Barnes, Staunton.

31 AUGUST 1991

FOOTBALL LEAGUE DIVISION ONE

LIVERPOOL	**3**
Burrows, Saunders, Houghton	
EVERTON	**1**
Newell	

Attendance: 39,072

Liverpool:
Grobbelaar, Ablett, Burrows, Nicol, Whelan (Marsh), Tanner, Saunders, Houghton, McManaman, Walters (Rosenthal), McMahon.

Everton:
Southall, Harper, Ebbrell, McDonald, Watson, Keown (Ratcliffe), Ward, Beardsley, Newell, Cottee (Warzycha), Sheedy.

28 DECEMBER 1991

FOOTBALL LEAGUE DIVISION ONE

EVERTON	1
Johnston	
LIVERPOOL	1
Tanner	

Attendance: 37,681

Everton:
Southall, Jackson, Harper, Ebbrell, Watson, Keown, Warzycha (Nevin), Beardsley, Johnston, Ward, Beagrie.

Liverpool:
Grobbelaar, Jones, Ablett, Nicol, Wright (McManaman), Tanner, Saunders, Houghton, Marsh, Molby, Thomas.

7 DECEMBER 1992

FA PREMIER LEAGUE

EVERTON	2
Beardsley, Johnston	
LIVERPOOL	1
Wright	

Attendance: 35,826

Everton:
Southall, Horne, Ablett, Snodin (Rideout), Watson, Keown, Kenny, Beardsley, Barlow, Johnston, Unsworth (Beagrie).

Liverpool:
Hooper, Marsh, Wright, Nicol, Piechnik, Hutchison (Stewart), McManaman, Redknapp, Rosenthal (Walters), Barnes, Jones.

20 MARCH 1993

FA PREMIER LEAGUE

LIVERPOOL	1
Rosenthal	
EVERTON	0

Attendance: 44,619

Liverpool:
James, Burrows, Harkness, Nicol, Wright (Molby), Whelan, McManaman (Rosenthal), Hutchison, Rush, Barnes, Walters.

Everton:
Southall, Jackson, Hinchcliffe, Snodin, Watson, Ablett, Ward (Radosavljevic), Beardsley, Cottee, Kenny (Barlow), Ebbrell.

18 SEPTEMBER 1993

FA PREMIER LEAGUE

EVERTON	2
Ward, Cottee	
LIVERPOOL	0

Attendance: 38,157

Everton:
Southall, Holmes, Hinchcliffe, Ebbrell, Jackson, Ablett, Ward, Horne, Cottee, Rideout, Beagrie (Radosavljevic).

Liverpool:
Grobbelaar, Nicol, Dicks, Whelan, Wright, Ruddock, Clough, Redknapp, Rush, Walters (Rosenthal), McManaman (Stewart).

GREATEST GAMES

22 SEPTEMBER 1990
FOOTBALL LEAGUE DIVISION 1

EVERTON	2
LIVERPOOL	3

Liverpool moved closer to Tottenham's record of 11 consecutive wins after a thrilling victory at Goodison Park. Bookmakers were offering odds of 20-1 against before kick-off, but Messrs Barnes and Beardsley were determined to keep the Reds in the hunt.

Everton battled all the way after being written off as underdogs, but had no answer to the two buzzing Bs. Goals from the pair had decided the year's other derby back in February, and there was no stopping Beardsley in particular as he notched two goals and set up the penalty for the third.

His first stemmed from a John Barnes free-kick in the 35th minute, a typical blind-side run and shot beating Southall. Barnes then scored himself from the penalty spot two minutes later after Rush was felled

when a Beardsley pass had put him through.

The provider on that occasion added a third himself 21 minutes before the end, and it looked as if the Reds were home and dry. But Everton dug deep, and left-back Andy Hinchcliffe charged forward to fire home in his first ever derby after a free-kick had been awarded for a foul on Sharp. The Scot had been receiving close attention from the Liverpool defence all afternoon, and this was some reward for his efforts.

With nothing to lose Everton then came forward in numbers, urged on by an increasingly vocal home crowd of nearly 40,000. They piled on the pressure, and when all-action Stuart McCall put the ball past visiting keeper Bruce Grobbelaar a hectic finish was ensured.

The Reds were unable to go on and beat Spurs' long-standing record and they failed to win the title that season, despite their good start and a second derby victory in February, this time by a 3-1 margin.

Above: Derby debutant and goalscorer Andy Hinchcliffe takes a throw.

Left: The match programme.

GREATEST GAMES

20 FEBRUARY 1991
FA CUP FIFTH ROUND REPLAY

EVERTON	**4**
LIVERPOOL	**4**

That this replay followed one of the more forgettable Merseyside derbies, a goalless draw at Anfield, shows how unpredictable derby games on Merseyside can be. It also preceded, if not prompted, Reds manager Kenny Dalglish's resignation.

'I had a little bit to do with that,' cracked Everton skipper Kevin Ratcliffe, for whom it would be one of his last derbies. 'There was a hell of an atmosphere, and some great goals.'

The first of these from Peter Beardsley (who ironically would soon be wearing a blue shirt) was scored when he latched onto Andy Hinchcliffe's goal-line clearance of an Ian Rush shot. But the thin Blue line held firm, refusing to concede a second that might have made the game safe, and two minutes after half-time got their reward when Graeme Sharp converted a centre from the overlapping Hinchcliffe.

Beardsley struck again with 20 minutes to go, a fine solo effort. But no-one in the 37,766 crowd was leaving Goodison just yet, and their patience was rewarded just three minutes later when Sharp was presented with the easiest of tap-ins after Grobbelaar collided with his own defender Steve Nicol.

Rush then notched a header to edge the Reds in front once more, but as time ran out Tony Cottee, Everton's pint-sized striker

who'd been on just minutes as sub for Pat Nevin, cracked a last-gasp equaliser. Extra time...

Next came perhaps the goal of the game, a John Barnes free-kick bent into the top corner of Southall's net. Then Cottee struck again from a quickly-taken Ratcliffe free-kick with just three minutes left to leave Liverpool on the carpet. Neither side had anything left to give, and Reds player-manager Dalglish, who watched from the dug-out, had clearly suffered with his fans. The dressing-room inquest was a heated one, and the next morning Liverpool chairman Noel White would be faced with the dilemma of finding a new manager.

For Everton, of course, it was joy unconfined – even if, having done the difficult bit, they were to lose to West Ham in the next round! 'I've never seen an atmosphere like it at the end of the match,' said Kevin Ratcliffe. 'We went to the dressing room at the end of the match as if we'd won... we'd come back every time after going down.'

The second replay was decided by a rare Dave Watson goal. 'Kenny had gone after that 4-4 game, and that didn't help their cause,' remarked Ratcliffe. 'The games were very close together and it took a lot out of both sets of players.' Spectators, too...

Left: Kenny Dalglish and David Speedie both suffered in different ways. Speedie was dropped after the first game for Peter Beardsley, while manager Dalglish resigned after the replay.

CHANGING COLOURS

While players may have supported the opposition in their youth – Steve McManaman is one current Red who spent many Saturdays on the Goodison Park terraces – Anfield legend Tommy Smith believes it runs in the blood.

'My old man was a Liverpudlian – I think that's how it almost always starts. Your dad supports Liverpool or Everton, and you follow him. There are rare exceptions, of course. But, in the main, that's what happens.

'Sometimes, I think a derby game affects the crowd more than the players. But, as a player, you don't like to lose – and you realise that, deep down, this feeling is well and truly there.'

GREATEST GAMES

21 NOVEMBER 1994
FA PREMIER LEAGUE

EVERTON	2
LIVERPOOL	0

Fairytales don't come any more unbelievable than Joe Royle's first match in charge as Goodison manager. Everton had been bottom of the table with only one win all season, and that the week before against fellow strugglers West Ham United. By contrast, their arch-rivals from across Stanley Park had won five of their last six League and Cup games.

And when Steve McManaman narrowly failed to bend his shot into the far right hand corner of Southall's net in the game's very first attack, it looked as if the points were heading for Anfield.

But Everton, keen to battle for their new boss, kept up an unbelievable tempo throughout the game, with wideman Andy Hinchcliffe's cultured left foot a particular and recurring danger from free-kicks and corners.

Not that Liverpool was to be outdone, McManaman following up his early near miss with a stunning piece of skill after Barnes found him with an outside-of-the-foot pass. The Liverpool winger switched the ball from one foot to the other, baffling his marker – only to find Neville Southall equal to the shot as he flung out a despairing but effective arm.

Play then swung to the other end and Daniel Amokachi, the Nigerian international bought by Mike Walker, only just missed out on his first derby goal when his shot took a deflection off Ruddock: James pushed the ball behind for a corner. But the danger was far from over. Hinchcliffe swung the flag kick into the area, where Duncan Ferguson – the controversial Glasgow Rangers striker, at Goodison on loan – outjumped two defenders and the keeper to head home.

Everton, spurred on by a capacity Goodison crowd, were buzzing, and Rideout hit the foot of the post with a shot from Ebbrell's pass. Liverpool moved up a gear in search of an equaliser and centre-back Ruddock, pushing up into midfield, picked out Jones on the right wing. But the England full-back, having found Hinchcliffe out of position, pulled his shot wide.

Hinchcliffe soon atoned for his error, playing a high ball into the Liverpool area which James could only punch clear. The ball hit Ferguson and fell kindly for his striking partner Paul Rideout, who slid the ball home for Everton's second.

The season would finish gloriously at Goodison, an FA Cup win combined with escape from seemingly inevitable relegation. Liverpool, under Roy Evans' shrewd leadership, beat Bolton to take the League (Coca-Cola) Cup and finish fourth.

Left: Although a veteran of many Rangers-Celtic clashes, this was Duncan Ferguson's first Merseyside derby – and he celebrated with a goal.

Far left: Joe Royle's decision to leave Oldham's homely Boundary Park to take up the Goodison hot seat brought immediate rewards and transformed Everton's season.

His arrival at Goodison coincided with an upturn in results that turned Howard Kendall's first season as manager into a respectable eighth following a gloomy start. Disputing the Number 1 jersey with Jim Arnold for two years, he returned from loan at Port Vale to make the position his own and see off not just Kendall but his successors.

An ever-present in 1984-85, when he was the football writers' Player of the Year, Southall was injured badly the following season and missed the 1986 derby FA Cup Final, Bobby Mimms deputising. He reclaimed his place part-way through the following term and has kept it ever since, establishing a League record of appearances that eclipsed Ted Sagar. Joe Royle's rumoured determination to bring Paul Gerrard from former club Oldham merely served to strengthen his resolve, and he continued undisputed through 1995, his 650th game in an Everton shirt.

Eccentric – he once staged a sit-down half-time pitch protest in the reign of Howard Kendall and motored home instead of attending the 1995 Cup Final banquet – Southall's nevertheless been Everton's most consistent player of the last decade. Commanding in the air, he can act like a spare centre-half (his boyhood position, in which he had trials for Bolton and Crewe) and is a deep thinker about the game. Wales manager Bobby Gould recognised the fact by appointing him coach, with Ian Rush, of the national team. Yet with the likes of Peter Shilton and John Burridge as his role models, it seemed unlikely that the player who first took up goalkeeping with Llandudno Swifts was about to hang up his gloves, either for club or country, in the near future.

Southall proved Everton's saviour on more than one occasion against Liverpool – 14 clean sheets tell their tale. And even when his heroics proved ineffectual, as in 1982 when five goals whistled past him at Goodison, he could still be his team's man of the match.

E nigmatic but effective – that's the verdict on Neville Southall, a former Llandudno hod-carrier snapped up by the Toffees after barely a season in League football with Bury. Fourteen campaigns later, Southall (born Llandudno, 16 September 1958) was still plying his trade for club and country, despite a reticence often interpreted as moodiness.

Everton record

Season	League Apps	League Goals	FA Cup Apps	FA Cup Goals	League Cup Apps	League Cup Goals	Total Apps	Total Goals
1981-82	26	—	1	—	—	—	27	—
1982-83	17	—	—	—	2	—	19	—
1983-84	35	—	8	—	11	—	54	—
1984-85	42	—	7	—	4	—	53	—
1985-86	32	—	5	—	5	—	42	—
1986-87	31	—	3	—	3	—	37	—
1987-88	32	—	8	—	7	—	47	—
1988-89	38	—	8	—	5	—	51	—
1989-90	38	—	7	—	4	—	49	—
1990-91	38	—	6	—	3	—	47	—
1991-92	42	—	2	—	4	—	48	—
1992-93	40	—	1	—	6	—	47	—
1993-94	42	—	2	—	4	—	48	—
1994-95	41	—	6	—	2	—	49	—
Total	494	—	64	—	60	—	618	—

Another Welsh international (with 59 caps to his credit between 1981-93), Kevin Ratcliffe played in front of Neville Southall for the majority of his 30 games against the old enemy from across Stanley Park – plus many hundreds more for club and country.

More than that, he became the most successful captain in Everton's history, collecting the League Championship, FA Cup and European Cup Winners' Cup trophies between May 1984 and May 1985: another League title came in 1987, but further European glory was unfortunately ruled out by the Heysel tragedy.

Nevertheless, Ratcliffe (born Deeside, 12 November 1960 and a fanatical Blues supporter as a youngster on the Goodison terraces) was not an immediate first choice when he broke into the Everton team under Gordon Lee – and this despite shutting out Joe Jordan in a 0-0 draw at Old Trafford on his debut.

He was often played out of position as full-back and only after he established himself as a central defender in Howard Kendall's reign, a transfer to Bobby Robson's Ipswich Town having meanwhile fallen through, that he took on the captain's role from the injury-stricken Mark Higgins: by February 1984 he was also Wales' skipper.

That year also saw him become the youngest man since Bobby Moore two decades earlier to hold the FA Cup. Thereafter the likable and influential 23 year old drove himself and his team on to greater heights.

Kevin spent much of his Goodison derby career attempting to subdue fellow Welshman Ian Rush. His last derby appearance was as sub for Martin Keown, the man bought from Aston Villa to replace him, in August 1991.

He moved on to Cardiff, helping them to promotion, but it was as (player and later) manager of Chester City that he would suggest he had the capability to reproduce his motivational abilities off the pitch.

Everton record

Season	League Apps	League Goals	FA Cup Apps	FA Cup Goals	League Cup Apps	League Cup Goals	Total Apps	Total Goals
1979-80	2	—	1	—	—	—	3	—
1980-81	21	—	5	—	2	—	28	—
1981-82	25	—	1	—	1	—	27	—
1982-83	29	1	5	—	4	—	38	1
1983-84	38	—	8	—	11	—	57	—
1984-85	40	—	7	—	4	—	51	—
1985-86	39	1	5	—	5	—	49	1
1986-87	42	—	3	—	5	—	50	—
1987-88	24	—	1	—	4	—	29	—
1988-89	30	—	8	—	4	—	42	—
1989-90	24	—	7	—	2	—	33	—
1990-91	36	—	6	—	3	—	45	—
1991-92	9	—	—	—	2	—	11	—
1992-93	—	—	—	—	—	—	—	—
Total	359	2	57	—	47	—	463	2

Royle, Neville Southall and Alec Troup – and none stemmed from their debut.

Taylor's derby record began promisingly with a 2-1 victory in October 1896. He scored the first of his five goals against the Reds in September the following year, this time a defeat. September 1899 saw his goal the decider as Everton left its former home with a 2-1 victory under its belt. They repeated the feat in January 1901, Taylor this time scoring both goals against a Liverpool defence that would see them to the Championship.

He scored a number of fine goals while playing up front, and in 1901 shared six goals with fellow hat-trick hero Jimmy Settle against Wolves – the second time two Everton players had scored three in the same game. Taylor had also crowned his first season at Goodison with an FA Cup Final appearance.

By the time Everton returned to the Crystal Palace, then the venue for such games, in 1906 he was the only team member left, picking up a winner's medal and a second loser's medal the following year. On both occasions he wore the Number 5 shirt, having dropped back as his pace failed him.

It was another FA Cup game, a semi-final against Barnsley, that brought his Everton career to a sad and untimely end. A shot hit him in the throat at close range, damaging his larynx, and he retired from League football.

He did so with a full trophy cabinet, comprising four Scotland caps, six appearances for the Scottish League and a Scottish League winner's medal with Dumbarton for season 1891-92 to add to his Everton honours.

The player, who like Graeme Sharp started his career at Dumbarton, ended his playing career with South Liverpool, for whom he signed in July 1912. He was to remain a Merseyside resident until his death in a motor accident on 21 February 1949 – and, though few are now alive who saw him in his prime, is still a Goodison legend.

In an era before specialisation was the norm, Scotsman John D Taylor (better known as Jack) clocked up a derby game appearance record that would remain unbeaten for over 70 years, simply by virtue of his ability to fill many different positions and roles. He was also highly regarded as a leader on the pitch.

Signed from St Mirren in 1896 as a right-winger, Taylor (born in Dumbarton on 27 January 1872) went on to establish a record that still stands today: he became the only player to clock up 100 consecutive League appearances after his debut (which he made against Sheffield Wednesday in September that year). Only four others have registered a consecutive century – Cyril Lello, Joe

Everton record

Season	League		FA Cup		League Cup		Total	
	Apps	Goals	Apps	Goals	Apps	Goals	Apps	Goals
1896-97	30	13	5	2	—	—	35	15
1897-98	30	3	5	3	—	—	35	6
1898-99	34	3	2	1	—	—	36	4
1899-1900	32	7	1	—	—	—	33	7
1900-01	25	11	2	1	—	—	27	12
1901-02	26	8	2	—	—	—	28	8
1902-03	33	3	3	1	—	—	36	4
1903-04	22	6	1	1	—	—	23	7
1904-05	34	4	6	—	—	—	40	4
1905-06	36	4	6	2	—	—	42	6
1906-07	34	1	8	2	—	—	42	3
1907-08	23	2	7	—	—	—	30	2
1908-09	27	1	1	—	—	—	28	1
1909-10	14	—	7	1	—	—	21	1
Total	400	66	56	14	—	—	456	80

PLAYERS' TOP TEN
GRAEME SHARP
1980-91 28 APPEARANCES

Another of Everton's long line of talented recruits from north of the border, Graeme Sharp would gain his greatest rewards in tandem with another Scottish striker, Andy Gray, in the mid 1980s – a period that saw him win international honours. Yet when Gordon Lee paid £120,000 for his services, the young Dumbarton striker (born Glasgow, 16 October 1960) was still to realise his potential.

Initially paired with Adrian Heath, Sharp would play in all three Merseyside Wembley Finals of the 1980s but scored in none, despite having notched in the win over Watford in 1984. He'd followed that with the equaliser against Bayern in the next season's Cup Winners' Cup semi-final, so there was nothing wrong with his nose for the big occasion. A single Under-21 appearance led to 12 full caps for his country, the first granted by Jock Stein in a World Cup qualifier against Iceland in 1985.

The most memorable of the six goals he scored in competitive derbies came in the title season of 1984-85 when he settled the game with a single piece of skill. As Gary Stevens' high ball through the channel dropped into his path, he controlled it with his left instep, throwing his marker Mark Lawrenson off balance in the process, before volleying a 25-yarder with his other foot that beat Bruce Grobbelaar all ends up. Little wonder Italian clubs were said to be taking a great interest in his future plans…

A double-figure League haul came to be expected of Sharp – he'd scored 30 in all competitions in 1984-85, but hit only nine in the second Championship-winning season two years later due to injury. Even so he came back to partner Wayne Clarke, the man who'd displaced him, having earlier formed a fruitful pairing with Gary Lineker. By the time his Everton career came to an end, he had established himself as the club's top postwar goalscorer.

In 1991 he moved to Oldham, ending an 11-year association with Goodison Park but joining another ex-Everton striker in Joe Royle. Though now 30, a fee of £500,000 reflected his value. And it was Royle he would replace in the manager's chair at Boundary Park when he returned to Merseyside to succeed Mike Walker in 1994.

Everton record

Season	League Apps	Goals	FA Cup Apps	Goals	League Cup Apps	Goals	Total Apps	Goals
1979-80	2	—	—	—	—	—	2	—
1980-81	4	—	—	—	—	—	4	—
1981-82	29	15	1	—	1	—	31	15
1982-83	41	15	5	2	4	—	50	17
1983-84	28	7	7	1	11	3	46	11
1984-85	36	21	6	2	4	3	46	26
1985-86	37	19	7	1	5	1	49	21
1986-87	27	5	1	2	5	2	33	9
1987-88	32	13	8	6	7	1	47	20
1988-89	26	7	6	3	4	2	36	12
1989-90	33	6	7	1	4	—	44	7
1990-91	27	3	6	2	3	3	36	8
Total	322	111	54	20	48	15	424	146

JACK SHARP
1899-1910 23 APPEARANCES

By coincidence, two international forwards named Sharp come fourth and fifth respectively in the Goodison Park derby roll of honour. Their careers were nearly seven decades apart, yet Jack Sharp's association with Goodison would last nearly 40 years as player and director.

Born in Hereford on 15 February 1878, he signed for Aston Villa in 1897 from local non-League team Hereford Thistle. A total of just 23 appearances in the claret and blue in two years suggested he had difficulty in making the transition to League football, but Everton's faith in signing him was to prove more than justified.

In the period from 1899 to 1910 Sharp clocked up exactly 300 League games in Everton's colours, as well as helping the team to consecutive Cup Finals in 1906 and 1907. Short but stocky in stature, he was deceptively quick, and his pinpoint centres proved meat and drink for the likes of Settle and Young (he created the latter's 1906 Cup-winning goal against Newcastle United).

His own favourite tactic of cutting inside the full-back helped him reach a personal double-figure tally of goals on three occasions, his most famous goal against Sheffield Wednesday in the lost 1907 Cup Final.

Sharp's derby career included three goals, and began with a win at Anfield in September 1899. The first goal was scored at the same venue two years later in a 2-2 draw, the last Everton's fourth in a 4-2 win in 1905. He bowed out five years later, again with a win in front of the Kop.

Capped twice by England, against Northern Ireland (in 1903) and Scotland (in 1905), Sharp also represented the Football League before hanging up his boots in 1910 to concentrate on his other sporting interest, cricket.

He'd already scored 105 against Australia in one of his three tests, and registered 38 centuries for his county side Lancashire in a total 22,015-run haul between 1899 and 1925. An all-rounder, he averaged 31.18 with the bat and took 434 wickets at 27.23 runs each with his fast-medium bowling. He also took 223 catches.

His brother Bert was also a professional footballer and his career exactly paralleled Jack's having played for Hereford Thistle, Aston Villa and Everton. To complete the family picture Jack's son was also at one time an Everton director.

Jack Sharp's sports goods shop in Liverpool's Whitechapel still trades today, keeping the name of an outstanding all-round sportsman alive despite his death on 28 January 1938 aged 59.

Everton record

Season	League Apps	League Goals	FA Cup Apps	FA Cup Goals	League Cup Apps	League Cup Goals	Total Apps	Total Goals
1899-1900	29	5	1	—	—	—	30	5
1900-01	25	7	2	—	—	—	27	7
1901-02	32	6	2	1	—	—	34	7
1902-03	27	6	2	1	—	—	29	7
1903-04	31	6	1	—	—	—	32	6
1904-05	21	8	6	2	—	—	27	10
1905-06	29	9	6	2	—	—	35	11
1906-07	27	7	6	3	—	—	33	10
1907-08	23	4	7	—	—	—	30	4
1908-09	31	6	2	1	—	—	33	7
1909-10	25	4	7	2	—	—	32	6
Total	**300**	**68**	**42**	**12**	**—**	**—**	**342**	**80**

5

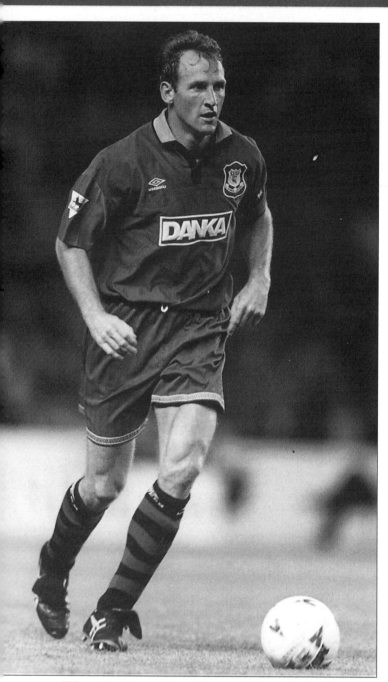

Hansen, he moved to Norwich for the considerable sum (for reserve) of £50,000 plus £50,000 after 25 appearances. This fe was to be doubled if he won an England cap, which he did i June 1984 when selected to tour South America. His debu ironically, was the historic win against Brazil where John Barne – then of Watford, later of Liverpool – scored his much-televise 'wondergoal'.

The return ticket to Merseyside (for a somewhat mor expensive £900,000) came in the 1986 close season, when Dere Mountfield contracted a long-term injury and Howard Kenda moved to cover the gap. But Watson was by this time a prove quantity, having notched 212 League games for the Canaries an proved himself an inspiring leader from the back.

His presence alongside Kevin Ratcliffe certainly helpe Everton claim the 1987 Championship and he managed to wi round supporters who had adopted his predecessor as a fo hero with his whole-hearted effort.

The following year also saw him an England regular, winnin five of his total 12 caps in the space of four months. In the en however, Mark Wright got the vote for the Europea Championships and Watson appeared only in the meaningles final fixture against the USSR.

The player's record against his first club began unpromising with a 3-1 reverse. He waited until 1991 to register his first go in the fixture – and what an momentous one it was, bein enough to decide the twice-replayed FA Cup Fifth Round th had encompassed a 4-4 draw and Kenny Dalglish's decision t quit as Anfield boss. (Unfortunately, the Toffees then contrive to lose to West Ham!)

Watson continued to clock up appearances against his firs club in the 1990s, having assumed the captaincy in succession t Kevin Ratcliffe in 1992. And while the team he led on the fiel was nowhere near as successful as Ratcliffe's side of the previou decade, consolations such as lifting the 1995 FA Cup after victor over favourites Manchester United made Watson's task mor than worthwhile.

Younger brother Alex also began his career on Merseyside making four League appearances for Liverpool between 1987-8 though he had to move to Bournemouth to enjoy an extende run in the first team.

A native Liverpudlian who started his professional career at Anfield, Dave Watson (born Liverpool, 20 November 1961 and no relation to the England, Leeds and Sunderland player who occupied the same position in the 1970s) crossed Stanley Park by a highly circuitous route.

Having failed to break into the Reds' first team due to the consistency of central defenders Phil Thompson and Alan

Everton record

Season	League		FA Cup		League Cup		Total	
	Apps	Goals	Apps	Goals	Apps	Goals	Apps	Goals
1986-87	35	4	3	—	2	—	40	4
1987-88	37	4	8	1	7	1	52	6
1988-89	32	3	7	—	4	1	43	4
1989-90	29	1	4	—	3	—	36	1
1990-91	32	2	6	2	3	—	41	4
1991-92	35	3	2	—	4	—	41	3
1992-93	40	1	2	1	6	—	48	2
1993-94	28	1	—	—	3	3	31	4
1994-95	38	2	6	1	2	1	46	4
Total	306	21	38	5	34	6	378	32

HARRY MAKEPEACE
1902-15 22 APPEARANCES

sportsmen to combine careers successfully.

Like Sharp, Harry (born Joseph William Henry Makepeace on 22 August 1881) was not a native Liverpudlian, having moved to the city at the age of ten from his birthplace, Middlesbrough. Swopping Tees for Mersey gave Everton the chance to sign him from Bootle Amateurs in 1902, and he was quickly on the first-team scene, making his debut in February the following year in an FA Cup win against Lancashire neighbours Manchester United.

At this stage, he was wearing the Number 10 shirt as an inside-forward, but though he failed to make a single appearance for the first team the following season, 1903-04, as they finished third in the First Division behind Sheffield Wenesday and Manchester City, he pushed his way into contention in 1904-05 as a tough-tackling wing-half.

He was happy to play on either side of the midfield, but it was as left-half that he won his four England caps, three against Scotland in 1906, 1910 and 1912 and one against Wales, again in 1912. He'd also represented the Football League in 1910.

Makepeace's first game against Liverpool was in the FA Cup First Round in 1905, and turned into a dream derby when he scored his side's only goal in a drawn game. He was also present, though did not score in, the 1906 semi-final win that took Everton to the FA Cup Final: he played in that, plus the losing Final a year later.

Though the First World War effectively ended his playing career (now in his thirties, his last derby was also Everton's last pre-war match against Liverpool, in 1915), Harry Makepeace returned to renew his long-running Goodison connection by becoming club coach after a spell in Holland.

His cricketing career continued to flourish, too, and he opened for England on four occasions, scoring a century against Australia in Melbourne.

Having remained on the Mersey, albeit the other side from the scene of his playing triumphs, Harry Makepeace died on 19 December 1952 at Bebington.

The careers of Harry Makepeace and his Everton colleague Jack Sharp had several parallels. Both represented their country at football and cricket, and both represented Lancashire in the County Championship in an era where less congested fixture lists permitted summer and winter

Everton record

Season	League		FA Cup		League Cup		Total	
	Apps	Goals	Apps	Goals	Apps	Goals	Apps	Goals
1902-03	3	—	1	—	—	—	4	—
1904-05	19	5	6	2	—	—	25	7
1905-06	27	2	6	2	—	—	33	4
1906-07	23	—	8	—	—	—	31	—
1907-08	31	2	7	—	—	—	38	2
1908-09	33	—	2	—	—	—	35	—
1909-10	32	4	7	2	—	—	39	6
1910-11	33	1	3	—	—	—	36	1
1911-12	34	1	5	1	—	—	39	2
1912-13	10	—	1	—	—	—	11	—
1913-14	16	—	1	—	—	—	17	—
1914-15	23	1	5	—	—	—	28	1
Total	284	16	52	7	—	—	336	23

PLAYERS' TOP TEN
ALEX 'SANDY' YOUNG
1901-11 22 APPEARANCES

The first of two Scots strikers to share the name, this Alex Young (born Alexander Simpson Young in Slamannan, Stirlingshire on 23 June 1880) was better known as Sandy – and, like his namesake almost 60 years later, became a proven goalscorer.

Though he ranks joint seventh in derby game appearances, Young's finest moment in a blue shirt undoubtedly came in the 1906 FA Cup Final at Crystal Palace in April. Mighty Newcastle were made to look foolish as he converted a Jack Sharp cross.

Only 21 when he arrived at Goodison in the 1901 close season, Young had already picked up experience with St Mirren and Falkirk, and it wasn't long before he was showing the goalscoring qualities that would win him two Scottish caps against England in 1905 and Wales two years later.

His League and Cup tally of 125 goals in 314 games is impressive, as is the dozen goals in 22 derby matches that puts him second only to the prolific Dixie Dean – who registered 19 goals in 17 matches against Liverpool – in the Everton listings and third, thanks to Ian Rush, overall.

He made his mark on derby history quickly, netting in both his first two games – a 4-0 League win and a 2-2 Cup draw, both in January 1902. In 1904, he produced one of the individual performances of the fixture by netting four of Everton's five – on April Fool's day, no less – in a 5-2 Goodison annihilation. He scored twice in a game on two occasions, in 1906 and an FA Cup tie in 1911, and both times his goals proved match-winners.

After helping Everton to fourth position in Division One in 1911, Young moved south to Spurs as he entered his thirties. His single season at White Hart Lane started well with three goals in five games, but he would move on first to Manchester City and then to non-League Burslem Port Vale the following season.

Relatively slight for a forward at five foot eight and three quarter inches and 11 stone, he was nevertheless lethal in front of goal and an excellent marksman. He emigrated to Melbourne, Australia in 1914, and died on 17 September 1959.

He may not have been the 'Golden Vision', but the first Alex Young made headlines with his Cup-winning goal to rival the San Francisco earthquake that had occurred just seven days earlier. His four goals in 1904 made Goodison Park move, too…

Everton record

Season	League Apps	League Goals	FA Cup Apps	FA Cup Goals	League Cup Apps	League Cup Goals	Total Apps	Total Goals
1901-02	30	6	2	1	—	—	32	7
1902-03	19	5	1	—	—	—	20	5
1903-04	22	10	—	—	—	—	22	10
1904-05	31	14	6	—	—	—	37	14
1905-06	30	12	5	2	—	—	35	14
1906-07	33	28	8	1	—	—	41	29
1907-08	33	16	6	5	—	—	39	21
1908-09	23	9	1	—	—	—	24	9
1909-10	24	2	7	3	—	—	31	5
1910-11	30	8	3	3	—	—	33	11
Total	275	110	39	15	—	—	314	125

9

COLIN HARVEY
1962-74 20 APPEARANCES

One of the accomplished midfield trio of Kendall, Harvey and Ball that proved the engine room of the 1970 Championship-winning side, Colin Harvey (born Liverpool, 16 November 1944) was also to serve the club as coach and manager in coming years, though never with as much success.

He combined skill with a prodigious workrate, pushing himself so hard that he had to have a hip replacement in the 1990s. Nevertheless a first-team career in blue and white that started in 1963 when he was pitched into European battle in the San Siro Stadium, Milan at the tender age of 18 went on until 1974 when he moved to Hillsborough in a £70,000 transfer. In between times his 380 games included 20 against Liverpool, the first a 4-0 win in September which saw his name on the scoresheet.

Indeed he could have been wearing red in that clash, for in 1962 he'd been invited for trials to Anfield. Liverpool told him to return in a week, but meanwhile he tried out for the Toffees and, when offered terms, accepted: an Everton-supporting family may well have influenced the decision!

Despite notching against the old enemy first time out, Harvey was not a prodigious goalscorer – indeed he wouldn't score again against the Reds. But in terms of aggression, box-to-box stamina and passing ability he was the complete player.

Harvey only gained one England cap, against Malta in 1971 – but that was one more than Kendall who, as manager, would promote his playing partner from youth team to first-team coach in 1983. Harvey proved a relative failure in the hot seat after Kendall's departure in June 1987, winning only the Charity Shield in three seasons, but was re-hired six days after his late-1990 sacking to resume as the returning Kendall's assistant. Harvey's ability as a coach was unquestioned, but he clearly was not cut out for overall command.

Since the end of Kendall's second spell in charge, Harvey has moved via Mansfield, where he was Andy King's lieutenant, to Oldham, where he's assistant to another former Goodison favourite Graeme Sharp.

Everton record

Season	League		FA Cup		League Cup		Total	
	Apps	Goals	Apps	Goals	Apps	Goals	Apps	Goals
1963-64	2	—	—	—	—	—	2	—
1964-65	32	2	4	1	—	—	36	3
1965-66	40	1	8	1	—	—	48	2
1966-67	42	1	6	—	—	—	48	1
1967-68	34	—	4	—	2	—	40	—
1968-69	36	4	4	—	4	—	44	4
1969-70	35	3	—	—	3	—	38	3
1970-71	36	2	5	1	—	—	41	3
1971-72	17	3	3	1	—	—	20	4
1972-73	26	—	—	—	1	—	27	—
1973-74	16	1	—	—	1	—	17	1
1974-75	4	1	—	—	—	—	4	1
Total	**320**	**18**	**34**	**4**	**11**	**—**	**365**	**22**

MICK LYONS
1969-82 20 APPEARANCES

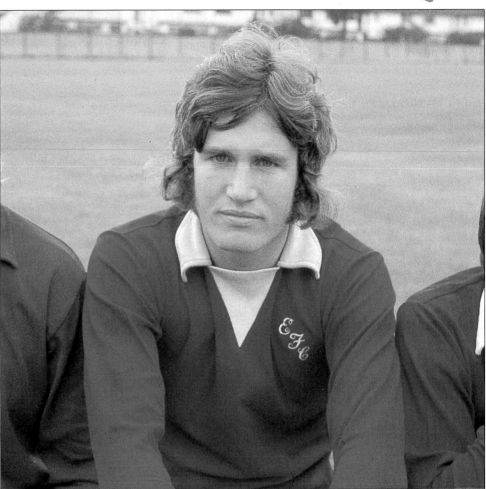

Rangy, enthusiastic and an indomitable leader, Merseysider Mick Lyons (born Croxteth, 8 December 1951) was the perfect player to have leading your side in a local derby. His willingness to move mountains for his team-mates made him a big fan favourite from his League debut in 1971 to his departure 11 years later, but the years were to be totally barren ones in terms of honours.

What was even stranger, in a dozen first-team years Lyons would never leave the field a winner against Liverpool: injury ruled him out of the only two Everton victories during that period!

Lyons had begun life as a striker, switching to central defence when David Johnson overtook him in the route to the first team. (Even so, he ended the 1973-74 campaign as top scorer, with nine goals.) A consistent run of appearances including two ever-present seasons brought him the captaincy, but he never managed to improve on five England Under-23 caps and B international recognition.

His derby debut came in the Number 10 shirt in March 1972, though neither he nor his fellow striker Johnson scored in a 0-4 reverse. The next game in October saw him on the subs' bench, a victim of his own versatility, but by 1975 he'd settled into a defensive role alongside Roger Kenyon and then Ken McNaught.

In 1979, Lyons notched one of the most spectacular strikes ever seen in a derby game... unfortunately the 40-yarder whistled past his own goalkeeper George Wood and would prove his only derby goal. Legend has it he was later approached in a pub by an overjoyed Everton fan who'd drawn his name as the first scorer and won £40!

Displaced by Billy Wright in early 1982 he took stock of his situation at 30, and a plethora of promising young centre-backs on the books persuaded him to cross the Pennines to Sheffield Wednesday later that year. Three seasons later, after helping Wednesday into the top flight, he joined Grimsby as player-manager, but was sacked in 1987 after their relegation from Division Two.

Everton re-engaged him to run their reserve team, but he left again in 1990, working at Wigan and then Huddersfield before becoming Brunei's national coach.

Everton record

Season	League Apps	League Goals	FA Cup Apps	FA Cup Goals	League Cup Apps	League Cup Goals	Total Apps	Total Goals
1970-71	2	1	—	—	—	—	2	1
1971-72	24	3	4	—	—	—	28	3
1972-73	25	2	—	—	1	—	26	2
1973-74	41	9	3	—	1	—	45	9
1974-75	38	8	4	3	2	—	44	11
1975-76	42	5	1	—	5	1	48	6
1976-77	40	4	7	1	9	2	56	7
1977-78	42	5	2	1	5	2	49	8
1978-79	37	6	1	—	2	—	40	6
1979-80	38	—	6	—	5	—	49	—
1980-81	33	2	1	1	—	—	34	3
1981-82	27	3	1	—	4	—	32	3
Total	**389**	**48**	**30**	**6**	**34**	**5**	**453**	**59**

his career in the Doncaster Senior League with Thorne Colliery, and seemed destined for nearby Hull City before Everton slipped in and obtained his signature. His first season in the top flight was a baptism of fire in a team destined to finish rock bottom, but he was to miss only one game as they bounced back at the first attempt – and kept his place as the 1930s unfolded.

His consistency was recognised by his country, and four England caps against Northern Ireland (1935), Scotland, Austria and Belgium (1936) followed. Without rivals between the sticks of the calibre of Vic Woodley and Harry Hibbs, the total would surely have been much higher.

An unimpressive figure in terms of stature, Sagar managed to evade shoulder-charging centre-forwards on the ground and, regularly, outjumped them in the air thanks to uncanny anticipation. Two League Championships in 1932 and 1939 and an FA Cup win in 1933 were a just reward for his efforts. The 1938-39 Championship win saw him register 18 clean sheets in 41 appearances: the one game he missed was lost 7-0!

He played little during the war years, but, under Everton's first manager Theo Kelly, regained his place midway through the first peacetime season from his wartime replacement Burnett and maintained it until Cliff Britton alternated the two in 1949-51. This was ironic since the former Goodison wing-half had shared a pitch many times with Ted in the 1930s.

Despite losing his place Sagar remained at Goodison, his 463rd and last League appearance a low-key, single-goal reverse at Plymouth in November 1952 in Division Two. He retired at the end of that season, having become the oldest player to represent the club.

Ted Sagar died on 16 October 1986, and didn't see Neville Southall beat his League appearance record – but his place in the Everton hall of fame is assured.

Though Gordon West and, now, Neville Southall have their supporters, Ted Sagar unarguably ruled from 1930s to 1950s as Everton's most accomplished custodian. While Dixie Dean was scoring at one end, Ted was stopping them at the other. And 1930s to 1950s is no great exaggeration: Sagar's spell of 24 years and one month at Goodison between 1929 and 1953 remains the longest any player has served a single League club. (For obvious reasons, it's unlikely ever to be rivalled.)

Born in Doncaster on 7 February 1910, Edward Sagar started

Everton record

Season	League		FA Cup		League Cup		Total	
	Apps	Goals	Apps	Goals	Apps	Goals	Apps	Goals
1929-30	8	—	1	—	—	—	9	—
1931-32	41	—	1	—	—	—	42	—
1932-33	42	—	6	—	—	—	48	—
1933-34	40	—	1	—	—	—	41	—
1934-35	35	—	4	—	—	—	39	—
1935-36	37	—	—	—	—	—	37	—
1936-37	29	—	4	—	—	—	33	—
1937-38	26	—	—	—	—	—	26	—
1938-39	41	—	5	—	—	—	46	—
1946-47	29	—	2	—	—	—	31	—
1947-48	42	—	5	—	—	—	47	—
1948-49	40	—	2	—	—	—	42	—
1949-50	18	—	—	—	—	—	18	—
1950-51	24	—	1	—	—	—	25	—
1951-52	10	—	—	—	—	—	10	—
1952-53	1	—	—	—	—	—	1	—
Total	463	—	32	—	—	—	495	—

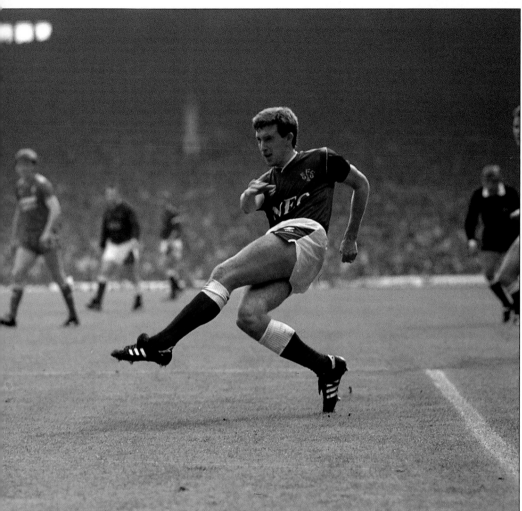

Reid and Paul Bracewell. His goal against Rapid Vienna in the 1985 Cup Winners' Cup win will long be remembered.

He only scored once against Liverpool, however, a consolation at Anfield in April 1987 in a 3-1 reverse. Nevertheless, his contribution was valued by players and supporters alike. The derby fixture saw him disputing midfield supremacy with Ronnie Whelan, with whom he was particularly friendly at Anfield.

The duo would serve side by side in Jack Charlton's Eire team, for which he played 45 times. His international career, which began with a sub appearance against Holland in 1984, ended nine years later with a similar role against Wales.

The Everton Number 11 shirt was his by right until the return of Howard Kendall from Manchester City in 1990. The claims of ex-City star Peter Beagrie were thenceforth pressed and Sheedy departed with a free transfer in recognition of his service.

After helping Newcastle to avoid a potentially catastrophic relegation, he played 26 games in their promotion season. His skills were later hawked to lower-division sides like Blackpool as he reached the veteran stage of his career.

A cultured midfielder with a sweet left foot, Kevin Sheedy was an integral part of the Everton and Eire teams of the early to mid 1980s. Prior to that, however, he'd spent four years in Liverpool's reserves, having never managed to break into the first team on more than three occasions.

A tribunal-fixed fee of £100,000 turned out to be a bargain as the Welsh-born player (his international qualification comes through his parents) gave his former rivals ten years of sterling service before taking advantage of a free transfer to become one of Kevin Keegan's first recruits at Newcastle United in February 1992.

Sheedy (born in Builth Wells, 21 October 1959) had moved to Anfield from Hereford in 1978, but only when he crossed the park in the first direct transfer between the clubs since another notable Number 11, Johnny Morrissey, in 1962, was he given space to develop.

And this he made full use of, becoming the midfield playmaker alongside the more combative likes of Steve McMahon, Peter

Everton record

Season	League		FA Cup		League Cup		Total	
	Apps	Goals	Apps	Goals	Apps	Goals	Apps	Goals
1982-83	40	11	5	2	3	—	48	13
1983-84	28	4	6	2	10	4	44	10
1984-85	29	11	6	4	2	—	37	15
1985-86	31	5	3	—	4	2	38	7
1986-87	28	13	1	—	4	1	33	14
1987-88	17	1	—	—	1	—	18	1
1988-89	26	8	8	4	2	—	36	12
1989-90	37	9	6	2	4	2	47	13
1990-91	22	4	3	1	1	—	26	5
1991-92	16	1	—	—	2	—	18	1
Total	274	67	38	15	33	9	345	91

GORDON WEST
1962-73 20 APPEARANCES

Manager Harry Catterick's first signing after he arrived at Goodison turned out to be inspired. Gordon West (born Barnsley, 24 April 1943) made an early mark by helping Everton to the Championship in his first full season, thereafter proving one of the club's longest-lasting custodians.

He'd made his debut in the top flight at just 17, displacing Blackpool's regular keeper Tony Waiters. And though he was unable to retain his place, Catterick had been impressed enough to pay what was then a record fee for a goalkeeper for the Yorkshireman's services. West now had better luck finding a first-team place, supplanting Albert Dunlop and quickly becoming a fan favourite with his instinctive saves and bravery in diving at opponents' feet.

Selected by Alf Ramsey to travel to Mexico in defence of the World Cup in 1970, West declined the invitation. As it happened, he might have found himself deputising for another goalkeeping Gordon, Banks, in that fateful quarter-final against Germany! Curiously it was in 1970 too that West's reign between the sticks at Goodison was threatened by Andy Rankin, the reserve keeper who had duelled for the Number 1 position the previous decade.

Even then, West saw off his rival and recorded another ever-present season – the third of his Everton career – before retiring in 1973 (a brief comeback across the Mersey at Prenton Park in 1975 proved less than successful, spanning just 17 games.)

His derby game record began in September 1962 when he took part in a free-flowing 2-2 draw. Then next game brought a clean sheet, the first of nine he'd record in the fixture, while his sense of humour endeared him to Liverpool fans as well as his own.

A weak kick, the result of a long-standing thigh injury, meant West favoured distributing the ball by hand. While this might have proved a liability in these days of the banned back-pass, he actually set up many attacking moves from the back with his powerful throws. Gordon West's record speaks for itself, and suggests he will be looked upon as the third member of the Goodison goalkeeping trinity along with Sagar and Southall.

Everton record

Season	League Apps	League Goals	FA Cup Apps	FA Cup Goals	League Cup Apps	League Cup Goals	Total Apps	Total Goals
1961-62	12	—	—	—	—	—	12	—
1962-63	38	—	3	—	—	—	41	—
1963-64	22	—	3	—	—	—	25	—
1964-65	20	—	4	—	—	—	24	—
1965-66	24	—	8	—	—	—	32	—
1966-67	36	—	5	—	—	—	41	—
1967-68	41	—	6	—	2	—	49	—
1968-69	42	—	5	—	4	—	51	—
1969-70	42	—	1	—	4	—	47	—
1970-71	12	—	1	—	—	—	13	—
1971-72	42	—	4	—	1	—	47	—
1972-73	4	—	—	—	—	—	4	—
Total	**335**	**—**	**40**	**—**	**11**	**—**	**386**	**—**

BRUCE GROBBELAAR
1981-94 33 APPEARANCES

A byword for eccentricity and entertainment, Bruce Grobbelaar was and remains simply a one-off. Following in the footsteps of two dependable performers in Tommy Lawrence and Ray Clemence, his idiosyncrasies stood out still more – yet his popularity with fans was underlined when bribes allegations broke after his departure. To a man and woman, Liverpool fans refused to countenance them.

The flamboyant Zimbabwean (born in Durban, South Africa, on 6 October 1957) had arrived at Anfield via Gresty Road, Crewe – but was not a graduate of that notable soccer academy. The fee of £250,000 was paid to Vancouver Whitecaps where former keeper Tony Waiters had guided his progress, and he was picking up League experience on loan when he came to the attention of Bob Paisley.

Clemence's shock decision to go south to Spurs in the close season of 1981 threw the newcomer in at the deep end after just three reserve games – but he never let down his fans or his manager, who claims he has 'probably dominated the area more than any other Liverpool goalkeeper.'

Grobbelaar's derby record, which began in November 1981 with a 3-1 win, includes 11 clean sheets, a 33 per cent success rate belying his supposed fallibility.

The three Wembley Finals – one League, two FA Cup, all of which he played in – were meat and drink to a man who'd habitually walk on his hands in the pre-match warm-up. (A save from Graeme Sharp during the League Cup Final arguably turned the tie.)

His Anfield career ended anti-climactically, Graeme Souness having publicly underlined his preference for rivals James and Hooper by loaning Grobbelaar out to Stoke City – the first time since his Crewe days that he'd played outside the top flight.

Yet he fought back to reclaim the Number 1 jersey in 1993-94 and play 29 games that included his final derby appearance, a 2-0 reverse at Goodison Park. Injury sustained against Leeds United in February ended his ever-present run and gave James the chance to make the keeper's shirt his own under new manager Roy Evans.

Grobbelaar retained his hold on top-flight football by signing for Southampton in 1994, and despite all adverse publicity and his continuing flamboyance remained Zimbabwe's Number 1. To date, his successor David James had failed to dislodge the legend.

Liverpool record

Season	League Apps	League Goals	FA Cup Apps	FA Cup Goals	League Cup Apps	League Cup Goals	Total Apps	Total Goals
1981-82	42	—	3	—	10	—	55	—
1982-83	42	—	3	—	8	—	53	—
1983-84	42	—	2	—	13	—	57	—
1984-85	42	—	7	—	3	—	52	—
1985-86	42	—	8	—	7	—	57	—
1986-87	31	—	3	—	9	—	43	—
1987-88	38	—	5	—	3	—	46	—
1988-89	21	—	5	—	—	—	26	—
1989-90	38	—	8	—	3	—	49	—
1990-91	31	—	7	—	3	—	41	—
1991-92	37	—	9	—	4	—	50	—
1992-93	5	—	—	—	2	—	7	—
1993-94	29	—	2	—	5	—	36	—
Total	440	—	62	—	70	—	572	—

IAN RUSH
1980-87 1988- 33 APPEARANCES

W e've all heard the joke: 'What will you do when Christ comes to Liverpool? Move St John to inside-left!' Staying in irreverent mode, it was the second coming of another Ian, this time Rush, from Juventus in June 1988 which helped revitalise Liverpool's fortunes after the anti-climax of FA Cup Final defeat by Wimbledon. Intriguingly, he was, for some while, both Liverpool's record sale and record purchase.

Rush (born St Asaph, Clwyd, Wales on 20 October 1961) had joined the Red ranks in time-honoured style, following the club policy of picking up players who'd shown promise in the lower divisions. Thompson, Clemence, Keegan, Lloyd and Neal were among the successes – and like them Rush, bought from Chester City for £300,000 in 1980, would have to serve his Anfield apprenticeship in the Central League side. His first eight first-team games late in the 1980-81 season brought no goals but after a brief return to the 'stiffs' Paisley gave him a second chance with the message to 'be more selfish in front of goal'.

Rush's impact second time round was immediate, bringing 28 goals in just 45 games. His combination with Dalglish was reminiscent of the Toshack-Keegan pairing that had brought so much success, but Rush was much more than a target man.

Rush's goals record in derbies is unparalleled, his 20 to the start of 1995-96 being the best of either side: to put it in context, only two other players have reached double figures.

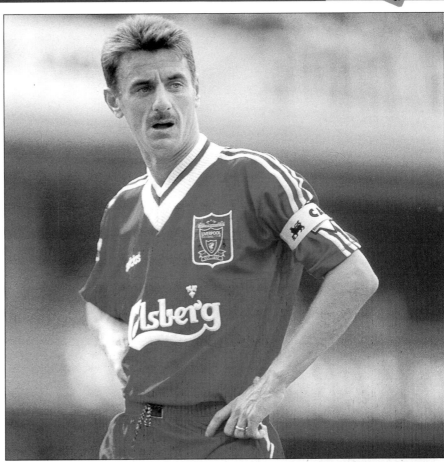

One was, of course, Dixie Dean whose record of 19 derby goals was equalled in the 1991 FA Cup Fifth Round Replay (the other was Everton's Sandy Young). Unlike his predecessors, Rush had the League Cup to swell his total though we have not counted other, 'spurious', competitions.

The first derby strike came in his first appearance in the fixture, a 3-1 win in November 1981. His best individual performance came exactly a year later in Liverpool's 5-0 humiliation of the old enemy at Goodison – his four-goal haul being only the third time this feat had been achieved after Sandy Young back in 1904 and Fred Howe in 1935.

The arrival of Stan Collymore for a UK record £8.5 million fee in the summer of 1995 seemed to signal the final curtain for Rush's Anfield dreams... but he and the young Robbie Fowler remained Roy Evans' first choice despite persistent rumours of a move to Celtic for the Welsh hitman.

National boss Bobby Gould wanted to make use of his experience on the coaching side, so it seemed likely the six-footer would continue to serve his country whichever club he chose to play with.

Liverpool record

Season	League Apps	League Goals	FA Cup Apps	FA Cup Goals	League Cup Apps	League Cup Goals	Total Apps	Total Goals
1980-81	7	—	—	—	1	—	8	—
1981-82	32	17	3	3	10	8	45	28
1982-83	34	24	3	2	8	2	45	28
1983-84	41	32	2	2	12	8	55	42
1984-85	28	14	5	6	1	—	34	20
1985-86	40	22	8	6	6	3	54	31
1986-87	42	30	3	—	9	4	54	34
1988-89	24	7	2	3	4	1	30	11
1989-90	36	18	8	6	3	2	47	26
1990-91	37	16	7	5	3	5	47	26
1991-92	18	4	5	1	3	3	26	8
1992-93	32	14	1	1	4	1	37	16
1993-94	42	14	2	1	5	4	49	19
1994-95	36	12	7	1	7	6	50	19
Total	449	224	56	37	76	47	581	308

All three arrived in a nine-month period, as building blocks in Bob Paisley's team restructuring plans following Kevin Keegan's departure to SV Hamburg. And though Hansen was the first he would take longest to become a regular choice. Once he'd established himself, dislodging the long-serving Emlyn Hughes, he quietly started turning himself into as big an Anfield legend as his predecessor.

Hansen had considered a career as a professional golfer before dedicating himself to football, and applied a golfer's analytical mind to every move he made. Superb anticipation gave him an all-important extra yard as he swept up anything that eluded larger defensive companion Phil Thompson. And though he scored few goals, those he did – notably an equaliser in the 1979 FA Cup semi-final against Manchester United – were often vital.

The highlight of Hansen's derby career was receiving the FA Cup after the first Merseyside Final in 1986 and again in 1989. He failed to score any of his ten career goals against the men from Goodison, but his battles with their strikers – ironically including future screen-mate Lineker – were certainly a feature of those he played in.

Hospitalised for much of the 1988-89 season, he reclaimed his place towards the end of the campaign but at 34 was clearly now counting the days. He announced his retirement in 1991 a week after Kenny Dalglish quit, emphasising that he was not a candidate to succeed his former team-mate. Alan Hansen bowed out at the top as one of the game's most honoured players, with a 17-medal haul that included eight Championships, four League Cups, three European Cups and two FA Cups.

Hansen only won 26 caps for Scotland between 1979-87 and was particularly disappointed not to go to Mexico in 1986, but even this failed to affect his club form. Yet it was one-time national manager Jock Stein who, while at Celtic, tipped off Bob Paisley that the player, though arguably too slight for the Scottish game, might flourish in the English League. Parkhead's loss was Anfield's gain.

The double act of Alan Hansen and Gary Lineker that may be seen on BBC-TV's *Match Of The Day* every Saturday links players who have seen life from both sides of Stanley Park. Yet while England's legendary goalpoacher stayed just one season, Hansen (born Alloa, 13 June 1955) spent almost all his career at Anfield, signing in April 1977 from Partick Thistle for £100,000. An obvious candidate for management, he chose instead to become a pundit – unlike team-mates and fellow Scots Dalglish and Souness who both took turns in the Anfield manager's chair and found it exacted a price.

Liverpool record

Season	League		FA Cup		League Cup		Total	
	Apps	Goals	Apps	Goals	Apps	Goals	Apps	Goals
1977-78	20	—	1	—	3	—	24	—
1978-79	34	1	6	1	—	—	40	2
1979-80	38	4	8	—	5	—	51	4
1980-81	36	—	—	—	8	1	44	1
1981-82	35	—	3	1	8	—	46	1
1982-83	34	—	3	—	8	—	45	—
1983-84	42	1	2	—	13	—	57	1
1984-85	41	—	9	—	2	—	52	—
1985-86	41	—	8	—	7	—	56	—
1986-87	39	—	3	—	9	—	51	—
1987-88	39	1	7	—	3	—	49	1
1988-89	6	—	2	—	—	—	8	—
1989-90	31	—	8	—	2	—	41	—
Total	436	7	60	2	68	1	564	10

PLAYERS' TOP TEN
IAN CALLAGHAN
1959-78 31 APPEARANCES

Half of an acclaimed wing partnership with Peter Thompson (both won England caps, though not in harness), Ian Callaghan proved his adaptability by slotting into a midfield role when wingers became obsolete and thus extended his useful life until three weeks short of his 40th birthday.

By this time Callaghan (born Liverpool, 10 April 1942) was playing with Fourth Division Crewe in front of 2,000 crowds,

having left Anfield for John Toshack's Swansea before playing in Ireland and Norway. But five years earlier he'd been recalled to England duty by Ron Greenwood after an 11-year gap that spanned the reigns of Alf Ramsey, Don Revie and Joe Mercer. Callaghan had played in the 1966 World Cup Finals against France, setting up the second goal of a 2-0 win for team-mate Roger Hunt, but was omitted in favour of Alan Ball as Ramsey pursued his admittedly successful policy of producing wingless wonders.

His other big career disappointment was a cartilage injury that ruled him out of much of the 1970-71 season. He returned to regain and retain his place for another five seasons, winning the football writers' vote as 1974 Player of the Year and Ron Greenwood's vote the following year – along with the award of the MBE for services to football.

Then younger talents in the shape of Terry McDermott and, eventually, Graeme Souness proved impossible to dislodge, and a free transfer was granted in grateful recognition of 17 years' honest service. His last match was a European Cup semi-final against Borussia Mönchengladbach.

The derby match atmosphere failed to inflame Callaghan, who was never sent off in his career and was booked only twice. He scored twice against Everton, both goals coming in the same match – a 2-1 win at Anfield on 28 September 1963 that was only his third exposure to the derby atmosphere.

Yet a man who was applauded off the field on his debut and applauded onto it on the occasion of his 800th game in a Liverpool shirt (against Derby County in 1977) should have been used to the plaudits.

Liverpool record

Season	League Apps	League Goals	FA Cup Apps	FA Cup Goals	League Cup Apps	League Cup Goals	Total Apps	Total Goals
1959-60	4	—	—	—	—	—	4	—
1960-61	3	—	—	—	2	—	5	—
1961-62	24	1	5	—	—	—	29	1
1962-63	37	2	6	—	—	—	43	2
1963-64	42	8	5	—	—	—	47	8
1964-65	37	6	8	1	—	—	45	7
1965-66	42	5	1	—	—	—	43	5
1966-67	40	4	4	—	—	—	44	4
1967-68	41	3	9	—	2	1	52	4
1968-69	42	8	4	1	3	1	49	10
1969-70	41	3	6	—	2	—	49	3
1970-71	22	—	4	—	1	—	27	—
1971-72	41	2	3	—	3	—	47	2
1972-73	42	3	4	—	8	1	54	4
1973-74	42	—	9	—	6	3	57	3
1974-75	41	1	2	—	3	—	46	1
1975-76	40	3	2	—	3	—	45	3
1976-77	33	1	5	—	2	1	40	2
1977-78	26	—	1	—	7	—	34	—
Total	640	50	78	2	42	7	760	59

PHIL NEAL
1974-86 29 APPEARANCES

Full-back has rarely proved a problem position for Liverpool, with the likes of Lawler, Moran, Byrne and Phil Neal in recent years. Yet Neal (born Irchester, Northamptonshire, 20 February 1951) was a striker as a schoolboy when he went for a trial with Spurs and was offered terms. He declined, deciding to continue his education and sign for his local side Northampton Town after leaving school. So instead of starting in the top flight, he graduated to it via a £60,000 transfer in October 1974.

By undergoing his education in the lower divisions he followed a similar path to Ray Clemence and Kevin Keegan, and like them would represent his country.

Neal would prove the ideal replacement for Tommy Smith, who'd moved to full-back in his twilight years – but he made his debut in a red shirt in the red-hot atmosphere of a Merseyside derby as deputy for left-back Alec Lindsay in a 0-0 draw at Goodison on 16 November 1974.

This switch of sides was no problem to a man who'd played in all 11 positions for Northampton including emergency goalkeeper.

Once established he proved a defensive fixture, missing only one game in the next ten seasons. This spoke volumes not only for his level of fitness but also an even temperament which also made him an ice-cool penalty taker. His three goals in derby fixtures all came from the spot, one being in the 1977 FA Cup semi-final replay.

An attacking full-back by instinct, he was never as prolific from open play as Chris Lawler. His captaincy was less demonstrative than an Emlyn Hughes, but remained effective.

Phil Neal left Anfield after 11 years in December 1985 to move into management with Third Division Bolton. He took them to the Freight Rover Final in his first season but lost his job in 1992, the year after they'd lost in the Third Division play-offs (Bruce Rioch his successor would profit from his work). He later managed Coventry City and played a coaching role with England under Graham Taylor.

Liverpool record

Season	League Apps	Goals	FA Cup Apps	Goals	League Cup Apps	Goals	Total Apps	Goals
1974-75	23	—	2	—	—	—	25	—
1975-76	42	6	2	—	3	—	47	6
1976-77	42	7	8	2	2	—	52	9
1977-78	42	4	1	—	9	1	52	5
1978-79	42	5	7	—	1	—	50	5
1979-80	42	1	8	—	7	—	57	1
1980-81	42	2	2	—	9	—	53	2
1981-82	42	2	3	—	10	1	55	3
1982-83	42	8	3	—	8	1	53	9
1983-84	41	1	2	—	12	1	55	2
1984-85	42	4	7	1	3	—	52	5
1985-86	13	1	—	—	2	—	15	1
Total	**455**	**41**	**45**	**3**	**66**	**4**	**566**	**48**

making his debut for Home Farm in the League of Ireland on his 16th birthday was soon bound for Anfield.

His rival as young pretender for the left midfield position soon to be vacated by Ray Kennedy was Kevin Sheedy, who'd ironically face him in the blue of Everton for so many of his derby games.

They shared 'digs', and both were at Aintree when Bob Paisley made the decision to pick Whelan for an eve of Grand National Friday night game. He played, scored and soon proved he couldn't be left out. After scoring twice in the Milk Cup Final of 1982 to equalise and then snatch the trophy from Spurs' grasp (he scored again in Liverpool's 1983 win), he wasn't to be omitted until the mid 1990s.

John Barnes' arrival saw Whelan take a more central role, but there was no diminution of his influence. Bob Paisley spotlighted Whelan as 'the man for the big occasion'… and aside from his Milk Cup heroics he proved a battler who relished derby games, ever since his debut in November 1981's 3-1 win.

Surprisingly he only scored once in the 29 fixtures he played, the opening goal in a 3-1 win at Goodison in 1982. He had less happy memories, though, of another 3-1 win in early 1991; the injury he sustained would keep him out for the rest of the season.

Whelan took over from Alan Hansen as captain, and would later take his leadership qualities into management with First Division Southend United. Having moved there as a player in 1994, he took the boss's chair in July the following year – even though former club and country team-mate Mark Lawrenson expressed public surprise that the easy-going Irishman had chosen the rocky road to management.

And though injury continued to dog his efforts to lead his team on the pitch, it seemed likely a player who never got the acclaim he deserved at Anfield would continue to make his own quiet mark.

'There's only one Ronnie Whelan' was a chant that must have rung out countless times – yet Bob Paisley, for one, realised that wasn't the case. And it was because his dad, also Ronnie, had played more than 15 seasons for St Patrick's Athletic and Drogheda after turning down Chelsea on the grounds of homesickness! Ronnie Junior (born Dublin, 25 September 1961) had no such qualms and, after

Liverpool record

Season	League Apps	League Goals	FA Cup Apps	FA Cup Goals	League Cup Apps	League Cup Goals	Total Apps	Total Goals
1980-81	1	1	—	—	—	—	1	1
1981-82	32	10	3	—	8	3	43	13
1982-83	28	2	1	—	6	2	35	4
1983-84	23	4	1	—	5	3	29	7
1984-85	37	7	7	4	3	1	47	12
1985-86	39	10	7	1	7	3	53	14
1986-87	39	3	3	—	8	2	50	5
1987-88	28	1	2	—	3	—	33	1
1988-89	37	4	5	—	6	—	48	4
1989-90	34	1	8	1	3	—	45	2
1990-91	14	1	1	—	1	—	16	1
1991-92	10	—	3	1	—	—	13	1
1992-93	17	1	—	—	—	—	17	1
1993-94	23	1	—	—	—	—	23	1
Total	**362**	**46**	**41**	**7**	**50**	**14**	**453**	**67**

was built. Bob Paisley admired the way Clemence 'could have nothing to do for 89 minutes, and then suddenly have the presence of mind to pull off a vital save.' Like his predecessor Lawrence and his successor Grobbelaar, he was a sweeper as much as a keeper, cajoling and organising his defence.

After a groin injury suffered while at Spurs in October 1987 ended his playing career, Ray Clemence moved into management with that club, but departed along with fellow coach and Anfield old boy Doug Livermore when the Terry Venables dynasty was swept out of White Hart Lane.

While Livermore returned to Anfield, Clemence (whose son Stephen was a promising Tottenham junior) elected to stay in north London with Barnet. There he attempted to combine the onerous task of finding success on a shoestring with a number of media commitments.

'You don't win trophies with a poor keeper' was Bob Paisley's belief – and though it was his managerial predecessor Bill Shankly who plucked Ray Clemence (born Skegness, 5 August 1948) from the lower-league obscurity of Scunthorpe 'Clem' would serve Paisley through to 1981, his last match the European Cup-clinching win against Real Madrid in Paris. The arrival of Bruce Grobbelaar appeared to persuade him to take on a new challenge, and he would enjoy six more seasons with Tottenham before hanging up his gloves.

He had the difficult task of succeeding Tommy 'The Tank' Lawrence in Shankly's team rebuilding process that was signalled by a shock 1970 FA Cup defeat by lowly Watford. Seven clean sheets in the last 13 games of the season confirmed the new boy had arrived. (His Anfield career statistic of 227 clean sheets in 470 First Division games makes equally breathtaking reading.) Yet though he would receive international recognition, the policy of alternating with the equally impressive Peter Shilton followed by national manager Ron Greenwood restricted his total of caps to a still-impressive 61.

In 1978-79 he was ever-present, conceded just 16 League goals and was unbeaten on 28 occasions – the rock on which success

Liverpool record

Season	League Apps	League Goals	FA Cup Apps	FA Cup Goals	League Cup Apps	League Cup Goals	Total Apps	Total Goals
1968-69	—	—	—	—	1	—	1	—
1969-70	14	—	1	—	—	—	15	—
1970-71	41	—	7	—	3	—	51	—
1971-72	42	—	3	—	3	—	48	—
1972-73	41	—	4	—	7	—	52	—
1973-74	42	—	9	—	6	—	57	—
1974-75	42	—	2	—	4	—	48	—
1975-76	42	—	2	—	3	—	47	—
1976-77	42	—	8	—	2	—	52	—
1977-78	40	—	1	—	9	—	50	—
1978-79	42	—	7	—	1	—	50	—
1979-80	41	—	8	—	7	—	56	—
1980-81	41	—	2	—	9	—	52	—
Total	470	—	54	—	55	—	579	—

TOMMY SMITH
1962-78 27 APPEARANCES

His first appearances were made, most inappropriately, in a Number 9 shirt, and he wore Number 10 in the 1965 FA Cup Final. Even so, he had more skill than critics credited him with. His size – five foot eight and 12 stone – won him a place in Liverpool's Central League team at the less than advanced age of 15, but he'd put on three more inches and another stone before he'd cemented his first-team place.

Smith's autobiography, titled *I Did It The Hard Way*, told many secrets including his dislike of Emlyn Hughes, the man who succeeded him as captain. This stemmed from events at the European Cup Final of 1978, a game Smith missed through injury (though it had been a rare Smith goal that had brought Liverpool back into the previous year's Final against Borussia Mönchengladbach).

Yet Hughes paid him the ultimate compliment in his life story. 'He is the greatest captain I have ever played under… although I never particularly got on with him as a man, I had nothing but admiration and respect for him as a captain on the pitch. He had powerful qualities of leadership.'

Despite Smith's widely recognised abilities, and the fact that he'd captained a successful England Under-23 side, he only won one full cap for his country, against Wales in 1971. Storey (19), Hunter (28) and Stiles (also 28) did markedly better. And it was to Wales, Swansea to be specific, that Smith moved in 1978 to play out his League career.

He briefly returned to Anfield as a youth coach after retirement, but eventually quit the game altogether to concentrate on outside interests.

His playing career has exacted a crippling physical toll, but Tommy Smith is still a big draw on the after-dinner speech circuit. And with two FA Cup, five Championship, two UEFA Cup and a European Cup medal to his name, he had many a story to tell.

In an era when hardmen were legion, Tommy Smith stood out among the Storeys, Stiles and Hunters as the most genuine of genuine articles. 'He was the sort of man you would want alongside you in the trenches' was how Bob Paisley put it.

In derby game terms Smith (born a wind-assisted goal kick from Anfield on 5 April 1945, just as the end of the war was in sight!) went into battle on 27 occasions. And, of course, it was a stage made for him.

Liverpool record

Season	League Apps	League Goals	FA Cup Apps	FA Cup Goals	League Cup Apps	League Cup Goals	Total Apps	Total Goals
1962-63	1	—	—	—	—	—	1	—
1964-65	25	4	8	—	—	—	33	4
1965-66	42	3	1	—	—	—	43	3
1966-67	42	1	4	—	—	—	46	1
1967-68	36	3	7	1	2	1	45	5
1968-69	42	6	4	1	3	—	49	7
1969-70	36	4	3	—	2	—	41	4
1970-71	41	2	7	—	3	1	51	3
1971-72	37	6	3	—	1	—	41	6
1972-73	33	2	2	—	4	—	39	2
1973-74	34	1	7	—	5	—	46	1
1974-75	36	2	—	—	4	—	40	2
1975-76	24	—	2	—	—	—	26	—
1976-77	16	—	4	—	—	—	20	—
1977-78	22	2	—	—	6	—	28	2
Total	**467**	**36**	**52**	**2**	**30**	**2**	**549**	**40**

EMLYN HUGHES
1966-79 26 APPEARANCES

He had to wait six months for his first taste of derby atmosphere, a 1-0 home win in September 1967. The first of four goals came two years and two months later as he opened the scoring in a 3-0 win at Goodison. Two more came in one memorable game in 1973 for which the score was Emlyn 2, Everton 0.

Hughes' last match in red was in April 1979, an FA Cup semi-final defeat against Manchester United depriving him of a Wembley send-off. He made up for this by leading his new club Wolves to a League Cup victory over Nottingham Forest, but after unsuccessfully managing Rotherham and periods with Hull, Mansfield and Swansea he turned his back on the game in favour of a media career.

These days, he's best known for his many appearances on BBC-TV's *A Question Of Sport*, but the award of an OBE in the 1980 New Year's Honours was well deserved.

Blackpool lost two great players to Merseyside in the course of the 1966-67 season. The best-known was Alan Ball, thanks to his role in the World Cup-winning England team, but it was the less heralded transfer of Emlyn Hughes (born Barrow, 28 August 1947) to Liverpool that would prove most influential on the long-term Merseyside scene.

He waited a matter of weeks for his first-team debut in March 1967, his transfer accelerated by the sacking of Tangerines manager Ron Suart. Having been promised first refusal, Shankly swooped to ensure he got his man.

And, when stopped for a minor traffic offence while driving him back to Liverpool, the manager asked the policeman if he knew who was in the car. 'The future captain of England,' burred Shankly – and his prediction came true. Joe Mercer, Don Revie and Ron Greenwood all made him their captain in succession, and he gained 62 caps.

Hughes' initial role was as a rangy left-half, in which position he succeeded Willie Stevenson. And though as time went by he dropped to centre and, in his last season, full-back, this did not prevent him from going on those rampaging runs that won him the nickname of Crazy Horse from the Kop.

Liverpool record

Season	League		FA Cup		League Cup		Total	
	Apps	Goals	Apps	Goals	Apps	Goals	Apps	Goals
1966-67	10	—	—	—	—	—	10	—
1967-68	39	2	9	—	2	—	50	2
1968-69	40	3	4	1	3	—	47	4
1969-70	41	7	6	—	2	—	49	7
1970-71	39	2	7	—	3	1	49	3
1971-72	42	8	3	—	3	—	48	8
1972-73	41	7	4	—	8	2	53	9
1973-74	42	2	9	—	6	—	57	2
1974-75	42	1	2	—	4	—	48	1
1975-76	41	2	2	—	3	—	46	2
1976-77	42	1	8	—	2	—	52	1
1977-78	39	—	1	—	9	—	49	—
1978-79	16	—	7	—	1	—	24	—
Total	**474**	**35**	**62**	**1**	**46**	**3**	**582**	**39**

A flying winger in the Callaghan, Thompson or Heighway mould, Arthur M. Goddard (born in Heaton Norris, and pictured *third from left foreground*) joined Liverpool during the course of the 1901-02 season from Glossop North End. It wasn't immediately apparent, but this was to be the start of a glowing career which would last until the outbreak of war.

Known as Artie, he'd started his career with local team Heaton Norris Albion before signing for Stockport and then Glossop, the latter in November 1889. His transfer value was rated at £250 – no mean fee then – but his value to Liverpool was beyond price.

A graceful, fast and fluent winger, he also captained the side, unusual from a player in his position. At five foot nine and a half inches and 11 stone seven, he was ideally built to attack at speed down the flanks.

His first season saw him miss just one game, and he would be absent just two dozen times in the next eight, so dependable was he, and he was a stalwart of the team that followed promotion in 1905 with a League Championship win.

Representative honours for the Football League against the Irish and Southern Leagues in 1910 and the Scottish League in 1913 were well deserved by a player whose right-wing forays set up many goals for strikers Joe Hewitt and Sam Raybould. His own strike rate was perhaps the Achilles heel of his game – only two seasons, 1902-03 and 1909-10, saw him reach double figures – but his value to the team was recognised by a long service benefit in 1914 which brought him £250.

The same year he was transferred to Cardiff City, whom he served until 1920, their last season outside the Football League before their greatest period of success. He then retired to return to Liverpool and go into business.

Liverpool record

Season	League		FA Cup		League Cup		Total	
	Apps	Goals	Apps	Goals	Apps	Goals	Apps	Goals
1901-02	11	2	—	—	—	—	11	2
1902-03	33	11	1	—	—	—	34	11
1903-04	33	7	1	—	—	—	34	7
1904-05	28	7	2	1	—	—	30	8
1905-06	38	7	5	2	—	—	43	9
1906-07	35	3	4	—	—	—	39	3
1907-08	35	4	4	—	—	—	39	4
1908-09	36	4	2	—	—	—	38	4
1909-10	35	13	1	—	—	—	36	13
1910-11	32	8	2	1	—	—	34	9
1911-12	28	2	1	—	—	—	29	2
1912-13	33	7	4	1	—	—	37	8
1913-14	11	—	—	—	—	—	11	—
Total	388	75	27	5	—	—	415	80

PLAYERS' TOP TEN
STEVE NICOL
1981-94 25 APPEARANCES

Alongside Alan Hansen and Graeme Souness, Steve Nicol (born Irvine, 11 December 1961) was perhaps Liverpool's most successful import from north of the border in recent decades. He might not court the attention his compatriots enjoyed both on and off the pitch, but his effectiveness on it was never doubted – least of all by his fellow professionals. And he made his presence felt in a number of different positions.

When he'd arrived at Anfield from home-town club Ayr United in October 1981, it was with the intention of succeeding Phil Neal as right-back. Three years later he'd played just two dozen games when he was sent on as substitute in the European Cup Final against AS Roma.

And irony of ironies, given Neal's reputation as an ice-cool penalty taker, Nicol was unfortunate enough to sky the Reds' first spot-kick in a shootout over the bar and into the opposition supporters.

Fortunately Neal and three other colleagues placed their kicks accurately to secure the silverware, but the fact that Nicol had stepped up to take the first was an early measure of his maturity and willingness to serve.

A genuinely two-footed player, Steve Nicol found his first first-team niche on the right of midfield before slipping back to right-back. He also thrilled a live TV audience if not Newcastle United fans by hitting a hat-trick in that cauldron of football fervour that is St James' Park in 1987. He only scored once in a derby game, and ironically it was his first, a 3-0 home win on 6 November 1983.

Yet Bob Paisley valued Nicol's 'special ability to dribble past a defender and cross the ball accurately with either foot' – even if he admitted 'I'm certain he would like to spend the rest of his days at right-back!'

Nicol also deputised in central defence for fellow Scot Alan Hansen when he was sidelined for much of the 1988-89 campaign, but had himself lost half a season, 1986-87, to injury.

Steve Nicol bade farewell to Anfield in 1994, stepping out of the top flight to First Division strugglers Notts County. In a traumatic first season at Meadow Lane which ended in relegation he served under four managers, including former Goodison boss Howard Kendall.

Yet 1995-96 saw him still giving his all for Sheffield Wednesday. Despite having the largest shoe size in the Anfield boot room, Nicol never got too big for his boots.

Liverpool record

Season	League Apps	League Goals	FA Cup Apps	FA Cup Goals	League Cup Apps	League Cup Goals	Total Apps	Total Goals
1982-83	4	—	—	—	—	—	4	—
1983-84	23	5	2	—	9	2	34	7
1984-85	31	5	6	—	2	—	39	5
1985-86	34	4	4	—	3	—	41	4
1986-87	14	3	—	—	5	1	19	4
1987-88	40	6	7	—	3	1	50	7
1988-89	38	2	6	—	6	—	50	2
1989-90	23	6	7	3	2	—	32	9
1990-91	35	3	7	—	2	—	44	3
1991-92	34	1	8	—	3	—	45	1
1992-93	32	—	1	—	4	—	37	—
1993-94	31	1	2	—	2	—	35	1
1994-95	4	—	—	—	1	—	5	—
Total	**343**	**36**	**50**	**3**	**42**	**4**	**435**	**43**

THE FIRST 100 LEAGUE GAMES

Liverpool and Everton played their 100th League derby on 8 October 1968 at Anfield. Suitably, perhaps, honours were even on the day, Smith and Ball the scorers. The record of the clubs at that point was as follows:

	P	W	D	L	F	A
Liverpool	100	31	28	41	137	149
Everton	100	41	28	31	149	137

DIXIE'S DOUBLE ACT

The Everton and Liverpool players have always been close. Everton legend Dixie Dean (*right*) was once walking along a road when he spotted Liverpool goalkeeper and fellow legend Elisha Scott (*below*)

passing on the other side. Dean nodded in acknowledgement and was astonished to see Scott dive full-length across the pavement as though he were trying to save an imaginary header!

EUROPE'S FOOTBALL CITY

Liverpool is, of course, the most successful English club side in Europe, having won four European Cups and two UEFA Cups. The only major European honour to have eluded them is the European Cup Winners' Cup, in which they were runners-up in 1966 against Borussia Dortmund, losing 2-1 after extra time. Everton's European record, by comparison, has seen them lift only one trophy; the European Cup Winners' Cup, when they beat Rapid Vienna 3-1 in 1985! Liverpool is therefore the only British city to have welcomed all three major European trophies.

CUP CLASH

In 1901 the Football Association announced that should the FA Cup Final between Spurs and Sheffield United require a replay, it would be held at Goodison Park one week after the first match. But, since Liverpool had a home game against Nottingham Forest the same day, the Anfield club protested.

The match was switched to Burnden Park, the home of Bolton Wanderers, and resulted in the lowest crowd for a Cup Final this century, only 20,447. Everton did, however, stage the Cup Final in 1894 (when Notts Country beat Bolton) and the replay in 1910 (when Newcastle United beat Barnsley). To date, Anfield has not been afforded the honour.

CHARITY BEGINS IN MERSEYSIDE

Aside from four Cup Finals (two FA Cup, one Milk Cup and one Screen Sport Super Cup, all of which were won by the Reds), Liverpool and Everton have met in three FA Charity Shields with the honours much more evenly spread; Liverpool winning once (in 1966, 1-0), Everton once (1984 1-0, pictured *below*) and a 1-1 draw in 1986. Everton had the pleasure of taking the Shield back to Goodison on four consecutive occasions from 1984-87 inclusive, even if the third was shared with their rivals.

As the FA Charity Shield did not begin until 1908, when Manchester United (the League Champions) met Queen's Park Rangers (the Southern League Champions) and won 4-0 after a replay, the Mersey clubs were denied a similar meeting in 1906 when Liverpool won the League and Everton the Cup.

CURIOSITY CORNER

Above: Legendary Anfield manager Bill Shankly.

Right: Kenny Dalglish cited the immense pressure on a Liverpool manager on his resignation in early 1991. He would eventually return to football to lead Blackburn Rovers to the Championship.

LIVERPOOL
Managers' Records

Manager	From	To	P	W	D	L	F	A	Success Rate
John McKenna	1892	August 1896	2	0	1	1	2	5	25%
Tom Watson	August 1896	May 1915	42	10	10	22	48	76	36%
David Ashworth	December 1919	February 1923	8	5	3	0	15	4	81%
Matt McQueen	February 1923	February 1928	10	4	3	3	18	13	55%
George Patterson	February 1928	May 1936	15	5	3	7	27	26	43%
George Kay	May 1936	February 1951	17	7	4	6	24	18	53%
Don Welsh	March 1951	May 1956	1	1	0	0	4	0	100%
Bill Shankly	December 1959	July 1974	27	11	8	8	31	24	56%
Bob Paisley	July 1974	June 1983	21	10	9	2	30	14	69%
Joe Fagan	June 1983	May 1985	7	2	2	3	5	4	43%
Kenny Dalglish	June 1985	February 1991	21	11	6	4	33	22	67%
Graeme Souness	April 1991	January 1994	5	2	1	2	6	6	50%
Roy Evans	January 1994		4	1	1	2	3	5	37%

EVERTON
Managers' Records

Manager	From	To	P	W	D	L	F	A	Success Rate
Selection Panel		May 1939	83	37	20	26	137	117	57%
Theo Kelly	May 1939	September 1948	5	1	2	2	2	8	40%
Cliff Britton	September 1948	February 1956	7	1	2	4	4	12	29%
Harry Catterick	April 1961	April 1973	25	8	7	10	24	30	46%
Billy Bingham	May 1973	January 1977	7	0	4	3	1	5	29%
Gordon Lee	February 1977	May 1981	12	2	6	4	11	15	45%
Howard Kendall	May 1981	June 1987	18	4	5	9	13	27	36%
Colin Harvey	June 1987	November 1990	10	2	2	6	9	15	30%
Howard Kendall	November 1990	December 1993	9	3	3	3	12	13	50%
Mike Walker	January 1994	November 1994	1	0	0	1	1	2	0%
Joe Royle	November 1994		3	2	1	0	4	1	83%

Left: Howard Kendall could not repeat initial success in his second spell in charge at Everton

Above: Joe Royle returned to Goodison after 12 years at Oldham.

DERBY DOUBLES:
Players who appeared for both sides in derby matches

Gary Ablett
Liverpool 1986-91, Everton 1992-
Tall Merseyside-born full-back or central defender who played over 100 League games for Liverpool. Loan spells at Derby and Hull preceded a 1992 transfer to Everton for £750,000, but despite exceeding his Anfield appearances in blue and winning an FA Cup medal at Goodison he was reportedly unsettled at the end of 1995.

Peter Beardsley
Liverpool 1987-91, Everton 1991-93
Mercurial ball-playing forward who'd been a folk hero at Newcastle before Liverpool prised him away in 1987. Discarded by Souness, he moved across the city to Goodison amid much supporter dissatisfaction, and regained his England place in his thirties after returning to his native north-east to play under Kevin Keegan.

David Burrows
Liverpool 1988-93, Everton 1994-95
Arrived at Anfield from West Bromwich and proved a solid and versatile if unspectacular defender. Spent less than a season at West Ham after leaving Liverpool during Graeme Souness's tempestuous tenure, but played only 19 times for Everton on returning north in 1994 and joined Coventry a year later.

Edgar Chadwick
Everton 1888-99, Liverpool 1902-04
This Blackburn-born England international transferred to Goodison from his home-town team in time for the first League season. After playing for Southampton in the 1902 FA Cup Final he returned to Merseyside for a spell with Liverpool before becoming one of the first Englishmen to coach abroad in Holland and Germany.

Dick Forshaw
Liverpool 1919-27, Everton 1927-29
An ever-present in the Liverpool Championship sides of 1921-23, Forshaw moved to Goodison and picked up a third medal in 1927-28. A skilful inside-forward, he scored 124 goals for Liverpool at a rate of nearly one every other game. He started his League career at Middlesbrough and ended it with Wolves.

David Johnson
Everton 1969-72, Liverpool 1976-82, Everton 1982-84
A tall, forceful centre-forward who led the line well, he spent four seasons at Ipswich in-between beginning his career at Everton and landing at Anfield in 1976. Returned to Everton in 1982, before winding down his career at Barnsley, Manchester City and Preston. Scored derby goals for both sides.

Tosh Johnson
Everton 1930-34, Liverpool 1934-36
Celebrated for his part in returning the Toffees to the top flight alongside Dixie Dean, Tommy 'Tosh' Johnson had signed from Manchester City with a reputation as a goalscorer. His spell at Anfield was brief and rather less glorious, but he ended his career with 222 League goals to his credit.

Billy Lacey
Everton 1908-12, Liverpool 1912-24
An early example of the player-exchange transfer deal took Lacey to Anfield as makeweight in a deal that sent Gracie and Uren the other way. Yet while that duo made only 37 appearances between them, the Eire international forward played over 250 games for the Reds before joining New Brighton.

Steve McMahon
Everton 1977-83, Liverpool 1985-91
Combative Liverpool-born midfielder who sandwiched two seasons at Villa Park between his Merseyside sojourns. Proved his worth with 17 England caps while at Anfield. Moved on to Manchester City before beginning a torrid spell in management at the County Ground, Swindon.

ve McMahon (opposite) and Tosh Johnson (above), two players who went on to y for Liverpool after their Goodison career.

CURIOSITY CORNER

WOMEN TAKE SIDES

The mini derby fought out by Liverpool and Everton's reserves in the Central (now Pontins) League is as fiercely contested as the real thing. But from September 1995 the Liverpool v Everton derby acquired a third dimension with the clubs adopting women's teams and kitting them out in the traditional strips.

Liverpool were first to move into the women's game, adopting the former Knowsley side and taking them all the way to the 1995 Cup Final.

Everton took over the Leasowe Pacific women's team earlier in year, following their neighbours' example, and found a home at non-League Marine. The stage was set for rivalry to commence in earnest.

Yet in echoes of the first Liverpool-Everton split in 1892, five Liverpool players were lured away to their rivals during the summer. But striker Maria Harper went back and her goal was enough to win the day in front of 100 fans. 'Merseyside are quite lucky to have two successful teams in the Premier League,' she said after the game. 'We play for pride and enjoyment: we don't get everything the men do.'

The Reds were coached by John Bennison, who passes his boot-room knowledge gained during years on the Anfield staff to a new set of players and admitted to being surprised at the standard.

PROGRAMME PALS

For a considerable period of time preceding World War I, Liverpool and Everton shared the same programme. Costing one penny and issued weekly from the offices of the *Bootle Times* where it was printed, it took in the first-team game of the week plus the other side's reserve fixture. Measuring nine inches by six, it could feature up to 12 pages.

The cover, from around 1907, featured a Liverpool and an Everton player shaking hands. The hostilities caused it to slim down to a single folded sheet of paper, but even when peace returned it wasn't until the early 1930s that the clubs decided to issue separate matchday programmes.

WAR BREAKS OUT ON PITCH

Billy Liddell's experience of the intense Mersey derby atmosphere began in the last years of World War II. The Dunfermline-born winger would clock up over 500 peacetime appearances from 1945, but cut his teeth in the wartime leagues. And one wartime derby game he played saw a very unusual pitch invasion.

'I have a vivid recollection of a game when I was marked by Billy Cook. Well, frankly, Billy was going at me pretty roughly, but, fortunately, I was getting out of the way.

'Nevertheless, Billy's tackling was enough to bring a soldier in uniform off the Anfield terraces and on to the pitch. He tried to have a go at Billy and when a policeman came along to remove him, Bill pleaded successfully that the soldier should be allowed to return to the crowd.'

OWN GOALS AND GAFFES

A total of six own-goals have been registered in derby games to date – although attribution, as ever, can be contested. As it stands, Everton have scored five times for the opposition, Liverpool only once. Yet that was undoubtedly the most public – Bruce Grobbelaar's in the 1984 Charity Shield in front of a sellout Wembley crowd (*below*).

Two were scored in one game on 4 March 1972 when Tommy Wright and John McLaughlin contributed to a 4-0 Anfield pasting. Full-back Wright was unfortunate enough to notch his own goal after just 35 seconds – and two weeks later, he compounded his error by scoring for the opposition again, Manchester City being the lucky recipients this time.

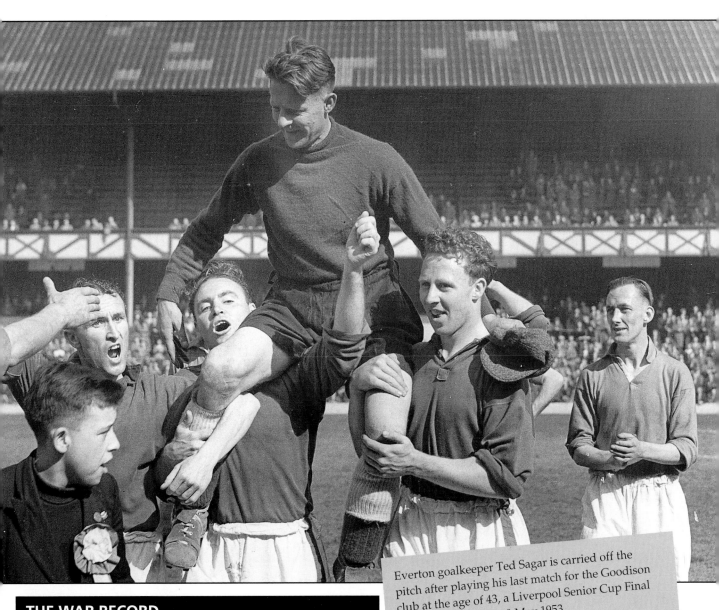

Everton goalkeeper Ted Sagar is carried off the pitch after playing his last match for the Goodison club at the age of 43, a Liverpool Senior Cup Final against Tranmere on 9 May 1953.

A fearless keeper renowned for throwing himself at attackers' feet regardless of the consequences, Sagar registered a total of 495 first-class appearances for the Toffeemen (despite having his career interrupted by the war) following his debut in the 4-0 win over Derby on 18 January 1930. His record has, of course, since been overtaken by current Blues custodian Neville Southall but his stay of 24 years and one month with the same club will be difficult for anyone to overhaul.

Sadly, Ted Sagar died in 1986.

THE WAR RECORD

Liverpool and Everton faced each other 51 times in wartime competition, details of which are recorded in Chapter 7. The summary of results is as follows:

WORLD WAR I

	P	W	D	L	F	A
Liverpool	16	7	3	6	35	32
Everton	16	6	3	7	32	35

WORLD WAR II

	P	W	D	L	F	A
Liverpool	35	19	6	10	76	65
Everton	35	10	6	19	65	76

CURIOSITY CORNER

FRIENDLIES AND TESTIMONIALS

SCREEN SPORT SUPER CUP

The Screen Sport Super Cup was introduced in season 1985-86 to compensate the six English clubs who had qualified for Europe but were banned by UEFA. The six teams were divided into two groups; Liverpool, Southampton and Tottenham Hotspur in one, Everton, Manchester United and Norwich City in the other, with the top two teams in each group advancing to the semi-final stage.

Everton, who beat Spurs in the semi-final and Liverpool, who knocked out Norwich, made it through to the Final, but this was held over to the following season, due in part to the lack of interest in the competition but also because Everton and Liverpool were meeting with regularity at this stage. They met in the FA Cup Final of 1986 and the following season's curtain-raising Charity Shield.

The Screen Sport Super Cup Final first leg was eventually played on 16 September 1986 at Liverpool, with the home side winning 3-1 thanks to two goals by Ian Rush and one from Steve McMahon against Everton's lone reply from Kevin Sheedy in a match watched by a crowd of 20,660. The line-ups were:

Liverpool: *Hooper, Venison, Beglin, Lawrenson, Whelan (Molby), Gillespie, Dalglish, Nicol, Rush, MacDonald, McMahon.*
Everton: *Mimms, Billinge, Power, Ratcliffe, Marshall, Langley, Adams, Wilkinson, Sharp, Steven, Sheedy (Aspinall).*

The return leg at Goodison was held on 30 September, with Liverpool winning 4-1 in front of 26,068 fans. Liverpool's goals came from Ian Rush (3) and Steve Nicol, Graeme Sharp scoring for Everton from the penalty spot. The line-ups:

Everton: *Mimms, Billinge, Power, Ratcliffe, Mountfield, Steven, Adams, Heath (Aspinall) (Pointon), Sharp, Wilkinson, Sheedy.*
Liverpool: *Grobbelaar, Gillespie, Beglin, Lawrenson, Whelan, Hansen, Wark, Nicol (Venison), Rush, Molby, McMahon (Walsh).*

This win (7-2 on aggregate) allowed the Reds to turn the previous season's Double into a treble, as the Liverpool programme pointed out! Rush's three goals in the second leg was the 10th hat-trick of his career.

As the trophy (and there was one to collect) has not since been contested, Liverpool are the reigning holders, although one suspects the tankards each player collected will have proved more useful!

TESTIMONIALS AND OTHER COMPETITIONS

A number of testimonial matches have been held between the two clubs over the years, one such being Liverpool's visit to Goodison Park on 13 March 1973 for recently retired Blues captain Brian Labone. In addition, local competitions like the Merseyside Floodlit Cup (*right*) have pitched the teams against each other. Interest in these clashes was at its highest when the clubs were separated by a League division, as in the years 1954-62 when Liverpool were exiled in the Second Division.

Ian St John arrived towards the end of that period and recalls the excitement a 'nothing' clash could generate.

'When I came to Liverpool in 1961 my first game was against Everton – and I scored a hat-trick. That was the Liverpool Senior Cup, played at the end of the season a couple of days after I signed. I was told there was a local Cup tie... and there were 60,000 at Goodison! They'd never met in the League because Liverpool at that time had been many years in the Second Division, so the fans were missing out on their derby matches.

'To get both teams together in the Liverpool Senior Cup was great, a chance for them to cross swords. And I'd just signed, so there was a lot of expectancy from our fans: "Who's this guy we've signed from Scotland?" We got beaten 4-3, but I scored the three goals!'

EVERTON FOOTBALL CLUB
OFFICIAL PROGRAMME
4D
LIVERPOOL FLOODLIGHT CUP
EVERTON
v
LIVERPOOL
Wednesday 18th October, 1961
Kick-off 7-30 p.m.

GOODISON PARK · LIVERPOOL

Left: The programmes for the first and second legs of the Screen Sport Super Cup Final in September 1986.

Below: Ian Rush, seen here with Ronnie Whelan, has constantly proved a thorn in Everton's side both in League and Cup competition.

Below left: The programme for the 1958 Floodlit Challenge Cup.

CURIOSITY CORNER

THE THOUGHTS OF CHAIRMAN SHANKLY

Bill Shankly was one of the greatest managers the game has ever seen and the man perhaps most responsible for putting Liverpool, the team, on the football map. He also did much to put Liverpool, the city, on the same map, although his comments about Everton were often said with his tongue very firmly in the side of his cheek. Here are a few of them.

He once said in an interview that there were two great teams in Liverpool, 'Liverpool', then he paused like a master comic before uttering the name of the second, 'and Liverpool Reserves.'

Another comment attributed to him concerned the 1966 FA Cup Final. Everton captain Brian Labone was being introduced to the member of the Royal Family in attendance, Princess Margaret. 'And where is exactly is Everton?' she is supposed to have asked. 'It's in Liverpool, ma'am.' 'Of course, we had your first team here last year!'

Labone had the last laugh, however, as Everton came from behind against Sheffield Wednesday to win the Cup 3-2 and ensure it remained in the city for another 12 months.

Despite his thinning thatch, Shankly was always fastidious about his hair and visited the barber regularly. On one occasion, he paid a call when his rivals were heading Division One. When asked 'Would you like anything off the top, Sir?' he simply responded 'Everton!'

The contrast between Bill Shankly and his taciturn counterpart Harry Catterick at Goodison during the 1960s was often remarked upon, and the source of many jokes. One undoubtedly apocryphal tale concerned the day Everton were struck by a 'flu bug and Catterick phoned his opposite number to suggest a training match, since there were too few fit Everton players to organise one 'in-house'.

Shankly declined, but suggested Catterick lay out 11 dustbin lids in a team formation for the players to dribble round as if they were the opposition.

Then minutes later, the phone rang again. 'So how's it going, Harry? Did you set it up alright?' burred the Scot.

'Yes, Bill,' came the anguished response. 'But I've got a problem… the dustbin lids are winning 2-0!'

SHANKS: A PLAYER REMEMBERS

Ian St John (Liverpool 1961-71) played all his derby games under Bill Shankly. He recalls the importance of the fixtures to a man who made half of Merseyside his own.

'When it came to derby games, Shanks was more keyed up than we were! He talked all the time anyway, so you couldn't say he talked more, but he really looked forward to the matches against Everton. I believe it was because as a player he was the kind that loves the big occasion, the atmosphere, he loved to get stuck in. So the derby match with its extra edge was always more appealing to him than an ordinary League game. He felt they were great occasions.

'The derby match had everything: winning it meant we were the top dogs in town. You could hold your head up till the next meeting, and that was vital to him. He always made us aware of the importance of the result for the fans, knowing that they had to go and face their pals at work, in the pubs or wherever. So it was crucial that the red side was the one with smiles on their faces!'

Left: Bill Shankly, pictured in 1966-67, proudly shows off the silverware won by his Liverpool team in the background.

Right: Ian St John made 336 League appearances in a Liverpool shirt following his 1961 transfer from Motherwell.

CURIOSITY CORNER

SUBSTITUTE SANDY

When Sandy Brown came on and scored at Goodison in a 3-1 win against Liverpool on 27 August 1966 he became Everton's first goal-scoring substitute. Though nominally a full-back, the ex-Partick Thistle player who came to the club after the 1963 Championship win was versatile enough to be named as substitute no less than 33 times in League games. Unfortunately, it will be his headed own goal in December 1969, since much-compiled as a classic footballing 'gaffe', that at least half of Merseyside will remember him for!

The first subs to be deployed in a derby were both introduced in the same game, a 25 September 1965 match at Anfield which the home side won 5-0. Alf Arrowsmith took Geoff Strong's place for the rampaging Reds, while the shell-shocked visitors replaced defender Brian Labone with midfield man Gerry Glover.

Glover, a product of the youth team, played only three times for the League side – two full appearances and this sub's spot – and two were against Liverpool, which must also be some sort of record.

ONCE AND OUT

Over the history of the fixture, only three players have made a single appearance for one of the clubs in a derby game. They are:

Marshall   **Liverpool**   **11 January 1902**

A goalkeeper whose Christian name went unrecorded. He stood in for regular custodian Bill Perkins whose only absence of the season was for a derby at Goodison. Everton won 4-0 and Perkins' return saw the nameless newcomer consigned to obscurity.

Harold McNaughton   **Liverpool**   **23 October 1920**

Another goalkeeper, a Scot who found another Scot(t), Elisha, impossible to displace. His single game came when his rival was on international duty. Newspaper reports called him 'a cool customer, quite undisturbed by the size of the crowd' and he kept a clean sheet in a 1-0 win.

Glenn Keeley   **Everton**   **6 November 1982**

On loan from Blackburn Rovers, a former club of manager Howard Kendall, the towering centre-half blotted his copybook by holding back Kenny Dalglish and being dismissed. He returned to Ewood Park to serve his suspension.

DERBY DEBUTANTS:
Players who made their League debuts in derby matches

Player	Team	Match	Player	Team	Match
R Menham	Everton	21 November 1896	Stanley Kane	Liverpool	20 March 1935
Jack Parkinson	Liverpool	23 September 1899	Harman Van Den Berg	Liverpool	16 February 1938
George Bowen	Liverpool	14 September 1901	William Higgins	Everton	21 September 1946
W White	Liverpool	14 September 1901 – scored 1	Bernie Wright	Everton	4 March 1972
Marshall	Liverpool	11 January 1902	Terry McDermott	Liverpool	16 November 1974
R Turner	Everton	9 April 1909 – scored 1	Phil Neal	Liverpool	16 November 1974
J Allan	Everton	12 February 1910	Glenn Keeley	Everton	6 November 1982
Walter Scott	Everton	12 February 1910	Julian Dicks	Liverpool	18 September 1993
J Houston	Everton	8 February 1913			
George Harrison	Everton	20 September 1913			
Phil Bratley	Liverpool	3 October 1914			
Harold McNaughton	Liverpool	23 October 1920			
Bobby Irvine	Everton	12 November 1921			
J Kelly	Everton	12 February 1927			
Ted Taylor	Everton	12 February 1927			
E Common	Everton	9 February 1929			
John McFarlane	Liverpool	9 February 1929			
Lachlan McPherson	Everton	4 January 1930			

Right: Julian Dicks, the most recent derby debutant, was unable to stake a first-team claim at Anfield and returned to West Ham United a year after his arrival from Upton Park in 1993.

THE RECOLLECTIONS OF PLAYERS AND MANAGERS FROM LIVERPOOL AND EVERTON ON THE NORTH'S MOST PRESTIGIOUS FIXTURE

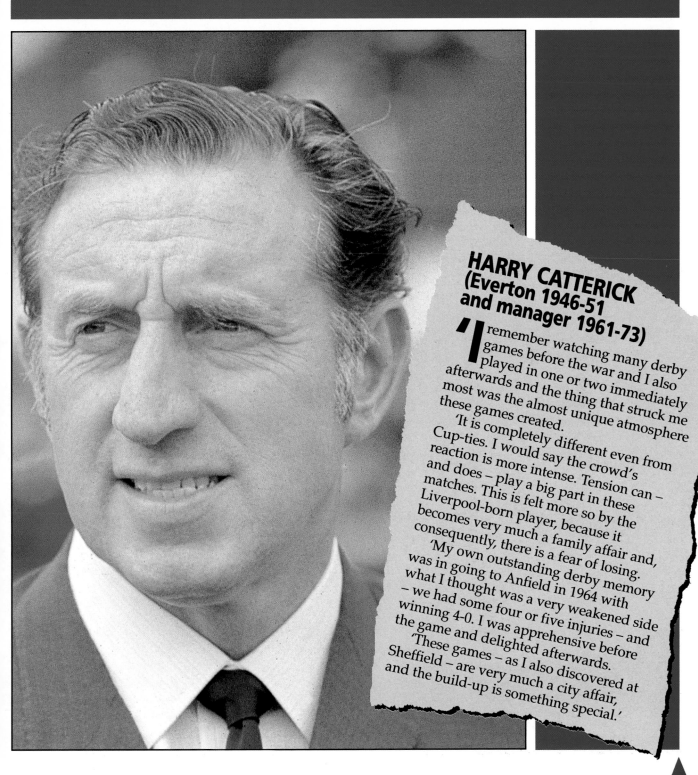

HARRY CATTERICK (Everton 1946-51 and manager 1961-73)

'I remember watching many derby games before the war and I also played in one or two immediately afterwards and the thing that struck me most was the almost unique atmosphere these games created.

'It is completely different even from Cup-ties. I would say the crowd's reaction is more intense. Tension can – and does – play a big part in these matches. This is felt more so by the Liverpool-born player, because it becomes very much a family affair and, consequently, there is a fear of losing.

'My own outstanding derby memory was in going to Anfield in 1964 with what I thought was a very weakened side – we had some four or five injuries – and winning 4-0. I was apprehensive before the game and delighted afterwards.

'These games – as I also discovered at Sheffield – are very much a city affair, and the build-up is something special.'

MEMORIES

JOEY JONES
(Liverpool 1975-78)

'Liverpool and Everton games are unique because of the mixture of passion, rivalry and friendship in one big city.

'I have relatives in Liverpool, some wear red and some wear blue. I wish every derby game in the country was filled with the same good spirit as this one.

'The sight of Reds and Blues travelling together gave my biggest pre-match buzz. The build-up in newspapers, on the radio and television was all part of the occasion. I loved the fuss. Every professional should do – then be fully prepared for the contest.

'Nobody wants to become the villain of the piece, because a bad mistake is remembered forever. An own goal for instance, is recalled more often than a winner from these games.

'I stood on the Kop as a lad. No other game in the world had any meaning while Liverpool and Everton were in action. They were great games to play in once the butterflies had settled down.'

WILLIE STEVENSON
(Liverpool 1962-67)

'There will be good laugh lines and plenty of banter, but stomachs will be churning at the same time. It is a form of escapism from the tensions which this very special match produces and always will do.

'We had tremendous battles with Everton and my personal ones were always with Roy Vernon. But we would leave the game behind at five o'clock and pop out for a drink together.

'We did not share the same social life in Glasgow. We went our different ways after the final whistle. Don't get me wrong, though. The rivalry is intense – and, while players say they take one match at a time, this one is no exception to the rule.

'The pressure begins to build up two weeks before the fixture and relief doesn't come until the game is over. The players know what the results means to their fans but win or lose, there is no bitterness.

'They will fear the thought of a mistake early on, but it only takes five minutes for good players to come to terms with big occasions.'

RON YEATS
(Liverpool 1961-71)

'I did not know what hit me. I wondered what it was all about. The banter and the build-up began two weeks beforehand and really got to me. It was something I had never experienced before.

'Frankly, I was pleased when they came to an end with the referee's whistle. They were full of tension, they were too heavily charged, too many people lived or died by one result.

'Where I would play a simple ten-yard pass in a normal game, I would hoof the ball to safety in derbies and breathe a sigh of relief afterwards. Other players may have enjoyed them – I didn't!

'The meetings were unique. Full of fire but never bad feeling. Everton's Alex Young was a close friend: we'd played in the same national service team.

'I would telephone him on the day before a game and say "I'll be looking after you tomorrow." He would reply; "I will have scored twice before you find me."

'There was always good humour between Liverpool and Everton players as well as the supporters.'

GLENN KEELEY
(Everton 1982)
His one and only game for Everton was a derby while on loan from Blackburn.

'Yes, you could describe it as great fun, certainly a memorable occasion. And for all the wrong reasons. I'd played in a "mini derby" (reserve fixture) the week before and had looked forward to the big one.

'My debut lasted around 25 minutes, then I was walking after being given my marching orders. Someone had played a through ball, and it took a bit of a skid off the pitch, so I had to spin and turn.

'Kenny Dalglish was a couple of yards or so behind me, and didn't have to turn quite so much. He got to the ball first and I caught hold of his jersey.

'The incident was treated as a professional foul – referees were being pretty strict about that sort of thing, at that stage of the season, though I feel I was unfortunate in that it was rated a sending-off offence.

'Admittedly you're pulling someone back by the shirt when he's breaking through with only the keeper to beat, but it's 50-50 whether or not he'll score. And I suppose it's an instinctive reaction on the defender's part. I know it was mine.'

ALAN BALL
(Everton 1966-71)

'I would give 15 years of my life to play in one again. Wherever I am at seven o'clock on the night of a game, I think of the players who took part and saying inwardly: "You lucky lads."

'I also played in London derbies for Arsenal but those games were not in the same league as the Merseyside derbies. The morning of a match reminded me of Christmas as a kid. The excitement and the build-up were almost unbearable.

'It's the supporters of both clubs who make these games what they are. The people of the city create that very special stage.

'Anfield became a lucky ground for me, and not many players can say that. They were wonderful days on Merseyside. I never wanted the 90 minutes to end. Yet the fear of losing was there until the closing moments. It was football on the knife edge and that's how I liked it.

'The Kop fans inspire their team but also applauded good opposing play and gave me a determination to do well. For me, they created an atmosphere like Wembley and I believe we had a respect for each other.'

MEMORIES

BILLY LIDDELL
(Liverpool 1945-61)

'Of all the derby games I played in, one stands out above all – the time when Liverpool, then in the Second Division, went to Goodison in the Cup in 1955 and won 4-0. I scored the first goal, and the thrill of winning so convincingly was even more than that of the 1950 semi-final when we beat Everton 2-0 at Maine Road.

'Although the papers and radio used to build up the derby so much, I never found it a great deal harder than any other. Perhaps I was lucky, because I didn't seem to suffer from nerves.

'There has always been tension surrounding the fixture. That's one of the troubles – no-one wants to get beaten in this particular match. Even so, there has always been a close link between the players of both clubs. I remember I used to see Peter Farrell quite a lot – speaking at youth clubs together – but friendship had to be put aside at least twice a year.

'Maybe I'm prejudiced, but I have always said that the Mersey derby is the best in the country. There often seems to be trouble among the fans in Manchester and, of course, a different type of fervour causes problems in the Rangers-Celtic match.

'I find that Anfield is a little better than Goodison for atmosphere – maybe it is because the ground is more compact compared with the high stands at Everton. But the supporters are equal in the sense that they seem more mature than at most other grounds.

'Though there are younger supporters, the average age seems higher than in most places – and, above all, everyone seems to appreciate good football.'

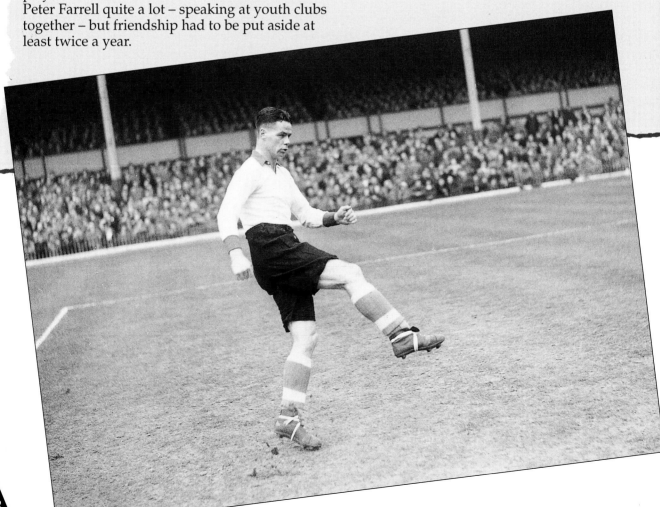

JIMMY GABRIEL
(Everton 1960-67)

'They have never lost their edge. They never change. And the difference between winning and losing is like a wedding and funeral. If we won, we wanted the next one to hurry around. If we lost we wanted it quicker still.

'The atmosphere and the big stage was everything a player could imagine. And the build-up to the day was colossal: the major enemy was coming!

'I suppose there was an extra edge for people like Brian Labone, Colin Harvey, Tommy Wright and Brian Harris because they were local lads and knew the feelings on the terraces from school days.

'I can remember Bill Shankly being asked about a certain player he had sold. I was at this particular function and listening to this question and answer session.

'Bill refused the question point-blank, but later took me aside and gave me a private explanation. "See, the player I was asked about – if I had broken him in half he would have smelled of perfume."'

119

BOB PAISLEY
(Liverpool 1939-54
and manager 1974-83)

'I've been on Merseyside long enough to consider myself a Liverpudlian (he said in 1976). The years condition you – but it doesn't matter how cool you try and play it, as the manager you always feel an obligation to your own supporters. You want your team to produce something from the game, for them.

'I know what goes on in the homes of the Merseyside football fans, when the derby game is coming up. And it would be the same, if one team were in the Second Division and one in the First, or if one were in Division Four and the other were in the top flight.

'There's still that quality about derby meetings, the opposition still feel that, on the day, despite the difference in division, they would have every right to lick you. You get keyed-up, because this is the most difficult game of the season to get over.

'You can talk about favourites and underdogs, but there are no favourites or underdogs when you kick off a derby game. It's 11 men against 11. And they all want to win.'

DAVE HORRIDGE
(Former *Daily Mirror* sportswriter)

'Of all the national newspaper soccer writers I have seen more Everton v Liverpool games than most. I believe my first was during the war, although I cannot remember most about it – except that, supported by my father, I sat on a crash barrier at Goodison.

'The first one I recollect was a 2-2 draw a few days after Christmas 1945, again at Goodison. I saw that from the boys' pen and I don't think I have missed one since except for the two years I spent in Egypt and Cyprus on a "holiday" paid for by the government... khaki suit and rifle provided!

'Derby day in Liverpool is a great day no matter what the result or the standard of the game. I have seen some bad ones. But most of my derby day memories have little to do with what happened on the pitch.

'In June 1947, I saw Liverpool beat Everton 2-1 in the Liverpool Senior Cup Final at Anfield. I "sagged" the school sports day to be there.

'On Monday morning my teacher trying to be clever, said to me in front of the whole class, "How did the game go, Horridge? I would like to have been there but had to attend the sports meeting."

'Me, being equally clever and knowing he had no proof of where I had been, replied, "Good. You should have been there."

'"I'm glad," said the teacher. "Perhaps you could write 1,000 words after school describing the game for me?"

BRIAN LABONE
(Everton 1957-71)

'I know I rarely looked forward to derby games. In fact, I didn't like them. The build-up starts about two weeks before the match and it becomes a bit of a strain two or three days before the game, when the tension gets inside you. It's not a very pleasant feeling.

'I don't think there are too many players who really relish them – there's too much at stake. To win is very, very pleasing and you walk ten feet tall for a week. To lose is hell. It's as simple as that and you know it will be one thing or the other when you go out for the kick-off.'

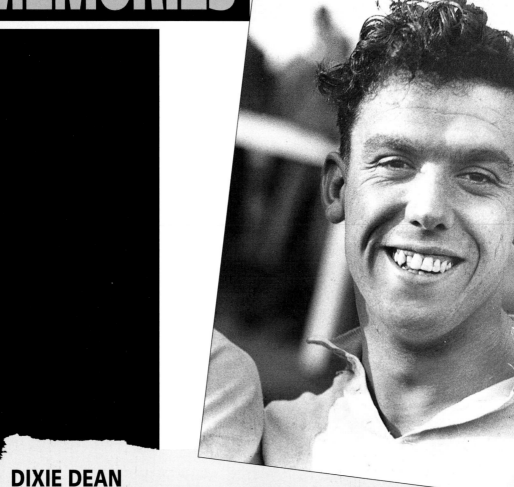

DIXIE DEAN
(Everton 1925-38)

'While the two sides were naturally great rivals, some grand friendships developed between the players off the field. It was the custom, for instance, that if we had played at Goodison Park, the teams would go to Anfield after the match to mix together socially – and vice versa when we played over there.

'The Everton team of my period was a far better footballing side than Liverpool. The Everton board were very strict in their demand for skilful football.

'To me, the derby game was just another fixture. I had contracted derby fever when I was quite young, so I knew what was coming and the build-up didn't affect me like it did some of the others. As skipper, however, it was my job to make the others forget it.

'Elisha Scott – the greatest goalkeeper in the world – was a great friend of mine, but we used to try to needle each other out there on the park. In 1931, I hadn't scored in five matches prior to the derby game and, just before the kick-off, Elisha cracked: "You aren't going to end that run this afternoon, you black-haired so-and-so!"

'I put three past him in the first nine minutes and asked him: "How's that suit you, you Irish so-and-so?" That very same evening we went out and had a couple of drinks and I think Elisha and I were the only two people in the city who weren't talking football.

'I used to post a little tube of aspirins to him on Thursday, so that he would get them on Friday morning. I used to put a note in which read: "Get yourself a good night's sleep – I shall be there again on Saturday!"

'Oh, but he was a good 'un. We were the best of friends off the field – and that's the way it should be, too.'

HOWARD KENDALL
(Everton 1967-74 and manager 1981-87, 1990-93)

'When I joined Everton from Preston, I had little idea of what to expect in derby week. I think the nearest to it that I had experienced was in Cup-ties – especially against Manchester United. It is something really special and, while one does get tense beforehand, you can take it from me that everyone who takes part loves it purely because of the atmosphere.

'I think the tension is determined more by the fans than it is created by the players. The local lads really get keyed-up and, clearly, if they are on the losing side, they feel it more than others – though no-one likes losing matches of this sort.

'Everyone gets upset when they have lost, but imported players – especially from places where they don't have this conflict of club loyalty within the city – do not suffer as deeply as the locals.

'There is a tremendous build-up for these games by the press and other media and players cannot help but notice the accumulation of pressures. But, in general, players love playing in this atmosphere, for it is truly electric.

'My outstanding memory from a derby game (as a player) was when I scored the only goal to beat Liverpool at Goodison Park in 1968. While it was by no means a great goal, it still delighted me and, believe me, I was walking ten feet tall afterwards!'

MEMORIES

GRAEME SHARP
(Everton 1980-91)

'With no disrespect to Manchester, I would say the Merseyside derby is probably on a par or second to the Rangers-Celtic one. It's certainly the biggest derby in England. It's a great experience for players, and I'm fortunate enough to have played in a few! The first memory is that you can't hear yourself speak for the first 20 minutes, the noise is so incredible. The fans are great and there's no animosity – they can go together to the game.

'Goals? Yes, you ask any Evertonian and it's the goals they scored against Liverpool that they remember. One I scored in 1985 against Bruce Grobbelaar, that's the one that stands out – even though we lost 3-2!

'There've been some good games along the way. The atmosphere's great and it's always nice to play in them. The Cup Finals stand out. The first one at Wembley, the Milk Cup Final we drew, was probably the best result for everyone travelling down to Wembley: all families together.'

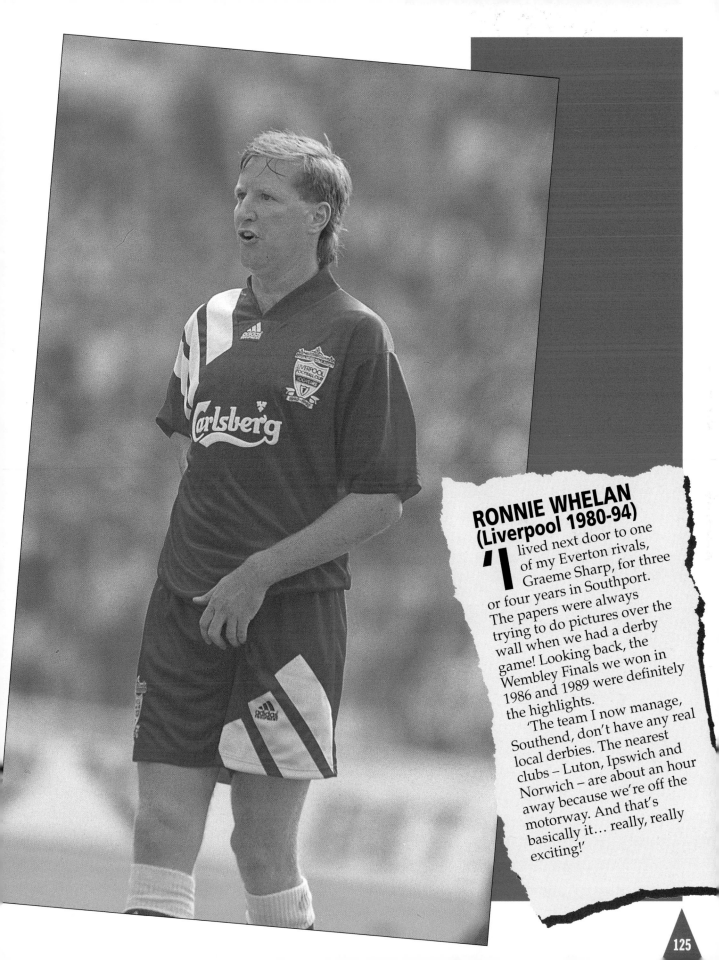

RONNIE WHELAN
(Liverpool 1980-94)

'I lived next door to one of my Everton rivals, Graeme Sharp, for three or four years in Southport. The papers were always trying to do pictures over the wall when we had a derby game! Looking back, the Wembley Finals we won in 1986 and 1989 were definitely the highlights.

'The team I now manage, Southend, don't have any real local derbies. The nearest clubs – Luton, Ipswich and Norwich – are about an hour away because we're off the motorway. And that's basically it… really, really exciting!'

RAY CLEMENCE
(Liverpool 1968-81)

'If other derby matches could learn anything from the Merseyside games, it is the way the fans can take defeat or success. I have seen Glasgow matches, Manchester derbies and played in the London games and I think they could all do with a little more humour. All the matches are as intense on the field. The players try just as hard in all the games to win for their respective sets of fans.

'Any victory in a derby match is good. It means so much to the fans out there. They are the ones who have to live with their friends' teasing for six months.'

IAN ST JOHN
(Liverpool 1961-71)

'I played my first League derby in 1963, after we came up from the Second Division. I scored two goals in 16 games – not a lot, I admit, but I remember scoring one in the 5-0 game in 1965, at the beginning of the Cup-winning season. We'd lost 4-0 the year before, so revenge was sweet.

'When I went to Liverpool, I didn't know any of their players – but I knew Alex Young, Alex Parker, Jimmy Gabriel, and Alex Scott from Everton. These are guys I'd played with for the Scotland team, and Sandy Brown was in the Scottish League team I'd played in, so I knew all those fellas at Goodison. In Liverpool I knew nobody, because as a Second Division team they didn't have any internationals.

'I don't think there's an awful lot to home advantage because the games rarely go to form. The expectancy of the home team is always greater, which adds a wee bit more pressure. The fans all think because they're at home they're going to win it, that they've got that advantage, but it doesn't always work that way. I've seen Liverpool go to Goodison and outplay Everton there so I don't think it really applies.

'I've seen games where the football has been terrific and I've seen some very tense, very tight nil-nillers, but I have to say in Merseyside derbies over the years the odds have always favoured attacking play. Yet if you look at the statistics elsewhere in this book you'll find there have been spells when things have been a bit tedious, particularly around the 1970s.'

MEMORIES

TOMMY SMITH
(Liverpool 1962-78)

'It's something different. During the week leading up to the match, you try to treat it as an ordinary game... but it's hard to do this. The game ahead is always at the back of your mind.

'You have different feelings about every side you play against, but the derby game gives you a special sort of feeling. You visit grounds like Old Trafford, and you remember certain games that you won or lost, and you have grounds for thinking that you can pull off a victory – but with a derby game, you just don't know how the result will go.

'It makes no difference that one team might be riding high, and the other not having such a good run; you know that this one game is different... and anything can happen. In that respect, it's just like the FA Cup, where you go into a tie knowing that anything can happen. And derby games of the past have turned up some shock results.

'You do your training during the days before the match, and you try to treat it as an ordinary week. But you get your wife to answer the phone calls, because of the clamour for tickets! People you haven't heard of for ages suddenly come on for tickets... which, unfortunately, you haven't got.'

DAVE JONES
(Everton 1974-79)

'Being a local lad made it a special fixture – my family was split straight down the middle on a derby day. My brother wouldn't speak to me because he was a Liverpudlian – he wouldn't speak to me for the whole day. You can't remember much about them because they were a hundred miles an hour. If you lost you daren't go into the town as an Evertonian.

'I had some great memories of playing against Liverpool – particularly my first one in 1976. I was only 18 or 19 and I was against Dave Fairclough who was a mate of mine. It was his first derby as well and that was special. We ended up losing 1-0.

'There were many funny moments. Five minutes before you were due to go out, the door was banged on and a load of toilet roll was thrown in – that's the way they were.

'The piece of humour I most remember was one when there was a pigeon with a broken wing on the pitch while we were warming up. Terry Darracott picked it up and was carrying it off the pitch, and as he did so one of the Liverpool staff said: "Jesus Christ, Terry, you've got quicker – you're catching pigeons now!"'

PAUL BRACEWELL
(Everton 1984-89)

'My Everton debut was in a Mersey derby at Wembley in the Charity Shield but the one which gave me the most pleasure was when we won at Anfield and went on to win the League. Graeme Sharp scored the only goal of the game which we felt really made people believe we could win the Championship.

'I've also played in Sunderland v Newcastle derbies but they are very different affairs to Merseyside ones, mainly because there is more hostility between the supporters. Unlike in Liverpool you can't imagine followers of the respective sides going to the match together. Perhaps if both clubs become successful the hostility might be reduced.'

PAUL WALSH
(Liverpool 1984-87)

'Brian Kidd and myself are the only two players, as far as I understand it, who have played in all three of the big derbies: Merseyside, Manchester and north London.

'Of these, the Merseyside derbies were by far and away the most exciting. The north London one came second and Manchester third – maybe because I played in three and lost them all: 2-0, 3-0 and 5-0!

'They're always very helter-skelter. When I played for Liverpool, Everton and Liverpool were the best two teams in the country. They were obviously very big derby matches and the tension was there, but a great atmosphere. These were certainly the biggest games I ever played in.'

131

PETER REID
(Everton 1982-89)

'I played in many Mersey derbies but undoubtedly the one which sticks in my mind above all others was Everton's 1-0 win at Anfield in 1984. It was Everton's first victory there for 14 years and it really gave us all the self-belief and confidence to know that we could go on to win the League – which we did. We had already beaten them in the Charity Shield, but the League win showed we had arrived as a major force. 'Graeme Sharp scored the goal at the Anfield Road End where the Evertonians were gathered which was absolutely great for them as Liverpool had been the dominant force in recent years. We were really up for it that day.'

WAR GAMES

27 NOVEMBER 1915

LIVERPOOL   **4**
Pagnam 3, Watson

EVERTON   **1**
Clennell

Attendance: 20,000

Liverpool:
E Scott, Longworth, Middlehurst, Bradley, Goddard, McKinlay, Pinkney, Watson, Pagnam, Banks, Metcalfe.

Everton:
Fern, Thompson, Maconnachie, Fleetwood, Wareing, Grenyer, Chedgzoy, Kirsopp, Nuttall, Clennell, Harrison.

26 FEBRUARY 1916

EVERTON   **0**

LIVERPOOL   **1**
Metcalfe

Attendance: 18,000

Everton:
Mitchell, Thompson, Simpson, Brown, Fleetwood, McNeal, Chedgzoy, Jefferis, Wareing, Grenyer, Harrison.

Liverpool:
Taylor, Longworth, Middlehurst, Bamber, Goddard, McKinlay, Pinkney, Watson, Pagnam, Metcalfe, Cunliffe.

1 APRIL 1916

EVERTON   **1**
Clennell

LIVERPOOL   **0**

Attendance: 25,000

Everton:
Fern, Thompson, Simpson, Brown, Fleetwood, Wareing, Chedgzoy, Kirsopp, Williamson, Clennell, Roberts.

Liverpool:
Taylor, Longworth, Middlehurst, Bamber, Goddard, McKinlay, Pinkney, Watson, Pagnam, Metcalfe, Cunliffe.

21 APRIL 1916

LIVERPOOL   **5**
Banks, Pagnam 3 (*2 pens*), Watson

EVERTON   **2**
Kirsopp 2

Attendance: 27,000

Liverpool:
Taylor, Longworth, Middlehurst, Bamber, Goddard, Wadsworth, Pinkney, Watson, Pagnam, Banks, Cunliffe.

Everton:
Bromilow, Thompson, Maconnachie, Brown, Fleetwood, Wareing, Williamson, Kirsopp, Clennell, Rigsby, Harrison.

Above: Brought to Goodison during the 1910-11 season, Sam Chedgzoy had to wait until 1920 for the first of his eight England caps. In 1924, however, his goal dribbled direct from a corner against Spurs led directly to a change in the rules.

2 DECEMBER 1916

LIVERPOOL   **2**
Metcalfe, Bennett

EVERTON   **1**
Kirsopp

Attendance: 22,000

Liverpool:
Swann, Longworth, Lucas, Bamber, Wadsworth, McKinlay, Goddard, Bennett, Pagnam, Metcalfe, Cunliffe.

Everton:
Mitchell, Smith, Thompson, Fleetwood, Wareing, Grenyer, Jefferis, Kirsopp, Bradbury, Clennell, Harrison.

17 MARCH 1917

EVERTON   **2**
Gault 2

LIVERPOOL   **2**
Bennett, Wadsworth

Attendance: 24,000

Everton:
Mitchell, Thompson, Maconnachie, Fleetwood, Wareing, Grenyer, Chedgzoy, Jefferis, Gault, Clennell, Donnachie.

Liverpool:
Campbell, Longworth, Lucas, Bamber, Wadsworth, McKinlay, Goddard, Metcalfe, Bennett, Lewis, Cunliffe.

7 APRIL 1917

EVERTON   **4**
Gault 2, Clennell, Donnachie

LIVERPOOL   **0**

Attendance: 16,000

Everton:
Mitchell, Smith, Thompson, Fleetwood, Wareing, Grenyer, Murray, Jefferis, Gault, Clennell, Donnachie.

Liverpool:
Houghton, Longworth, Lucas, Lowe, Wadsworth, McKinlay, Goddard, Pagnam, Bennett, Metcalfe, Cunliffe.

WAR GAMES

21 APRIL 1917

LIVERPOOL   **0**

EVERTON   **5**
Gault 3, Clennell 2

Attendance: 25,000

Liverpool:
Houghton, Longworth, Lucas, Bamber, Wadsworth, McKinlay, Goddard, Page, Bennett, Lewis, Cunliffe.

Everton:
Fern, Smith, Thompson, Fleetwood, Wareing, Grenyer, Murray, Jefferis, Gault, Clennell, Donnachie.

29 SEPTEMBER 1917

EVERTON   **2**
Clennell, Gault

LIVERPOOL   **2**
Bennett, Metcalfe

Attendance: 25,000

Everton:
Mitchell, Thompson, Robinson, Fleetwood, Wareing, Grenyer, Kirsopp, Jefferis, Gault, Clennell, Donnachie.

Liverpool:
Lovell, Longworth, Lucas, Bamber, W Wadsworth, McKinlay, Waine, Metcalfe, Bennett, Lewis, Cunliffe.

Right: Fondly known as 'Big Waddy' to differentiate from his brother Harold, Walter Wadsworth won the League title twice with Liverpool in 1922 and 1923.

W. WADSWORTH.

6 OCTOBER 1917

LIVERPOOL   **6**
McKinlay, Lewis 4, Bennett

EVERTON   **0**

Attendance: 25,000

Liverpool:
Campbell, Longworth, Lucas, Bamber, W Wadsworth, McKinlay, Waine, Metcalfe, Bennett, Lewis, Cunliffe.

Everton:
Mitchell, Thompson, Robinson, Williams, Fleetwood, Grenyer, Murray, Jefferis, Gault, Clennell, Donnachie.

1 JANUARY 1918

LIVERPOOL   **4**
Lewis 2, Waine, Bennett

EVERTON   **1**
Gault

Attendance: 25,000

Liverpool:
Campbell, Longworth, Speakman, Bamber, Jenkinson, McKinlay, Waine, Metcalfe, Bennett, Lewis, Schofield.

Everton:
Fern, Bull, Robinson, Challinor, Wareing, Grenyer, Murphy, Gault, Wright, Clennell, Donnachie.

29 MARCH 1918

EVERTON   **3**
Jefferis 2, Gault

LIVERPOOL   **2**
Lewis, Green

Attendance: 28,000

Everton:
Mitchell, Collins, Scott, Cotter, Fleetwood, Grenyer, Wadsworth, Jefferis, Gault, Clennell, Burgess.

Liverpool:
Connell, Longworth, Jenkinson, Bamber, W Wadsworth, McKinlay, Waine, Green, Bennett, Lewis, Schofield.

5 OCTOBER 1918

LIVERPOOL   **2**
Metcalfe, H Wadsworth

EVERTON   **4**
Grenyer 2, Gault, Miller

Attendance: 30,000

Liverpool:
Connell, Longworth, Jenkinson, Bamber, W Wadsworth, McKinlay, H Wadsworth, Metcalfe, Bennett, Lewis, Schofield.

Everton:
Mitchell, Robinson, Thompson, Fleetwood, Wareing, Grenyer, Miller, Jefferis, Gault, Clennell, Donnachie.

12 OCTOBER 1918

EVERTON   **4**
Clennell, Donnachie, Miller, Opposition og

LIVERPOOL   **2**
Green, Wareing og

Attendance: 35,000

Everton:
Mitchell, Smith, Robinson, Fleetwood, Wareing, Grenyer, Miller, Jefferis, Gault, Clennell, Donnachie.

Liverpool:
Connell, Longworth, Jenkinson, Bamber, W Wadsworth, McKinlay, H Wadsworth, Green, Bennett, Lewis, Schofield.

1 JANUARY 1919

EVERTON   **1**
Jefferis

LIVERPOOL   **2**
Metcalfe, Lewis

Attendance: 30,000

Everton:
Mitchell, Smith, Robinson, Fleetwood, Wareing, Williams, Kirsopp, Jefferis, Gault, Clennell, Donnachie.

Liverpool:
W Scott, J Page, Jenkinson, Bamber, W Wadsworth, McKinlay, H Wadsworth, Metcalfe, Miller, Lewis, Phillips.

WAR GAMES

18 APRIL 1919

LIVERPOOL   1
Pearson

EVERTON   1
Gault

Attendance: 36,955
Liverpool:
W Scott, Longworth, Jenkinson, Bamber,
W Wadsworth, McKinlay, H Wadsworth, Forshaw,
Matthews, Lewis, Pearson.
Everton:
Fern, J Page, Robinson, Peacock, Wareing,
Grenyer, Miller, Jefferis, Gault, Clennell, Evans.

2 DECEMBER 1939

LIVERPOOL   2
Nieuwenhuys, Fagan

EVERTON   2
Davies, Stevenson

Attendance: 8,000
Liverpool:
Riley, Cooper, Tennant, Busby, Bush, McInnes,
Nieuwenhuys, Taylor, Fagan, Balmer, Van Den
Berg.
Everton:
Sagar, Jackson, Saunders, Lindley, TG Jones,
Watson, Davies, Bentham, Bell, Stevenson, Boyes.

30 MARCH 1940

EVERTON   1
Lawton

LIVERPOOL   3
Nieuwenhuys 2, Liddell

Attendance: 12,896
Everton:
Sagar, Jackson, Greenhalgh, Lindley, TG Jones,
Watson, Wyles, Catterick, Lawton, Stevenson,
Boyes.
Liverpool:
Riley, Harley, Tennant, Busby, Bush, Paisley,
Liddell, Taylor, Nieuwenhuys, Carney,
Van Den Berg.

25 DECEMBER 1940

LIVERPOOL   3
Carney 2, Nieuwenhuys

EVERTON   1
Bentham

Attendance: 5,000
Liverpool:
Bartram, Harley, Stuart, Lambert, Turner, Spicer,
Paisley, Carney, Nieuwenhuys, Polk, Liddell.
Everton:
Sagar, Cook, Greenhalgh, Jackson, TG Jones,
Watson, Arthur, Bentham, Lawton, Simmons, Lewis.

4 JANUARY 1941

LIVERPOOL   1
Paisley

EVERTON   2
Lawton, Lyon

Attendance: 3,000
Liverpool:
W Teasdale, Stuart, Owens, Lambert, Turner, Spicer,
Nieuwenhuys, Paisley, Fagan, Polk, Liddell.
Everton:
Sagar, Cook, Greenhalgh, Mercer, TG Jones,
Watson, Arthur, Bentham, Lawton, Lyon, Boyes.

11 JANUARY 1941

EVERTON   4
Jackson 4

LIVERPOOL   1
Shafto

Attendance: 5,000
Everton:
Sagar, Cook, Greenhalgh, Mercer, TG Jones,
JE Jones, Arthur, Bentham, Jackson, Stevenson,
Penlington.
Liverpool:
Bartram, Stuart, Owens, Lambert, Turner, Spicer,
Nieuwenhuys, Paisley, Shafto, Patterson, Liddell.

8 FEBRUARY 1941

LIVERPOOL   1
Done

EVERTON   3
Catterick 3

Attendance: 3,000
Liverpool:
G Jackson, Stuart, Owens, Lambert, Turner,
Spicer, Nieuwenhuys, Paisley, Done, Polk, Liddell.
Everton:
Sagar, Cook, Greenhalgh, Bentham, TG Jones,
JE Jones, Arthur, Simmons, Catterick, Stevenson,
Boyes.

31 MAY 1941

LIVERPOOL   2
Liddell, Done

EVERTON   2
Mercer, Stevenson

Attendance: 6,000
Liverpool:
Hobson, Lambert, Seddon, Kaye, Cook, Spicer,
Liddell, Paisley, Fagan, Done, Hanson.
Everton:
Lovett, Cook, Greenhalgh, Bentham, TG Jones,
Watson, Boyes, Mercer, Catterick, Stevenson,
Lyon.

*Top right: Bob Paisley was a regular fixture of
the Liverpool side during the Second World War.*

2 JUNE 1941

EVERTON 3

Boyes 2, Jackson

LIVERPOOL 1

Jones og

Attendance: 4,000

Everton:
Lovett, Cook, Greenhalgh, Bentham, TG Jones, Hill, Boyes, Simmons, Jackson, Owen, Lyon.

Liverpool:
Hobson, Seddon, Lambert, Kaye, Cook, Spicer, Liddell, Farrow, Done, Polk, Hanson.

25 OCTOBER 1941

LIVERPOOL 3

Liddell 2, Bush

EVERTON 2

Cook, Lyon

Attendance: 12,989

Liverpool:
Hobson, Taylor, Lambert, Whitaker, Bush, Kaye, Nieuwenhuys, Ainsley, Done, Polk, Liddell.

Everton:
Burnett, Cook, Greenhalgh, Bentham, H Jones, Keen, Anderson, Owen, Lawton, Stevenson, Lyon.

1 NOVEMBER 1941

EVERTON 5

Bentham 3, H Jones, Lyon

LIVERPOOL 3

Done 2, Liddell

Attendance: 20,000

Everton:
Burnett, Cook, Greenhalgh, Mercer, TG Jones, Watson, Owen, Bentham, H Jones, Stevenson, Lyon.

Liverpool:
Hobson, Lambert, Ramsden, Carney, Whitaker, Kaye, Nieuwenhuys, Fagan, Done, Dorsett, Liddell.

11 APRIL 1941

LIVERPOOL 0

EVERTON 2

Anderson, TG Jones

Attendance: 33,445

Liverpool:
Hobson, Gutteridge, Lambert, Taylor, Bush, Kaye, Nieuwenhuys, Carney, Done, Haycock, Liddell.

Everton:
Burnett, Cook, Jackson, Bentham, Keen, Curwen, Owen, Mercer, TG Jones, Stevenson, Anderson.

18 APRIL 1942

EVERTON 0

LIVERPOOL 1

Balmer

Attendance: 33,780

Everton:
Burnett, Cook, Jackson, Bentham, Keen, Curwen, Anderson, Owen, TG Jones, Stevenson, Caskie.

Liverpool:
Hobson, Gutteridge, Owen, Kaye, Bush, Haycock, Nieuwenhuys, Balmer, Done, Jones, Taylor.

30 MAY 1942

LIVERPOOL 4

Done 2, Carney, Wharton

EVERTON 1

Lawton

Attendance: 13,761

Liverpool:
Hobson, Gutteridge, Owen, Shankly, Woodruff, Kaye, Liddell, McLaren, Done, Carney, Wharton.

Everton:
Burnett, Cook, JE Jones, Bentham, H Jones, Keen, Owen, Mutch, Lawton, Stevenson, Watson.

Right: Everton winger Wally Boyes scored two goals in the June 1941 win.

WAR GAMES

12 SEPTEMBER 1942

LIVERPOOL	1
Mills

EVERTON	0

Attendance: 17,131

Liverpool:
Hobson, Gutteridge, Lambert, Kaye, Bush, Spicer, Liddell, Dorsett, Mills, Done, Taylor.

Everton:
Burnett, Cook, JE Jones, Bentham, TG Jones, Watson, Jackson, Mutch, H Jones, Grant, Anderson.

19 SEPTEMBER 1942

EVERTON	4
H Jones 2, Jackson, Mutch

LIVERPOOL	4
Done, Dorsett 2, Liddell

Attendance: 17,000

Everton:
Burnett, Cook, JE Jones, Bentham, TG Jones, Watson, Jackson, Mutch, H Jones, Stevenson, Anderson.

Liverpool:
Hobson, Westby, Gutteridge, Kaye, Keen, Pilling, Liddell, Dorsett, Mills, Done, Hulligan.

9 JANUARY 1943

EVERTON	1
Mutch

LIVERPOOL	3
Hulligan 2, Shepherd

Attendance: 18,206

Everton:
Burnett, Cook, Greenhalgh, Bentham, Humphreys, Mercer, Jackson, Mutch, H Jones, Stevenson, Fowler.

Liverpool:
Hobson, Gutteridge, Lambert, Kaye, Westby, Pilling, Shepherd, Fagan, Done, Haycock, Hulligan.

16 JANUARY 1943

LIVERPOOL	2
Balmer, Done

EVERTON	1
Lawton

Attendance: 20,400

Liverpool:
Hobson, Bush, Gutteridge, Kaye, Charlesworth, Pilling, Hall, Eastham, Balmer, Done, Hulligan.

Everton:
Birkett, Cook, Greenhalgh, Mercer, Humphreys, Curwen, Bentham, Mutch, Lawton, Stevenson, Jackson.

26 APRIL 1943

LIVERPOOL	4
Fagan, Balmer, Done, Nieuwenhuys

EVERTON	1
McIntosh

Attendance: 17,000

Liverpool:
Hobson, Pope, Westby, Kaye, Low, Pilling, Nieuwenhuys, Balmer, Done, Fagan, Hulligan.

Everton:
Burnett, Jackson, Greenhalgh, Bentham, Humphreys, Watson, Linaker, Stevenson, McIntosh, Beattie, JE Jones.

9 OCTOBER 1943

EVERTON	4
Lawton, McIntosh, Stevenson, Opposition og

LIVERPOOL	6
Done 4, Harley, Welsh

Attendance: 28,835

Everton:
Burnett, JE Jones, Greenhalgh, Bentham, TG Jones, Scott, Grant, Wainwright, Lawton, Stevenson, McIntosh.

Liverpool:
Hobson, Westby, Gulliver, Kaye, Hughes, Pilling, Harley, Balmer, Done, Welsh, Hanson.

Left: Jack Balmer, nephew of Everton's full-back brothers Robert and Walter at the turn of the century, began his career as a Goodison amateur before commencing his 12-year stay with Liverpool in 1935.

WAR GAMES

22 JANUARY 1944

LIVERPOOL   **1**
Fagan

EVERTON   **4**
Wainwright 2, Lawton, Wyles

Attendance: 34,221

Liverpool:
Hobson, Westby, Gulliver, Nieuwenhuys, Hughes, Pilling, Balmer, Beattie, Fagan, Done, Liddell.

Everton:
Burnett, Jackson, JE Jones, Grant, TG Jones, Watson, Wyles, Wainwright, Lawton, Tatters, McIntosh.

29 JANUARY 1944

EVERTON   **2**
Lawton, Wyles

LIVERPOOL   **3**
Nieuwenhuys, Balmer, Welsh (*pen*)

Attendance: 45,820

Everton:
Burnett, Jackson, JE Jones, Grant, TG Jones, Mercer, Wyles, Wainwright, Lawton, Stevenson, McIntosh.

Liverpool:
Hobson, Westby, Gulliver, Busby, Hughes, Pilling, Nieuwenhuys, Balmer, Welsh, Done, Liddell.

10 APRIL 1944

EVERTON   **3**
Grant, TG Jones, McIntosh

LIVERPOOL   **0**

Attendance: 40,000

Everton:
Burnett, Jackson, Greenhalgh, Britton, TG Jones, Watson, Grant, Gillick, Lawton, Boyes, McIntosh.

Liverpool:
Hobson, Jones, Gulliver, Polk, Hughes, Pilling, Campbell, Beattie, Done, Welsh, Hulligan.

15 APRIL 1944

LIVERPOOL   **3**
Hulligan 2, Done

EVERTON   **0**

Attendance: 25,062

Liverpool:
Hobson, Westby, Gulliver, Polk, Hughes, Pilling, Campbell, Nieuwenhuys, Done, Beattie, Hulligan.

Everton:
Burnett, JE Jones, Greenhalgh, Grant, TG Jones, Watson, Jackson, Bentham, Lawton, Wainwright, McIntosh.

22 APRIL 1944

LIVERPOOL   **4**
Done 3 (*1 pen*), Polk

EVERTON   **2**
TG Jones, Wyles

Attendance: 24,404

Liverpool:
Hobson, Westby, Gulliver, Whiteside, Hughes, Pilling, Campbell, Polk, Done, Beattie, Dougal.

Everton:
Burnett, JE Jones, Greenhalgh, Grant, TG Jones, Watson, Rogers, Astbury, Wyles, Bentham, McIntosh.

21 OCTOBER 1944

EVERTON   **0**

LIVERPOOL   **2**
Smith 2

Attendance: 33,199

Everton:
Burnett, Jackson, Greenhalgh, Grant, Lindley, Watson, Rawlings, Wainwright, Wyles, Stevenson, Peters.

Liverpool:
Kemp, Harley, Gulliver, Busby, Hughes, Pilling, Nieuwenhuys, Taylor, Smith, Balmer, Cumner.

16 OCTOBER 1943

LIVERPOOL   **5**
Harley, Done, Balmer 2, Nieuwenhuys

EVERTON   **2**
McIntosh, Stevenson

Attendance: 25,000

Liverpool:
Hobson, Westby, Gulliver, Kaye, Hughes, Pilling, Harley, Balmer, Nieuwenhuys, Done, Hanson.

Everton:
Burnett, JE Jones, Greenhalgh, Bentham, TG Jones, Hallard, Roberts, Caskie, Murphy, Stevenson, McIntosh.

Top: The war interrupted Berry Nieuwenhuys' Anfield career which began in 1933 and finished in 1947 after 239 League games. The South African wing forward, however, was an all-round sportsman, playing cricket, golf, tennis and baseball.

WAR GAMES

28 OCTOBER 1944

LIVERPOOL   0

EVERTON   0

Attendance: 26,008

Liverpool:
Hobson, Harley, Gulliver, McInnes, Hughes, Pilling, Nieuwenhuys, Taylor, Smith, Welsh, Liddell.

Everton:
Burnett, Jackson, Greenhalgh, Grant, Lindley, Watson, Rawlings, Wainwright, Catterick, Stevenson, TG Jones.

26 DECEMBER 1944

EVERTON   2
Stevenson, Wainwright

LIVERPOOL   2
Liddell 2

Attendance: 35,226

Everton:
Burnett, Jackson, Greenhalgh, Grant, Lindley, Watson, Humphreys, Wainwright, TG Jones, Stevenson, McIntosh.

Liverpool:
Hobson, Seddon, Gulliver, Kaye, Hughes, Spicer, Liddell, Nieuwenhuys, Rawcliffe, Taylor, Patterson.

3 FEBRUARY 1945

EVERTON   4
Bentham, McIntosh, Rawlings, Wyles

LIVERPOOL   1
Taylor

Attendance: 26,780

Everton:
Burnett, Jackson, Greenhalgh, Grant, TG Jones, Watson, Rawlings, Bentham, Wyles, Stevenson, McIntosh.

Liverpool:
Hobson, Westby, Gulliver, Kaye, Hughes, Pilling, Campbell, Taylor, Blood, Kinghorn, Hulligan.

10 FEBRUARY 1945

LIVERPOOL   3
Cumner 2, Nieuwenhuys

EVERTON   1
Lawton

Attendance: 33,235

Liverpool:
Hobson, Harley, Gulliver, Kaye, Hughes, Pilling, Campbell, Nieuwenhuys, Welsh, Taylor, Cumner.

Everton:
Burnett, Jackson, Greenhalgh, Grant, Lindley, Watson, Boyes, Bentham, Lawton, Stevenson, McIntosh.

24 MARCH 1945

LIVERPOOL   1
Liddell

EVERTON   0

Attendance: 39,640

Liverpool:
Hobson, Harley, Gulliver, Kaye, Hughes, Pilling, Nieuwenhuys, Taylor, Liddell, Welsh, Cumner.

Everton:
Burnett, Jackson, Greenhalgh, Grant, Morris, Watson, Catterick, Bentham, Wyles, Stevenson, Boyes.

31 MARCH 1945

EVERTON   0

LIVERPOOL   1
Liddell

Attendance: 51,512

Everton:
Burnett, Jackson, Greenhalgh, Grant, Mercer, Watson, Wainwright, Gillick, Lawton, Stevenson, McIntosh.

Liverpool:
Hobson, Westby, Gulliver, Busby, Hughes, Kaye, Campbell, Nieuwenhuys, Liddell, Welsh, Cumner.

2 APRIL 1945

LIVERPOOL   1
Shannon

EVERTON   3
Grant, Jackson, Wyles

Attendance: 22,815

Liverpool:
Hobson, Jones, Gulliver, Kaye, Hughes, Pilling, Campbell, Taylor, Shannon, Welsh, Kinghorn.

Everton:
Burnett, Jackson, Greenhalgh, Grant, Mercer, Watson, Wainwright, Gillick, Wyles, Stevenson, McIntosh.

Left: Outside-left Bill Kinghorn's Liverpool League career lasted just one season, 1938-39, though he made further appearances for the Reds during wartime football.

WAR GAMES

LIVERPOOL	**2**
Liddell, Shannon	

EVERTON	**1**
Wyles	

Attendance: 25,446

Liverpool:
Hobson, Westby, Gulliver, Kaye, Easdale, Pilling, Taylor, Balmer, Shannon, Welsh, Liddell.

Everton:
Burnett, Jackson, Greenhalgh, Bentham, Bell, Watson, Bond, Wainwright, Wyles, Boyes, Makin.

EVERTON	**2**
Boyes, Catterick	

LIVERPOOL	**2**
Baron, Liddell	

Attendance: 60,296

Everton:
Burnett, Jackson, Greenhalgh, Bentham, Mercer, Watson, Rawlings, Stevenson, Catterick, Fielding, Boyes.

Liverpool:
Nickson, Harley, Lambert, Finney, Hughes, Paisley, Balmer, Baron, Fagan, Nieuwenhuys, Priday.

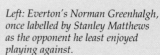

Left: Everton's Norman Greenhalgh, once labelled by Stanley Matthews as the opponent he least enjoyed playing against.

Above: Billy Fagan cost Liverpool £7,000 from Preston North End on his arrival in October 1936. He would go on to give sterling service to the Anfield club until 1952 before joining Belfast Distillery and later becoming player-manager of Weymouth.

8:STATISTICS

DERBY APPEARANCES

LIVERPOOL	EVERTON
37	
	Neville Southall 1981-
33	
Bruce Grobbelaar 1981-94 Ian Rush 1980-87, 1988-	
32	
Alan Hansen 1977-90	
31	
Ian Callaghan 1959-78	
30	
	Kevin Ratcliffe 1977-93
29	
Phil Neal 1974-86 Ronnie Whelan 1980-94	Jack Taylor 1896-1910
28	
	Graeme Sharp 1980-91
27	
Ray Clemence 1968-81 Tommy Smith 1962-78	
26	
Emlyn Hughes 1966-79	
25	
Arthur Goddard 1901-14 Steve Nicol 1982-94	
24	
Alex Raisbeck 1898-1909	

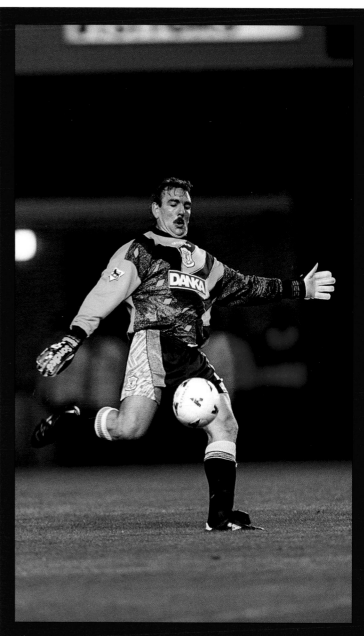

Above: Everton custodian Neville Southall is fast approaching 40 competitive appearances against Liverpool since his 1981 arrival at Goodison Park.

DERBY APPEARANCES

LIVERPOOL	EVERTON
23	
	Jack Sharp 1899-1910
	Dave Watson 1986-
22	
Kenny Dalglish 1977-90	Harry Makepeace 1902-15
	Alex 'Sandy' Young 1901-11
20	
John Barnes 1987-	Colin Harvey 1962-74
Chris Lawler 1962-76	Mick Lyons 1969-82
Donald McKinlay 1909-29	Ted Sagar 1929-53
Elisha Scott 1912-34	Kevin Sheedy 1982-92
	Gordon West 1962-75
19	
Jack Cox 1897-1909	Walter Abbott 1899-1908
Ron Yeats 1961-71	Brian Labone 1957-71
	Tommy Wright 1963-73
18	
Billy Dunlop 1894-1909	Adrian Heath 1982-89
Steve Heighway 1970-81	John Hurst 1964-76
Mark Lawrenson 1981-88	Trevor Steven 1983-89
Ephraim Longworth 1910-28	
Steve McMahon 1985-91	
17	
Tom Bromilow 1919-30	Bill 'Dixie' Dean 1925-38
Jan Molby 1984-	Johnny Morrissey 1962-72
	Gary Stevens 1979-88

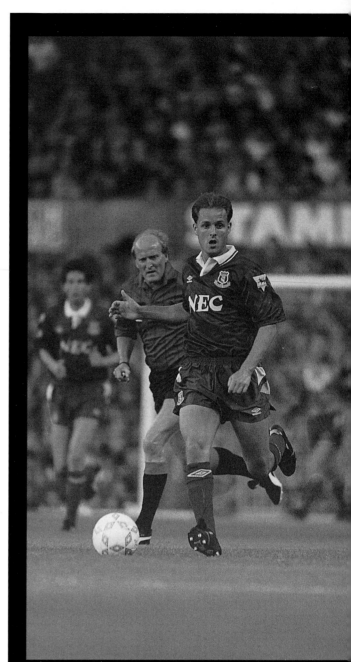

Above: John Ebbrell has so far been a one-club man, spending seven years at Goodison since his 1988 League debut.

Opposite: Pictured during 1977-78, his first season at Anfield, Kenny Dalglish was bought to replace Kop idol Kevin Keegan.

DERBY APPEARANCES

LIVERPOOL	EVERTON
16	
Gordon Hodgson 1925-36 Roger Hunt 1959-70 Ray Kennedy 1974-82 Tommy Lawrence 1962-71 Jimmy McDougall 1928-38 Jack Parkinson 1899-1914 Ian St John 1961-71 Phil Taylor 1935-54 Phil Thompson 1971-83	Walter Balmer 1897-1908
15	
Fred Hopkin 1921-31 Craig Johnston 1981-88 Robert Robinson 1903-12 Graeme Souness 1977-84 Peter Thompson 1963-72	Sam Chedgzoy 1910-26 Alan Harper 1983-88, 1991-93 Billy Scott 1904-12
14	
Peter Beardsley 1987-91 Billy Lacey 1912-24	John Bailey 1979-85 Alex 'Sandy' Brown 1963-71 Hunter Hart 1922-29 Alex Stevenson 1934-48
13	
Jack Balmer 1935-52 Harry Chambers 1919-28 Sam Hardy 1905-12 Kevin Keegan 1971-77 Sammy Lee 1977-86 Terry McDermott 1974-83 Tom Morrison 1927-35 Sam Raybould 1899-1907	Alan Ball 1966-71 Robert Balmer 1902-11 John Ebbrell 1988- Tom Fern 1913-24 Tom Fleetwood 1911-23 Howard Kendall 1967-74 Roger Kenyon 1966-79 John Maconnachie 1907-20

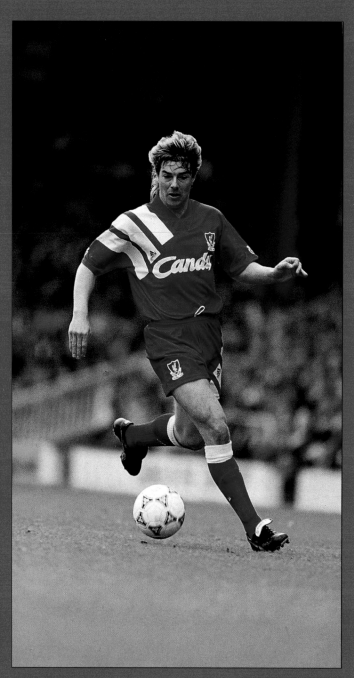

Above: Barry Venison followed his time at Liverpool with spells at Newcastle and Galatasaray before signing for Southampton in late 1995.

Opposite: Scottish international Stuart McCall, scorer of some vital Everton goals during his ten derby appearances.

DERBY APPEARANCES

LIVERPOOL	EVERTON
13	
Arthur Riley 1925-39 Barry Venison 1986-92	Peter Reid 1982-89 Jimmy Settle 1899-1908
12	
Gary Ablett 1986-91 Tom Bradshaw 1929-38 Jimmy Case 1974-81 Dick Forshaw 1919-27 Bill Goldie 1897-1903 Alan Kennedy 1978-85 Billy Liddell 1945-61 Berry Nieuwenhuys 1933-47 Walter Wadsworth 1914-26	Warney Cresswell 1927-36 Martin Dobson 1974-79 Val Harris 1907-14 Andy King 1976-80, 1982-84 Bob Latchford 1974-81 Alec Troup 1923-30 Pat Van den Hauwe 1984-89
11	
James Bradley 1905-11 Gerry Byrne 1957-69 Ray Lambert 1945-56 Tommy Lucas 1919-33 Jock McNab 1919-28 Maurice Parry 1900-09 Willie Stevenson 1962-68	John Bell 1892-98, 1901-03 Cliff Britton 1930-45 Billy Cook 1932-45 Tony Cottee 1988-94 Tommy Eglington 1946-57 Bobby Irvine 1921-28 John McDonald 1920-27 Ian Snodin 1987-94 Jock Thomson 1930-39
10	
Joe Hewitt 1903-10 James Jackson 1925-33 Bill Jones 1946-54 Gordon Milne 1960-67 Bob Paisley 1945-54	Tom Booth 1900-07 Richard Boyle 1890-1902 Peter Farrell 1946-57 Wally Fielding 1946-59 Jimmy Gabriel 1960-67

DERBY APPEARANCES

LIVERPOOL	EVERTON
10	
Cyril Sidlow 1946-51	Harold Hardman 1903-08
John Toshack 1970-78	Tommy G Jones 1936-50
	Stuart McCall 1988-91
	Neil McDonald 1988-91
	Pat Nevin 1988-92
	Jack O'Donnell 1925-30
	Joe Royle 1966-74
	Jimmy Stein 1928-36
	Sam Wolstenholme 1897-1904
9	
David Burrows 1988-93	Paul Bracewell 1984-89
Brian Hall 1968-76	Jack Crelley 1899-1907
Ray Houghton 1987-92	Ted Critchley 1926-34
David Johnson 1976-82	Charlie Gee 1930-40
Alec Lindsay 1969-77	George Harrison 1913-23
Steve McManaman 1990-	Derek Mountfield 1982-88
Tommy Robertson 1897-1902	Kevin Richardson 1979-86
Albert Stubbins 1946-53	Derek Temple 1956-67
Alfred West 1903-11	Eddie Wainwright 1944-56
	Tommy White 1927-37
	Billy Wright 1974-83
	Alex Young 1960-68
8	
Robert Crawford 1908-15	Terry Darracott 1968-79
Dick Edmed 1926-31	Andy Hinchcliffe 1990-
Willie Fagan 1937-52	Joe Mercer 1932-46
David Fairclough 1975-83	Jim Pearson 1974-78
Gary Gillespie 1983-91	Alex Scott 1963-67
Archie Goldie 1895-1900	

DERBY APPEARANCES

LIVERPOOL	EVERTON
8	
Alfred Hanson 1932-38	
Larry Lloyd 1969-74	
William Perkins 1898-1903	
John Walker 1897-1902	
7	
Jim Beglin 1984-88	G Beare 1910-14
Kenneth Campbell 1911-20	Mike Bernard 1972-77
Tom Chorlton 1904-11	William Brown 1914-28
Tom Cooper 1934-39	Jimmy Cunliffe 1930-46
Laurie Hughes 1945-58	Jimmy Dunn 1928-35
Glenn Hysén 1989-92	Albert Geldard 1932-38
Harry Lowe 1911-20	Brian Harris 1954-66
Ronald Orr 1907-12	Jimmy Husband 1964-73
Jackie Sheldon 1913-21	Matt Jackson 1991-
James Stewart 1909-14	Frank Jefferis 1911-20
Geoff Strong 1964-70	Tommy Johnson 1930-34
	Martin Keown 1989-92
	GW Kitchen 1898-1904
	David Lawson 1972-78
	Steve McMahon 1977-83
	Billy Muir 1897-1902
	Joe Peacock 1919-27
	Trevor Ross 1977-82
	George Saunders 1939-51
6	
John Aldridge 1986-89	Stanley Bentham 1934-48
Phil Boersma 1969-76	Mick Buckley 1971-78
Harry Bradshaw 1893-98	Bertie Freeman 1907-11
Peter Cormack 1972-76	Torry Gillick 1935-45

DERBY APPEARANCES

LIVERPOOL	EVERTON
6	
Robert Done 1926-35	Alan Grenyer 1910-24
James Harrop 1907-12	Mark Higgins 1976-84
Dick Johnson 1919-25	Johnny Holt 1888-98
Rob Jones 1991-	Gary Jones 1968-76
John McCartney 1893-98	J Kelly 1927-29
Jimmy Payne 1948-56	Mike Newell 1989-91
Steve Staunton 1988-91	Mike Pejic 1977-79
William Steel 1931-35	Paul Power 1986-88
Harry Storer 1895-1900	J Proudfoot 1898-1901
Charlie Wilson 1897-1905	Paul Rideout 1992-
Dave Wright 1929-34	W Stevenson 1907-13
Mark Wright 1991-	George Telfer 1972-81
	Albert Virr 1924-29
	George Wood 1977-80
5	
Harold Barton 1929-34	Gary Ablett 1992-
Matt Busby 1935-40	Peter Beagrie 1989-94
Robert Ferguson 1912-15	T Browell 1911-13
George Fleming 1901-06	Edgar Chadwick 1888-99
Fred Howe 1934-38	Wilf Chadwick 1922-25
David James 1992-	John Connolly 1972-76
Joey Jones 1975-78	Dai Davies 1970-77
Andy McGuigan 1900-02	Norman Greenhalgh 1938-48
Tom Miller 1911-21	Barry Horne 1992-
Ronnie Moran 1952-65	Alan Irvine 1981-84
Bob Pursell 1911-20	Jack Jones 1933-45
Jamie Redknapp 1991-	Cyril Lello 1947-57
Neil Ruddock 1993-	Neil McBain 1923-25
Harold Uren 1907-12	T McDermott 1903-05
Vic Wright 1933-37	Ken McNaught 1972-77

T. COOPER

Above left: Tom Cooper made 150 League appearances prior to the intervention of World War II, but was killed in a motorcycle accident in December 1940 while with the Military Police.

Left: Jackie Sheldon's total of seven derby games for Liverpool was restricted by the fact that he was suspended for match-rigging in 1915 until after the First World War.

Above: Goodison hero Gary Jones found first-team opportunites limited and moved to Birmingham City in 1976. He later returned to Merseyside, after a spell in the USA, to become a publican.

DERBY APPEARANCES

LIVERPOOL	EVERTON
5	
	Eric Moore 1949-57
	Fred Pickering 1964-67
	Neil Pointon 1985-90
	David Raitt 1922-28
	Dennis Stevens 1962-65
	R Thompson 1913-20
	Alan Whittle 1967-72
	GG Williams 1929-35
	Ray Wilson 1964-69
4	
John Carlin 1902-07	**Ray Atteveld** 1989-92
Benjamin Dabbs 1933-38	**Peter Beardsley** 1991-93
Alun Evans 1968-72	**H Bolton** 1906-08
Robbie Fowler 1993-	**F Bradshaw** 1911-14
John Glover 1900-03	**George Brewster** 1920-22
Gordon Gunson 1929-33	**George Burnett** 1946-51
Mike Hooper 1986-93	**Wayne Clarke** 1987-89
'Rabbi' Howell 1897-1901	**Dave Clements** 1973-76
Harry Lewis 1919-22	**Jack Cock** 1923-25
John McConnell 1909-12	**Tim Coleman** 1907-09
Archie McPherson 1929-35	**AL Davies** 1926-30
Joe McQue 1893-98	**Peter Eastoe** 1979-82
Malcolm McVean 1893-97	**J Gourlay** 1909-13
Jimmy Melia 1955-64	**Jackie Grant** 1942-56
Hugh Morgan 1897-1900	**A Hartley** 1892-97
David Pratt 1922-27	**Jack Hedley** 1947-50
John Robertson 1900-02	**David Johnson** 1969-72, 1982-84
Michael Robinson 1983-85	**David Jones** 1974-79
Ronny Rosenthal 1990-94	**Tommy Lawton** 1937-45
Percy Saul 1906-09	**Duggie Livingstone** 1921-26

Above: Super striker Robbie Fowler burst onto the first-team scene with 37 goals in his first 70 League appearances for Liverpool.

Opposite: Ian Wilson made his name with Leicester City in the early 1980s but made just 34 League appearances after his 1987 transfer to Goodison.

DERBY APPEARANCES

LIVERPOOL	EVERTON
4	
Bill Shepherd 1948-52	Joe McBride 1978-82
Danny Shone 1921-26	John McLaughlin 1971-76
Eddie Spicer 1945-54	Henry Newton 1970-73
Harold Wadsworth 1919-24	Eamonn O'Keefe 1979-82
Jimmy Walsh 1923-28	Bobby Parker 1913-21
Mark Walters 1991-	Bruce Rioch 1976-77
Thomas Wilkie 1895-99	Steve Seargeant 1968-78
	Billy Stewart 1893-97
	Dave Thomas 1977-79
	David Unsworth 1992-
	Roy Vernon 1960-65
	Mark Ward 1991-94
	Paul Wilkinson 1985-87
	Ian Wilson 1987-89
	R Young 1910-11
3	
George Allan 1895-99	L Bell 1897-98
Alf Arrowsmith 1961-68	W Bocking 1931-34
Phil Babb 1994-	Wally Boyes 1938-49
John Bamber 1919-24	Ted Buckle 1949-55
Kevin Baron 1945-54	J Cameron 1895-97
Frank Becton 1894-98	Harry Catterick 1946-51
Ernie Blenkinsop 1933-38	Joe Clennell 1914-21
Tom Bush 1933-47	Jackie Coulter 1934-37
Bill Cockburn 1924-27	Charlie Crossley 1920-22
David Davidson 1928-30	W Davidson 1911-13
Ned Doig 1904-08	Dicky Downs 1920-23
Cyril Done 1939-52	GS Eccles 1898-1902
Harry Eastham 1936-47	John Gidman 1979-81
Sam English 1933-35	Ronnie Goodlass 1971-77

Above: England striker Gary Lineker stayed just one season at Goodison Park following his transfer from Leicester City.

Opposite: Steve Harkness found a first-team place difficult to hold on to and spent periods on loan at Huddersfield and Southend following his arrival from Carlisle United.

DERBY APPEARANCES

LIVERPOOL	EVERTON
	3
Thomas Fairfoul 1913-15	AL Harland 1922-25
Sam Gilligan 1910-13	Asa Hartford 1979-81
Bobby Graham 1964-72	W Holbem 1911-13
Jim Harley 1935-48	George Jackson 1934-47
Tony Hateley 1967-69	Tony Kay 1962-64
James Holmes 1895-98	W Kirsopp 1914-21
John McDonald 1909-12	Bill Lacey 1908-12
Kevin MacDonald 1984-89	Gary Lineker 1985-86
Mike Marsh 1988-93	Paul Lodge 1977-83
Robert Marshall 1897-99	Duncan McKenzie 1976-78
Arthur Metcalfe 1912-15	Mick Meagan 1952-64
Ernest Peake 1908-14	G Molyneux 1896-99
Henry Race 1927-30	Geoff Nulty 1978-79
Archie Rawlings 1923-26	W Palmer 1913-14
Frederick Rogers 1934-39	Joe Parkinson 1994-
Ian Ross 1966-72	Aubrey Powell 1948-50
Jimmy Ross 1894-97	Predrag 'Preki' Radosavljevic 1992-94
Robert Savage 1931-38	Andy Rankin 1961-71
John Scales 1994-	D Reid 1920-27
Nigel Spackman 1986-89	Harry Ritchie 1928-30
David Speedie 1991	Garry Stanley 1979-81
Harold Taylor 1932-37	D Storrier 1893-97
Jack Tennant 1933-35	RF Turner 1908-10
Michael Thomas 1992-	Tommy 'Gordon' Watson 1933-48
Peter Wall 1967-70	A Weldon 1927-30
Paul Walsh 1984-87	GW Wilson 1906-07
John Wark 1983-87	

DERBY APPEARANCES

LIVERPOOL	EVERTON
2	

LIVERPOOL	EVERTON
Alan A'Court 1952-65	Neil Adams 1986-89
Augustus Beeby 1909-11	Alan Ainscow 1981-83
Stig Bjornebye 1992-	James Arnold 1981-85
Sam Bowyer 1907-12	Smart Arridge 1893-96
Lance Carr 1933-36	David Bain 1924-28
James Clarke 1927-31	GH Barlow 1908-10
Thomas Cleghorn 1895-99	Stuart Barlow 1990-95
Avi Cohen 1979-81	Arthur Berry 1909-10
Daniel Cunliffe 1897-98	J Blythe 1898-1901
Julian Dicks 1993-94	Brian Borrows 1977-83
Tommy Gracie 1911-14	A Bowman 1901-02
Andrew Hannah 1893-95	T Cain 1894-95
Steve Harkness 1991-	JH Caldwell 1912-13
David Hodgson 1982-84	Archie Clark 1931-36
John Hughes 1903-06/09	Robert Clifford 1908-10
John Hunter 1899-1902	Joe Donnachie 1906-08, 1919-20
Don Hutchison 1991-94	S Fazackerley 1920-22
Colin Irwin 1979-81	Duncan Ferguson 1994-
Dirk Kemp 1936-40	Dick Forshaw 1927-29
Kevin Lewis 1960-63	Jimmy Galt 1914-20
George Livingstone 1902-03	Gerry Glover 1964-67
Jimmy McInnes 1937-40	Andy Gray 1983-85
John McLaughlin 1969-75	Bryan Hamilton 1975-77
Duncan McLean 1893-95	HJ Hardy 1925-28
Richard Morris 1901-05	Joe Harper 1972-74
Jimmy Nicholl 1913-15	W Henderson 1902-03
Peter Platt 1902-04	William Higgins 1946-49
Bernard Ramsden 1937-48	Oscar Hold 1950-52
Tom Reid 1925-29	John Humphreys 1946-50
Thomas Rogers 1906-11	Ernie Hunt 1967-68
Charlie Satterthwaite 1899-1902	Mo Johnston 1991-93

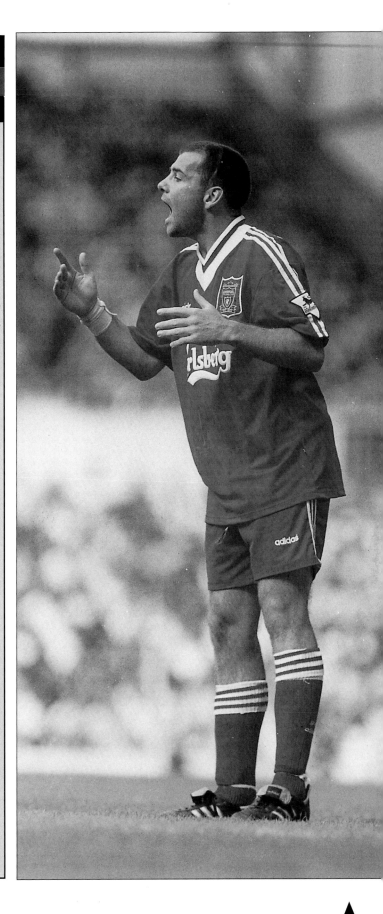

LIVERPOOL	EVERTON
	2

LIVERPOOL	EVERTON
Dean Saunders 1991-92	**GW Jones** 1919-23
Jimmy Smith 1929-32	**Tommy E Jones** 1948-61
Paul Stewart 1992-	**F Kennedy** 1924-27
Nicky Tanner 1989-93	**Billy Kenny** 1992-94
Harman Van Den Berg 1937-40	**Brian Kidd** 1979-80
	John Kirwan 1898-99
	Kevin Langley 1986-87
	Alex Latta 1889-95
	Clarence Leyfield 1934-36
	Anders Limpar 1994-
	JH McClure 1929-33
	James 'Seamus' McDonagh 1980-81
	R McFarlane 1897-98
	John McIlhatton 1946-48
	T McInnes 1894-95
	James McIntosh 1949-52
	L McPherson 1930-32
	Ian Marshall 1985-87
	P Meecham 1897-97
	Willie Miller 1935-36
	Mike Milligan 1990-91
	Alfred Milward 1888-96
	Bobby Mimms 1985-88
	Keith Newton 1969-72
	Jimmy O'Neill 1949-60
	Alex Parker 1958-65
	Charlie Parry 1889-95
	Harold Potts 1950-56
	George Rankin 1948-56
	Arthur Rigby 1929-32

...t: Everton's Nigerian import Daniel ...iokachi.

...ow: Dean Saunders followed in the ...otsteps of his father Roy when he signed for ...verpool in July 1991.

DERBY APPEARANCES

LIVERPOOL	EVERTON
2	
	H Robertson 1895-97
	Leigh Roose 1904-05
	Bert Sharp 1899-1901
	J Sheridan 1902-03
	Graham Stuart 1993-
	Ted Taylor 1927-28
	Colin Todd 1978-79
	JH Turner 1898-1900
	Imre Varadi 1979-81
	W Wareing 1912-19
	Robert Warzycha 1991-92
	J Watson 1899-1901
	LC Weller 1909-21
	Wattie White 1908-10
	Norman Whiteside 1989-90
	WD Williams 1922-25
1	
Eric Anderson 1952-57	J Adams 1894-95
William Banks 1913-15	H Adamson 1907-09
John Bovill 1911-14	J Allan 1909-12
George Bowen 1901-02	Daniel Amokachi 1994-
Philip Bratley 1914-15	Brett Angell 1993-95
Ken Brierley 1947-53	Ian Atkins 1984-85
Joseph Brough 1910-11	BH Baker 1920-26
Frederick Buck 1903-04	G Barker 1896-97
Jimmy Carter 1991	Alan Biley 1981-82
Ernest Chadwick 1902-04	Billy Bingham 1960-63
Nigel Clough 1993-	W Black 1905-06
Charles Cotton 1903-04	J Brearley 1902-03
Russell Crossley 1950-54	HF Briggs 1895-96

DERBY APPEARANCES

LIVERPOOL	EVERTON
1	
J Davies 1900-03	**David Burrows** 1994-95
James Dawson 1913-14	**H Clarke** 1898-99
William Devlin 1926-28	**Thomas Clinton** 1948-55
John Drummond 1894-95	**Billy Coggins** 1930-33
John Evans 1953-57	**EW Common** 1928-33
Phil Ferns 1962-65	**HE Cook** 1905
Jim Furnell 1961-64	**Peter Corr** 1948-49
Fred Geary 1895-99	**G Couper** 1906-07
Robert Glassey 1935-37	**T Crompton** 1898-99
Jack Haigh 1950-52	**S Davies** 1921
Davy Hannah 1894-97	**J Divers** 1897-98
Charlie Hewitt 1907-08	**Ephraim 'Jock' Dodds** 1946-48
Jack Heydon 1950-53	**AA Dominy** 1926-28
Alfred Hobson 1936-46	**PG Dougal** 1937-38
Alan Irvine 1986-88	**Gordon Dugdale** 1947-49
Brian Jackson 1951-58	**WC Easton** 1927-30
Tom 'Tosh' Johnson 1934-36	**David Falder** 1949-50
Stanley Kane 1934-36	**Mike Ferguson** 1981-82
Neil Kerr 1894-95	**FJ Forbes** 1922-25
Hector Lawson 1923-25	**WE Gault** 1912-20
Tommy Leishman 1959-63	**E Gee** 1897-99
Doug Livermore 1967-71	**R Gray** 1899-1900
Norman Low 1934-37	**Tom Griffiths** 1926-31
Jason McAteer 1995-	**Patrick Heard** 1978-79
John McBride 1893-95	**Dave Hickson** 1948-55, 1957-50
W McCann 1894-95	**Martin Hodge** 1979-83
Andrew McCowie 1896-99	**Paul Holmes** 1992-
John McFarlane 1928-30	**J Houston** 1913-14
Jimmy McLean 1894-96	**D Hughes** 1898-99
John McLean 1903-04	**Thomas Jackson** 1968-70

Above: Tommy Leishman helped return Liverpool to the top flight in 1961-62 but was released by Bill Shankly after just 11 League appearances the following season, never again to play in English League football.

Opposite: Andrei Kanchelskis scored two goals in his first Everton-Liverpool fixture to give the Goodison Park outfit a 2-1 win in November 1995.

DERBY APPEARANCES

LIVERPOOL	EVERTON
1	
David McMullan 1925-28	WC Jordan 1911-12
Harold McNaughton 1920-21	Andrei Kanchelskis 1995-
William McPherson 1906-08	Glenn Keeley 1982
Hugh McQueen 1893-95	Bob Kelso 1888-89, 1891-95
Matthew McQueen 1893-99	J Kerr 1923-27
Daniel McRorie 1930-33	FO King 1933-36
Marshall 1901-02	Maurice Lindley 1946-51
William Michael 1896-97	A McDonald 1899-1900
Richard Money 1980-81	J McGourty 1932-34
David Murray 1904-06	E Magner 1910-12
Robert Neill 1894-97	George Martin 1928-32
Cyril Oxley 1925-26	RC Menham 1896-97
Frederick Pagnam 1914-20	FW Mitchell 1913-19
Edward Parry 1920-25	H Morton 1937-39
Albert Pearson 1919-21	W Owen 1898-99
Torben Piechnik 1992-94	J Page 1913-20
George Pither 1926-28	T Parker 1926
Bob Priday 1945-49	Stefan Rehn 1989-90
Syd Roberts 1931-37	H Rigsby 1919
Doug Rudham 1954-60	T Robson 1929-30
William Salisbury 1928-29	A Schofield 1895-99
Roy Saunders 1952-59	Walter Scott 1909-11
John Shafto 1937-39	Craig Short 1995-
Les Shannon 1947-49	David Smallman 1975-80
Albert Shears 1925-29	Jack Southworth 1893-94
Samual Speakman 1912-20	Arthur Styles 1967-74
Trevor Storton 1972-74	George Thomson 1960-63
Bobby Thomson 1962-64	W Toman 1899-1901
Geoff Twentyman 1953-60	Mike Trebilcock 1965-68
Alan Waddle 1973-77	Douglas Trentham 1936-49

Above: Ian Rush celebrates one of his 20 successful strikes against Everton – this time scoring his second and Liverpool's third in the 1986 FA Cup Final.

Opposite: Everton's top marksman Dixie Dean needed just 17 derby games to register his 19 goals, compared to Rush's 33 appearances.

DERBY APPEARANCES

LIVERPOOL	EVERTON
1	
Gordon Wallace	Rob Wakenshaw
1962-67	1983-85
W White	Mike Walsh
1901-02	1978-79
Albert Whitehurst	W Williams
1928-29	1894-97
Don Woam	Bernie Wright
1950-51	1972-73

DERBY GOALSCORERS

LIVERPOOL	EVERTON
20	
Ian Rush	
1980-87, 1988-	
19	
	Bill 'Dixie' Dean
	1925-38
12	
	Alex 'Sandy' Young
	1901-10
8	
Harry Chambers	Jimmy Settle
1919-28	1899-1908
Jack Parkinson	
1899-1914	
7	
Dick Forshaw	
1919-27	
6	
Jack Balmer	Bobby Parker
1935-52	1913-21
Peter Beardsley	Graeme Sharp
1987-91	1980-91
Gordon Hodgson	
1925-36	
5	
Kenny Dalglish	Alan Ball
1977-90	1966-71
Willie Fagan	Jack Taylor
1937-52	1896-1909
Fred Howe	
1934-38	
Roger Hunt	
1959-70	
Own goals	

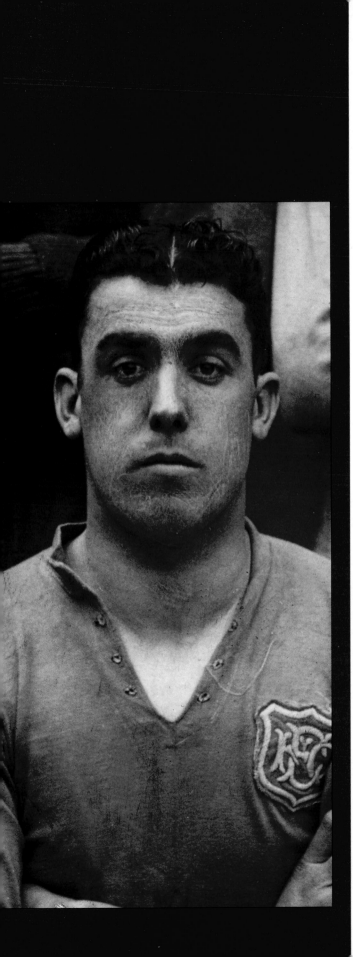

DERBY GOALSCORERS

LIVERPOOL	EVERTON
4	
John Barnes 1987-	Bertie Freeman 1907-11
Emlyn Hughes 1966-79	Tommy Lawton 1937-45
Sam Raybould 1899-1907	Roy Vernon 1960-65
3	
Harold Barton 1929-34	Walter Abbott 1899-1907
Jimmy Case 1974-81	Sam Chedgzoy 1910-26
Jack Cox 1897-1909	Joe Clennell 1914-21
Arthur Goddard 1901-14	Tony Cottee 1988-94
Ray Houghton 1987-92	Ted Critchley 1926-34
Billy Liddell 1945-61	Harold Hardman 1903-08
Steve McMahon 1985-94	Andy King 1976-80, 1982-84
Phil Neal 1974-86	Gary Lineker 1985-86
Tommy Robertson 1897-1902	Stuart McCall 1988-91
Tommy Smith 1962-78	Harry Makepeace 1902-14
Albert Stubbins 1946-53	Johnny Morrissey 1962-72
	Jack Sharp 1899-1909
	Alex Stevenson 1934-48
	Tommy White 1927-37
2	
Tom Bromilow 1919-30	G Beare 1910-14
Ian Callaghan 1959-78	John Bell 1892-98, 1901-03
Dick Edmed 1926-31	Stanley Bentham 1934-48
John Evans 1953-57	T Browell 1911-13
Robbie Fowler 1992-	Wilf Chadwick 1922-25
Gordon Gunson 1929-33	Wayne Clarke 1987-89
Alfred Hanson 1932-38	Tim Coleman 1907-09
Steve Heighway 1970-81	Peter Eastoe 1979-82
Joe Hewitt 1903-10	Tommy Johnson 1930-34
Fred Hopkin 1921-31	Mo Johnston 1991-93

DERBY GOALSCORERS

LIVERPOOL	EVERTON

2

LIVERPOOL	EVERTON
John Hunter 1899-1902	Andrei Kanchelskis 1995-
David Johnson 1976-82	Alex Latta 1889-1895
Dick Johnson 1919-25	Jimmy McIntosh 1949-52
Craig Johnston 1981-88	Mike Newell 1989-91
Ray Kennedy 1974-82	Joe Royle 1966-74
Billy Lacey 1911-24	J Sheridan 1902-03
Chris Lawler 1962-76	Derek Temple 1956-67
Andrew McCowie 1896-99	Alec Troup 1923-30
Tom Miller 1911-21	Dave Watson 1986-
Richard Morris 1901-05	Alan Whittle 1967-72
Berry Nieuwenhuys 1933-47	W Williams 1894-97
Alex Raisbeck 1898-1909	
Jimmy Ross 1894-97	
Ian St John 1961-71	
John Shafto 1937-39	
Danny Shone 1921-26	
Graeme Souness 1977-84	
David Speedie 1991	
Willie Stevenson 1962-68	
Harold Taylor 1932-37	
John Toshack 1970-78	
Jimmy Walsh 1923-28	
Dave Wright 1929-34	

1

LIVERPOOL	EVERTON
Alan A'Court 1952-65	GH Barlow 1908-10
John Aldridge 1986-89	Peter Beardsley 1991-93
Kevin Baron 1945-54	L Bell 1897-98
Frank Becton 1894-98	J Blythe 1898-1901
Ken Brierley 1947-53	Wally Boyes 1938-49
David Burrows 1988-94	J Brearley 1902

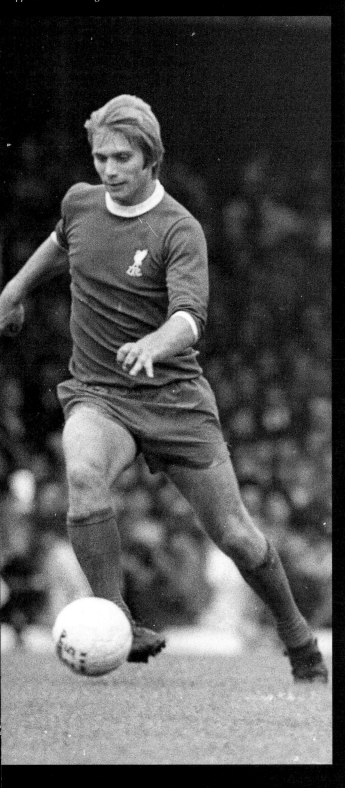

Opposite: Joe Royle, scorer of two Everton goals against Liverpool between 1966 and 1974.

Below: Alun Evans' £100,000 transfer from Wolves in 1966 established a new record for a teenager, but his early potential failed to materialise and he moved on to Aston Villa for £70,000 in 1972 after 79 League appearances and 21 goals.

DERBY GOALSCORERS

LIVERPOOL	EVERTON
1	

LIVERPOOL	EVERTON
Peter Cormack 1972-76	George Brewster 1920-22
Daniel Cunliffe 1897-98	Alex 'Sandy' Brown 1963-71
Sam English 1933-35	Jack Cock 1923-25
Alun Evans 1968-72	Martin Dobson 1974-79
David Fairclough 1975-83	Ephraim 'Jock' Dodds 1946-48
Sam Gilligan 1910-13	Tommy Eglington 1946-57
Bobby Graham 1964-72	Peter Farrell 1946-57
Brian Hall 1968-76	Duncan Ferguson 1994-
Davy Hannah 1894-97	Mike Ferguson 1981-83
Charlie Hewitt 1907-08	Jimmy Gabriel 1960-67
Mark Lawrenson 1981-88	WE Gault 1912-20
Sammy Lee 1977-86	J Gourlay 1909-13
Harry Lewis 1919-22	Tom Griffiths 1926-31
Kevin Lewis 1960-63	Alan Harper 1983-88, 1991-93
Terry McDermott 1974-83	Asa Hartford 1979-81
Jimmy McDougall 1928-38	A Hartley 1892-97
Jock McNab 1919-28	Colin Harvey 1962-74
Archie McPherson 1929-35	Adrian Heath 1982-89
Joe McQue 1893-98	Andy Hinchcliffe 1990-
Arthur Metcalfe 1912-15	Bobby Irvine 1921-28
Jan Molby 1984-	Frank Jefferis 1911-20
Tom Morrison 1927-35	David Johnson 1969-72, 1982-84
Jimmy Nicholl 1913-15	Bob Kelso 1888, 1891-95
Steve Nicol 1982-94	Howard Kendall 1967-74
Cyril Oxley 1925-26	F Kennedy 1924-27
Frederick Pagnam 1914-20	Brian Kidd 1979-80
Bob Paisley 1945-54	Joe McBride 1978-82
Henry Race 1927-30	T McDermott 1903-05
Archie Rawlings 1923-26	A McDonald 1899-1900
Syd Roberts 1931-37	T McInnes 1894-95

DERBY GOALSCORERS

LIVERPOOL	EVERTON
	1

LIVERPOOL	EVERTON
Michael Robinson 1983-85	**Duncan McKenzie** 1976-78
Robert Robinson 1903-12	**George Martin** 1928-32
Ronny Rosenthal 1990-94	**Alfred Milward** 1888-96
Dean Saunders 1991-92	**Pat Nevin** 1988-92
Jackie Sheldon 1913-21	**Jack O'Donnell** 1925-30
James Stewart 1909-14	**Fred Pickering** 1964-67
Nicky Tanner 1989-93	**J Proudfoot** 1898-1901
Alan Waddle 1973-77	**Kevin Ratcliffe** 1977-93
John Walker 1897-1902	**Paul Rideout** 1992-
Alfred West 1903-11	**Bruce Rioch** 1976-77
Ronnie Whelan 1980-94	**Kevin Sheedy** 1982-92
W White 1901-02	**Jimmy Stein** 1928-36
Mark Wright 1991-	**Gary Stevens** 1979-88
	Douglas Trentham 1936-49
	RF Turner 1908-10
	Imre Varadi 1979-81
	Eddie Wainwright 1944-56
	Mark Ward 1991-94
	W Wareing 1912-19
	Wattie White 1908-10
	Paul Wilkinson 1985-87
	WD Williams 1922-25
	Sam Wolstenholme 1897-1903
	Own Goals

Above: Everton skipper Kevin Ratcliffe scored his only derby goal at Anfield in February 1986.